100 YEARS OF ROYAL NAVY SUBMARINES

100 YEARS OF ROYAL NAVY SUBMARINES

JoPalmer 2005

Jeremy Flack

Airlife
England

Copyright © 2002 Jeremy Flack

First published in the UK in 2002
by Airlife Publishing Ltd

British Library Cataloguing-in-Publication Data
A catalogue record for this book
is available from the British Library

ISBN 1 84037 300 8

This book contains rare photographs and the publisher has made
every endeavour to reproduce them to the highest quality. Some,
however, have been technically impossible to reproduce to the standard that we normally demand, but have been included because of
their rarity and interest value.

Typeset by Rowland Phototypesetting Ltd, Bury St Edmunds, Suffolk
Printed in China

Airlife Publishing Ltd

101 Longden Road, Shrewsbury, SY3 9EB, England
E-mail: airlife@airlifebooks.com
Website: www.airlifebooks.com

Acknowledgements

A number of people have been instrumental in helping me put this book together and I would like to thank them. It was David Healey at Fleet Media Ops who planted the idea of this book in my mind and Andrew Johnston of Airlife who helped to see it come to life. I have sought and received assistance from various directions, including the officers and men of the various boats that I have visited, especially those of HMS *Vanguard* and HMS *Sovereign*, the Imperial War Museum at London and John Delaney at Duxford, Steve Wilmott and Shaline Groves together with the MoD Police at Faslane, Peter Duppa-Miller, Mike Edwards and Mike Smith of BAE Systems, Andrew Rice of Rolls Royce, Kate Hall of Lockheed Martin, John Constantine and Wendy Smith of DML, Ralph Dunn of DPA, Neil Ruenzel of General Dynamics Electric Boat, Sue Kennard of Alenia Marconi and Wendy Gulley at the Submarine Force Museum.

Special thanks to Cdr Jeff Tall, together with Debbie and Maggie, for putting up with me on my frequent visits and access to the photo archive.

I would also like to thank Loretta who assisted with some of the photography, and a big thank you to my wife Julie, without whose cooperation and assistance this book would not have happened: not only putting up with my invading most rooms around the house with piles of papers and photographs, she also helped with the photography and research, as well as keeping me fed and watered.

Contents

Introduction

Thoughts of how to build a vessel capable of sailing beneath the waves have vexed man over the centuries. Designers have made various proposals, and although some may have been attempted it was only in the last couple of centuries that these ideas began to be constructed.

Unfortunately, it is conflict which tends to make ideas happen, and it was the American Revolution which kick-started the submarine. David Bushnell designed and built a craft which on the face of it was little more than a barrel with a few bits and pieces. However, it was one of the early attempts to put theory into practice. Named the Turtle, its wooden shell was large enough for one person. It was pedal powered and had a snorkel for fresh air. It carried an explosive charge and had a drill with which to attach it to the hull of a ship. No actual drawing survives of the craft (if it ever existed), but a representation of the Turtle is on display at the RN Submarine Museum at Gosport.

The Turtle was built and an attempt to attach the charge was made in September 1776 against a Royal Navy ship that was blockading New York. It failed because Bushnell was unable to drill into the wooden warship owing to it having a copper-plated hull.

Despite the failure, it proved a concept and the ideas progressed. During the American Civil War a 7.5 ton craft named the *Huntley* became the first to actually sink an enemy boat. Unfortunately, it was lost in the explosion. In 1995 she was located and is the subject of a recovery and preservation project.

For some reason men of the cloth appeared to influence submarine development on this side of the Atlantic. One was a curate named George William Garrett. He designed and was awarded patents for his craft in 1878. Named *Resurgam*, his 14 ft (4.27 m) craft had pistons to draw water in and out for ballast, a hand crank for power and ports with leather gloves to handle the explosives. Following the success of *Resurgam*, he commenced work on *Resurgam II*. This was a 30 ton boat, launched at Birkenhead in 1879. It was powered by a steam engine which used its latent heat to run for a couple of miles submerged. It was lost when he attempted to take it to Portsmouth to show a Swedish arms dealer.

Despite this set-back, the arms dealer – Thorsten Nordenfelt – formed a partnership with Garrett, and several boats were built and sold, including two built by the Barrow Shipbuilding Company (later to become Vickers Sons and Maxim) in 1885 for the Turkish Navy.

About the same time, a monk with the Christian Brothers in Cork was having similar thoughts. In 1873 he was becoming so obsessed with these ideas that he left the order. He decided to join a large number of people who emigrated to the USA at the time of the Famine. There, John Holland became a teacher, but the submarine idea continued to occupy his thoughts so much that he even sent a proposal to the American government. This was turned down, but because of his Irish background a backer came forward. Known as the Fenian Brotherhood, this backer dreamed of an Irish Republican Navy submarine which would attack British shipping and so help in their struggle to gain Irish independence.

Over the next seven years, the Holland Torpedo Boat Company built three boats of moderate success, but Holland was always struggling for funds. Isaac Rice was a storage battery manufacturer and could see potential in Holland's ideas and became a partner injecting vital funds.

Gradually Rice took control of the business and it became the Electric Boat Company. In April 1900 Rice had persuaded the American government to order the *Holland IV*, which became USS *Holland*.

Considering Holland's past supporters, it is interesting to learn that Rice then went to London in an attempt to sell his boat to the Admiralty. They scoffed at the idea – it was ungentlemanly and the type of war machine that would be used by the weaker nation, which Great Britain could never be! According to Rear Admiral A. K. Wilson, the submarine was 'underhand, unfair, and damned un-English'.

However, submarines were entering service with a growing number of countries, and it was becoming felt that perhaps some should be purchased in order to develop anti-submarine techniques. Consequently, the Admiralty advised Rice in December 1900 of their requirement for five of his boats. Arrangements were made with Vickers Sons and Maxim at Barrow to build the boats at a cost of £35,000 each.

HM Submarine *Torpedo Boat No 1* was laid down on 4 February 1901. Despite problems with drawings, she was launched on 2 October 1901 and underwent her sea trials in April 1902.

Although the Royal Navy had been involved with submersible craft over a century earlier, albeit potentially on the receiving end, the potential was ignored and it had fought shy of owning its own. Although by this time a number were in service, especially in France, most were pretty innocuous, with poor performance, range and weaponry. For most of the time they had required considerable expenditure with little to show for it, leaving further requests for development funding rather limited.

On the other hand, the Royal Navy decided to acquire the submarine as they were starting to have some potential. The US Navy had already ordered and received several earlier Holland models, and in August 1900 ordered six of the more advanced Holland No. 10 design as the Adder Class. It was this same model which was ordered by the Admiralty.

Some modifications were required as a result of the trials, and at last the Royal Navy had a satisfactory submarine with limited capabilities. In those early days to leave Portsmouth and navigate around the Isle of Wight and return was a major adventure.

During their first fleet manoeuvres, the five Hollands were assigned to defend Portsmouth. Much to the surprise of almost everybody, these small, seemingly incapable boats attacked and 'sank' four warships.

The new boats had made their mark and their potential could be appreciated. Already the design was being developed, and the A Class were being built and entering service. It wasn't long before the dangerous petrol engines were replaced by the diesel. In no time the Royal Navy had gone from a service that had no wish for the submarine to having one of the largest fleets. By 1906 she was only just behind France, which had sixty boats.

However, the submarine service had a stigma which kept it separate from the rest of the Navy. On board ship, and especially ashore, the Royal Navy demanded a high standard of discipline, including personal hygiene. On board a submarine life was very different, with very limited and cramped conditions. Equipment was usually covered in a film of grease and there was often water inside the hull. With washing facilities minimal, the boats often had a unique smell of man and machine. When these boats came home from their patrols their crew would often look worse for wear and would be excluded from mainstream naval society almost to the extent of becoming a separate society. The implication of this was that the branch did not have proper representation within the Admiralty.

Being a new service, the Admiralty planners had limited or no knowledge of submarines, and there were no experienced representatives at the appropriate level to plead their case. Consequently, they frequently made inappropriate decisions for the little-understood submarine force as the role for the K Class typified.

When war broke out in 1914, Great Britain had over a hundred submarines either in service or being built, France had seventy, Germany forty-five, the USA forty and Japan just sixteen.

During the early days of the war, the boats and their crews rapidly matured as they found what they were really capable of. British and German boats had major successes but also suffered many losses. Problems with torpedo failures plagued them. The British Grand Fleet, which had been against submarines from the start, demanded that the submarine should come under its control and sail within its formations. The small boats could never have the necessary power to keep up with the the large surface ships. These demands kept rearing their head into the 1930s with the Thames Class and wasted valuable resources.

The effect of the submarine on the operation of the large capital ships was to restrict a substantial amount of their time at sea to reduce their possible exposure to attack. When the German U-18 was rammed near the 'safe' waters of Scapa Flow, panic mode went into operation within the Grand Fleet. Although she had not hit any of the sheltering battleships and cruisers, these waters had been considered beyond the range of the U-boats, and the ships were immediately moved.

As had originally been thought, as the British blockage of German ports was being felt, so the U-boats resorted, hesitantly initially, to breaking international law by attacking merchant ships and civilian liners such as the *Lusitania*, in which 1,198 men, women and children were killed. By 1917, Germany was building submarines on a huge scale, and in her desperation the attacks became unrestricted.

In 1914 there had been a report that the Germans were building a 22 knot submarine, and at the same time the Grand Fleet was pressing its demands for its submarines. This resulted in a design for the K Class, which entered service in 1917. These steam-driven monsters turned out to be monsters in more ways than one. They were huge – twice the length and three times the weight of most of their contemporaries. Although they were fast on the surface they were cumbersome and slow to react and became accident prone.

During this period the USA had remained neutral. Although some H Class boats had been built for Great Britain, she tried not to get involved, but on 6 April 1917 this changed when she joined Britain to fight the Germans.

R Class boats were the first anti-submarine warfare (ASW) boats with concentration on underwater speed and detection equipment. Unfortunately they became operational too late to have any success. Only one attack was made, and then the torpedoes failed to explode. As a result the idea of an ASW submarine was not pursued for many years.

When the war ended in 1919 the Germans had lost around two hundred of their U-boats, of which seventeen were to British submarines. The Royal Navy had lost a total of fifty-four submarines, and the other Allies thirty-five. Five commanding officers had been awarded VCs.

With the war over, British armed forces began a decline to what was considered to be a minimum size for home defence and overseas interests. The USA managed to get the first disarmament treaty off the ground, and on 6 February 1922 the Washington Naval Treaty was signed by the five principal maritime powers – Britain, France, Italy, Japan and the USA. A formula was devised that would reduce the overall number of warships. It would allow some new building at the expense of existing older ships but would restrict their size and guns. By 1930 the Royal Navy had fifty submarines and a further ten being built, but the recession was requiring investments to be made elsewhere. On 22 April a further agreement was made to curb the building of the replacement vessels for six years and to reduce the number of capital ships.

During these inter-war years, the Admiralty continued with its fixation on a fast boat which would be used with the Grand Fleet. It also experimented with submarine cruisers, aircraft carriers and minelayers, but all had been lost or scrapped by the time conflict in Europe was rearing its head once again.

In the Second World War, Royal Navy submarines were extensively used to combat Axis forces across the North Sea, in the Bay of Biscay, in the Mediterranean and later in the Far East.

The Porpoise Class were specially developed for the role as minelayers, and as a result often had to operate in the shallow enemy coastal waters where they were most vulnerable. As a result most were lost to enemy action.

Malta was a thorn in the side for Axis forces in the Mediterranean, and was subjected to continual attack by air and on the sea. Submarines played an important role in the supply of vital materials to help prevent the beleaguered island falling into enemy hands.

The landing of special agents or special forces became one of a number of new roles for these boats, usually conducted at night to ensure they were not seen. Modern boats are able to facilitate entry and exit while submerged, usually through the emergency escape, which means that they are virtually undetected. A number of the Royal Marine SBS (Special Boat Squadron) were landed by a Royal Navy submarine during the conflict in the Falklands. Submarines were also used for reconnaissance, and also as markers, where they played a vital role by guiding invasion forces to the correct beaches.

During the Second World War approximately one-third of Royal Navy submarines failed to return home to base. While some can be accounted for in enemy attacks, it is probable that about a third were lost due to mines.

Despite the atrocious conditions compared with surface ships, especially in the earlier boats, the submariners were a unique breed with their own form of discipline and a close society.

A special mini-submarine was developed to attack specific targets. Referred to as X Craft, these boat were responsible for a number of special operations, including attacks on the German *Tirpitz* and Japanese *Takao* which were causing the Allies major losses.

At the end of the Second World War Churchill said of them, 'Of all the branches of men in the Forces, there is none which shows more devotion and faces grimmer perils than the submarine. Great deeds are done in the air and on the land; nevertheless, nothing surpasses your exploits.'

As the world returned to peace the massive war machine was drastically cut. This time, although the cuts were harsh, the submarine service, which had now proved its worth, was not exposed to the same level of cuts as most other areas.

► John Holland in the hatch of one of his early submarines.

▼ Rear Admiral Rob Stevens CB – Flag Officer Submarines – with PO Thomas Gould VC, and veteran ex submariner Hugh Smith representing current and past submariners at the launch of the Royal Mail set of postage stamps by HMS *Holland* on 10 April 2001.

The Cold War brought about a change of emphasis, with anti-submarine warfare moving to the fore. Porpoise and Oberon Class diesel-powered hunter/killers (SSK) were introduced with greatly improved capabilities.

Speed had always been a problem for submarines, and attempts were made to improve this by using German-developed hydrogen-peroxide-fuelled engines, but like the early petrol engines this proved too unstable to be practical. The introduction of nuclear power brought about the true submarine with unlimited capabilities which were soon to be exploited to the maximum with the SSBN.

Now capable of operating at higher speed in any part of the world for indefinite periods, the new submarines were developed into highly effective hunters. The commissioning of HMS *Dreadnought* in April 1963 led to a major change in the fortunes of the Royal Navy Submarine Service. A series of nuclear-powered hunter killers (SSN = Fleet Attack Submarine Nuclear) were now built and were capable of seeking and destroying enemy ships more efficiently then ever before.

A further development, of fitting a nuclear-powered boat with long-range missiles by the USA, was adopted by the Royal Navy. Capable of hiding for lengthy periods undetected in any part of the world, armed with long-range, nuclear-armed strategic missiles, these mighty boats became the holder of the British deterrent.

In the meantime, the SSNs were upgraded with the Sub-Harpoon anti-ship missile to augment the shorter-range torpedoes which had also been significantly improved. A tactical role enhancement is currently being implemented with the introduction of the Tomahawk cruise missile, enabling these hunters to be able to project their might at specific land targets. The introduction of the Tomahawk filled the gap between the anti-ship and submarine operations of the SSN and the nuclear attack of the SSBN (= Ballistic Missile Submarine Nuclear). This was a conventional weapon fired with surgical accuracy by using the latest GPS navigation, as was seen when a number were launched operationally during operations against the Serbian armed forces attacking Kosovo.

Today the Royal Navy Submarine Service is at the forefront of British defence policy. In its first hundred years of operation it has leaped from being equipped with five small boats with marginal capabilities and with little status to being equipped with the most powerful boats in the Royal Navy and amongst the best in the world.

The current crews of the Royal Navy Submarine Service are extremely effective and capable in their current role with these powerful boats. However, one should reflect on the past crews who struggled, often in appalling conditions, to achieve what were often heroic results. Many paid the ultimate price to ensure that we have been able to keep our freedom. To them we should offer our thanks for the debt that society owes them but often forgets.

▶ A full-scale representation of the Turtle that was used to attack HMS *Eagle* in 1776.

Holland Class

The very first submarine to be purchased by the Royal Navy was HM Submarine *Torpedo Boat No 1*, later to be known as HMS *Holland 1*, which cost £35,000. She was built by Vickers Sons and Maxim at Barrow and launched in 1901. She was armed with a single 14 in (355 mm) torpedo tube.

Designed by John P. Holland, the Royal Navy model was a licence-built copy of those built for the US Navy as the Adder Class. Out of the water she looked like a short, fat cigar tube with a single propeller at the stern. She had a pair of vertically mounted rudders above and below the propeller for steering, and a further pair horizontally to control diving. Once the drawings arrived from America, work got under way at Vickers, and despite some problems with these drawings construction commenced in great secrecy. Initially, the Holland was very unstable, nearly turning on its end, but after nearly twelve months of trials and modifications it settled down.

The Holland boats did not have a conning tower in the now traditional form, or a periscope. They incorporated a small cylindrical protuberance big enough to fit the captain's head and shoulders, and this was fitted with windows. An experimental periscope was designed and fitted to one of the later Hollands, and HMS *Holland 2* had a slightly larger conning tower.

When surfaced, the Holland boats proved difficult to control because of the lack of structure outside the hull. The captain and the coxswain had difficulty hanging on to the wheel and masts while on deck with water washing around their feet. Once submerged, the boat changed from a nose-up attitude to nose-down, which was a little unnerving to those not used to it, as it would appear to be constantly diving. However, control was good and it actually appeared to have good manoeuvrability. HMS *Holland 2* recorded a dive of 78 ft (23.7 m) when she had accidentally taken on too much ballast.

HM S/m *No 1* was the first submarine completed for the Royal Navy, but being the first of type was subjected to lengthy and exhaustive trials lasting until 1903. As a consequence HM S/m *No 2* became the first to enter service when commissioned on 1 August 1903, and by the end of 1903 all five were in service.

As the crews adapted to their new environment, these primitive submarines, with a single torpedo tube and either three long or five short torpedoes, proved surprisingly effective. They rudely awoke the complacent captains of many warships to their presence with the crash of a practice torpedo against their ships' sides. Despite the steep learning curve for the early submariners in this new environment, none of the Holland boats were involved in a major incident in their ten years of service with the Royal Navy. Probably the worst was an explosion of petrol vapour, ignited by arcing in the electric motor, in which four were injured.

Despite the attitude of the Admiralty to the idea of submarine warfare, and the limited capability of these Hollands, sufficient support was gained for the future of submarines to be assured. The lessons learned during their early life prompted the Admiralty and Vickers to produce an improved design. As a result, the order for *Holland 6* was modified to become the first of the new larger A Class.

Although the Holland boats were extremely primitive and the crews had to adjust to a new and totally unfamiliar environment, none of the five boats were lost or suffered any fatalities during their service with the Royal Navy. Considering the fragility of the boats this was no mean feat, and a credit to their crews. This was not to say there were no incidents, as there were. On 18 March 1904 HMS *Holland 1* was taking part in manoeuvres when she sank off the Nab Lightship. Her crew was rescued safely and the boat salvaged a month later. After refurbishment she was returned to service.

All the Holland Class were paid off during 1912/13, and HMS *Holland 1* was sold to the shipbreaker T. W. Ward for scrapping for £410. She foundered while on tow to the breakers and was eventually discovered in 1981. She was salvaged in 1982 and now takes pride of place on public display in the RN Submarine Museum at Gosport.

Preserved
HMS *Holland 1*   1901   RN Submarine Museum, Gosport

Class	Holland Class	
Role	Coastal Submarine	
	IMPERIAL	METRIC
Sub Disp – surfaced	113 tons	114.8 tonnes
Sub Disp – submerged	122 tons	124 tonnes
Length	63 ft 10 in	19.5 m
Beam	11 ft 9 in	3.58 m
Draught	9 ft 11 in	3.02 m
Propulsion	1 × 160 bhp Wolseley petrol engine	
	1 × 70 ehp electric motor	
Speed	7.5 knots surfaced, 5 knots submerged	
Range	250 nm at 8 knots surfaced, 25 nm at 7 knots submerged	
Armament	1 × 14 in (355 mm) torpedo tube (bow)	
	3 long or 5 short torpedoes carried	
Complement (Officers/Men)	8 (2/6)	

Builder	Name	Class	Launched	Fate	Date
Vickers	Holland 1 (ex HM S/m No. 1)	Holland Class	2.10.1901	PO – Preserved	7.10.1913
Vickers	Holland 2	Holland Class	21.2.1902	PO – Scrapped	7.10.1913
Vickers	Holland 3	Holland Class	9.5.1902	PO – Scrapped	7.10.1913
Vickers	Holland 4	Holland Class	23.5.1902	PO – Expended as target	7.10.1912
Vickers	Holland 5	Holland Class	10.6.1902	PO – Foundered	8.8.1912
Vickers	Holland 6	Holland Class		Cancelled – Built as A.1	

▲ The start of it all – the launch of HM Submarine *Torpedo Boat No. 1* being launched by Vickers Sons and Maxim at Barrow-in-Furness on 2 October 1901. She was usually referred to as *Holland 1*. *(HM Submarine Museum)*

▼ HMS *Holland 1* under way. *(HM Submarine Museum)*

▲ *Holland* crew crowd the freeboard to pose for the camera while under way. *(HM Submarine Museum)*

▼ The wreck of HMS *Holland 1* was discovered in 1981, and now takes pride of place at the HM Submarine Museum at Gosport. *(Jeremy Flack)*

▲ As the Holland Class had no bulkheads they looked deceptively spacious inside. *(HM Submarine Museum)*

▼ The bow cap is partially open to reveal the 14 in (355 mm) torpedo tube behind. *(Jeremy Flack)*

A Class

The A Class of submarine was a development of the Holland Class in the light of the early experience. This first development was certainly a leap forward in size, with the hull length being 50 per cent greater, but the technology was still primitive.

HMS *A.1* was originally planned to be the sixth Holland Class, but with the rapidly increasing list of proposed design improvements it was decided that this boat would incorporate most of the proposals in an enlarged hull that was increased in length by 40 ft (12.2 m), and this led to the new class. A late change to double the number of torpedo tubes to two from HMS *A.2* onwards represented a further increase in size, by almost 2 ft (0.6 m), and became the standard for the rest of the class, although even then further improvements were incorporated. Despite the improved design and engine power, the performance in terms of speed changed little over that of the Hollands: the surface speed increased slightly, but submerged they remained almost the same. HMS *A.5* was the first of the Group 2 and was fitted with a 550 bhp 16-cylinder engine replacing the earlier 12-cylinder, but this still only increased the speed by half a knot and proved to be a less reliable engine.

A Class were still surface-powered by the petrol engine with its inherent dangers. An explosion aboard HMS *A.5* in February 1905 was caused by a build-up of petrol fumes after refuelling, and killed five of her crew. In an attempt to find a solution, HMS *A.13* was fitted with an experimental MAN-type (Maschinefabrik Augsburg-Nürnberg) heavy-oil-powered engine. Built by Vickers under licence, this engine would today be classified as a diesel engine. Although it used a vastly safer fuel, it was a much heavier engine and reduced the amount of fuel that could be carried. Consequently. it wasn't until the D Class towards the end of the decade that the improved diesel engine began to replace the petrol.

One of the first improvements was the conning tower, which served several roles. It featured two hatches – one leading onto the bridge, and a lower one sealing the conning tower from the control room. This virtually eliminated water entering the boat from larger waves, and enabled the boat to go to sea in rougher weather. It gave some protection to the captain and coxswain when on the casing, and the higher elevation gave them a better view. HMS *A.11* featured a further-enlarged conning tower. The longer hull gave a better passage than the Holland's when on the surface, but it was still poor. The story was the same with her endurance.

It was acknowledged early on that the firepower of the A boats was limited, and so a second tube was incorporated in HMS *A.2* onwards.

The technique for diving the Holland and A Class boats was to dive when they were stationary. Gradually, as experience was gained, it was discovered that it was possible to dive with care while under way. However, with only rudders at the tail, it was not easy to control. As a result HMS *A.7* was fitted with an experimental additional pair of hydroplanes on her conning tower.

Although the Hollands all survived until paid off, the A boats were soon to succumb to accidents, both major and minor, which are inevitable to almost every type of machine. Sadly, unlike ships and vehicles, the fate of submarines is more akin to that of aircraft, with even simple incidents leading to fatal results.

HMS *A.1* had the misfortune to be the first Royal Navy submarine lost when on 18 March 1904 she was participating in manoeuvres off Spithead. It would appear that her captain was so concentrating on making a submerged 'attack' on the cruiser HMS *Juno* that he failed to notice that the steamer *Berwick Castle* was bearing down on her. She was struck on her conning tower and sank with the loss of all her crew. *Berwick*'s master was unaware of any submarine activity and just reported that he thought he had been struck by a practice torpedo. When HMS *A.1* failed to return to Portsmouth the implications of the message were quickly realised. Following a search, the wreck was located and recovered the following month, but it was too late for the eleven crew.

However, prior to this, HMS *A.1* had already suffered less disastrous accidents. While still with Vickers, trapped hydrogen from the charging batteries had ignited, causing a small explosion. Once in service, sea water had got into the batteries, resulting in a cloud of choking chlorine inside the hull. Owing to this she had to be abandoned and was towed to port. *A.1* was eventually sunk as a target in August 1911.

A total of seven crew were killed and twelve injured in two petrol explosions aboard HMS *A.5* in February 1905. She was subsequently salvaged and returned to service following refurbishment.

HMS *A.7* and *A.8* departed Plymouth on 8 June 1905 for Looe, where they were to take part in an exercise. After passing the Plymouth breakwater *A.8* made a dive and returned to the surface shortly afterwards. The crew of an escorting torpedo boat noticed that she had a distinct list and then was gradually sinking. As the crew of the torpedo boat turned to come to her assistance the bow dipped and the stern lifted out of the water before she slid below the waves. Only four of those on or close to the conning tower had time to scramble clear. What had happened was that a hatch had failed to be sealed, and as the boat submerged water had poured in. The crew attempted to surface as quickly as they could, but the time taken to get back on the surface would have meant that several tons of water would have flooded the compartment, upsetting the trim of the boat. Although she managed to get to the surface, water continued to pour in, so that in a short time the weight of the water in the flooded bow swept through the boat. Valuable air would have been forced out as the crew tried to scramble out of the narrow hatch in the conning tower, hastening her demise. As she slipped below the waves a small explosion was heard as the battery exploded.

HMS *A.8* was raised on 8 June and brought back to Devonport, where the 14 dead crew members were removed. A funeral followed a few days later, and the towns of Plymouth, Devonport and Stonehouse came to a halt to pay respects to those lost. HMS *A.8* was refurbished and returned to service. However, the short range and small weapon load meant that the A Class was soon superseded, and she was then used mainly for training before being scrapped in 1920. Only a month before scrapping, HMS *A.8* had suffered internal explosions and sunk. It was thought that these might have been battery related and caused minimal damage, as she was rapidly put back into service.

HMS *A.4* took on a quantity of water during signal trials. This was not a major problem if only a small amount of water was taken in, as the ballast tanks could be adjusted to compensate. However, the effect of sea water on the batteries was a different and more lethal one. Sea water is a conductor of electricity and so shorts the batteries. Apart from a build-up of explosive hydrogen, choking chlorine gas is also produced. In the confines of a small submarine these can be lethal. Once surfaced, the crew of HMS *A.4* were all ordered on deck and the boat was towed to Portsmouth. As she entered the harbour an explosion was heard and the boat sank. Again, damage must have been minimal as she was soon put back into service.

HMS *A.9* foundered following a collision with SS *Coath* off Plymouth only a year after she was launched. She was able to resurface by releasing her drop keel. In July 1908 she suffered another deadly incident when some of her crew were suffocated through the effects of carbon monoxide poisoning from the petrol engine.

On 2 February 1912, HMS *A.3* was struck by HMS *Hazard* near the Isle of Wight She was on exercise when she surfaced just in front of the warship. The collision created a large hole in her side and she sank almost immediately with the loss of her crew. She was salvaged the following month, and as she was considered too bad to repair, she was finally expended as a target on 17 May.

HMS *A.7* was also lost during a training exercise. She was making practice torpedo attacks against HMS *Onyx* and *Pigmy* on 16 January 1914 in Whitsand Bay near Plymouth. She was seen to dive but failed to surface afterwards. Bad weather frustrated any rescue attempt, and although she was located six days later no attempt was ever made to salvage the boat.

When war broke out, the surviving A Class boats were mainly used to help provide local defence at various strategic locations. By 1916 they had been superseded and were relegated to the training role.

HMS *A.10* was alongside HMS *Pactolus* in March 1917 at Ardrossan when undetected leaking ballast tanks caused her to lose buoyancy, and she sank. She was salvaged but not repaired, and was finally scrapped in 1919.

Of the thirteen A Class boats built, a number suffered flooding accidents or petrol explosions, which, although they caused no structural damage, resulted in some 70 crew losing their lives. Most of these boats were refurbished and returned to service. Most ended their days in the training role and were finally paid off in 1916/7 and then held in reserve before being sold and scrapped in 1920. One further boat (*A.14*) was originally ordered, but was cancelled before construction began and replaced with the order for HMS *B.1*.

	Class	A Class, Group 1
	Role	Coastal Submarine

	IMPERIAL	METRIC
Sub Disp – surfaced	189 tons*	192 tonnes
Sub Disp – submerged	205.5 tons*	208.8 tonnes
Length	105 ft 0.5 in*	32.1 m
Beam	12 ft 8.75 in*	3.9 m
Draught	11 ft 6 in*	3.5 m
Propulsion	1 × 600 bhp Wolseley petrol engine 1 × 150 ehp electric motor	
Speed	11.5 knots surfaced, 6 knots submerged	
Range	500 nm at 30 knots surfaced, 10 nm at 5 knots submerged	
Armament	2 × 18 in (457 mm) torpedo tube (bow) (except A.1 with 1 tube) 3 torpedoes carried	
Complement (Officers/Men)	11 (2/9)	
Data note	*A.1 was slightly smaller	

Builder	Name	Class	Launched	Fate	Date
Vickers	HMS *A.1*	A Class, Group 1	9.7.1902	PO – Scrapped	7.1911
Vickers	HMS *A.2*	A Class, Group 1	16.4.1903	Damaged – PO – Scrapped	1.1920
Vickers	HMS *A.3*	A Class, Group 1	9.5.1903	PO – Expended as target	17.5.1912
Vickers	HMS *A.4*	A Class, Group 1	9.6.1903	PO – Scrapped	16.1.1920

	Class	A Class, Group 2
	Role	Coastal Submarine

		IMPERIAL	METRIC
Sub Disp – surfaced		190 tons	193.04 tonnes
Sub Disp – submerged		205.5 tons	208.8 tonnes
Length		105 ft	32 m
Beam		12 ft 8 in	3.9 m
Draught		10 ft	3 m
Propulsion		1 × 550 bhp Wolseley petrol engine	
		1 × 150 ehp electric motor	
Speed		11.5 knots surfaced, 6 knots submerged	
Range		500 nm at 10 knots surfaced, 30 nm at 5 knots submerged	
Armament		2 × 18 in (457 mm) torpedo tubes (bow)	
		4 torpedoes carried	
Complement (Officers/Men)		14 (2/12)	
Data note		*1 × 500 hp Hornsby-Ackroyd heavy oil (diesel) engine in A13	

Builder	Name	Pennant No.	Class	Launched	Fate	Date
Vickers	HMS *A.5*	I15	A Class, Group 2	3.3.1904	PO – Scrapped	1920
Vickers	HMS *A.6*	I16	A Class, Group 2	3.3.1904	PO – Scrapped	16.1.1920
Vickers	HMS *A.7*	I17	A Class, Group 2	23.1.1905	Sunk – Accident	16.1.1914
Vickers	HMS *A.8*	I18	A Class, Group 2	23.1.1905	PO – Scrapped	8.10.1920
Vickers	HMS *A.9*	I19	A Class, Group 2	8.2.1905	PO – Scrapped	16.1.1920
Vickers	HMS *A.10*	I10	A Class, Group 2	8.2.1905	PO – Scrapped	4.1919
Vickers	HMS *A.11*	I01	A Class, Group 2	8.3.1905	PO – Scrapped	5.1920
Vickers	HMS *A.12*	I02	A Class, Group 2	3.3.1905	PO – Scrapped	1.1920
Vickers	HMS *A.13*	I03	A Class, Group 2	18.4.1905	PO – Scrapped	1920
Vickers	HMS *A.14*		A Class, Group 2		Cancelled	

▲ HMS *A.13* was the first Royal Navy submarine to be fitted with the safer diesel engine which would become standard with the D Class onwards. *(HM Submarine Museum)*

▼ HMS *A.7* under way and featuring a conning tower which enabled a better view and greatly reduced the amount of water that entered the boat. *(HM Submarine Museum)*

B Class

The B Class represented a further development of the original Holland and the previous A boats, increasing in both size and weight. They were the first Royal Navy submarines to incorporate a casing which provided extra protection to the hull as well as improving their buoyancy when surfaced. They were also the first to be fitted with hydroplanes near the bow, which enabled them to dive easily while under way. Their surface speed was an improvement over the A Class, but submerged it remained much the same. HMS *B.1* was naturally the first of the class, but she was in fact modified during construction as she had originally been laid down as *A.14*.

Such were the range and speed of the B Class that they would normally be towed for a lengthy passage – to the Mediterranean for instance.

On 4 October 1912, HMS *B.2* was lost when she was accidentally run down and sunk by the SS *Amerika* off Dover, with the loss of 15 crew. She was not recovered so that her crew would be left undisturbed.

On 22 December 1914, Lt Norman Douglas Holbrook became the first submariner to be awarded a Victoria Cross. During his command of HMS *B.11*, Holbrook successfully attacked and sank the Turkish battleship *Messudieh* on 13 December. The attack involved diving under five rows of mines, then returning the same way safely despite being subjected to attacks by gunfire and torpedo boats. The attack and escape had required *B.11* and her crew to spend nine hours submerged – quite some feat for an early submarine! On their return, in addition to Holbrook's VC, all the crew were awarded DSCs or DSMs.

On 9 August 1916, HMS *B.10* had completed a patrol off Páola and returned to her base, which at that time was at Venice. The Italian cruiser *Marco Polo* was being used as a depot ship and *B.10* was alongside making some repairs. Without warning some aircraft of the Austrian Naval Air Service attacked the port and *B.10* was hit and sank. She was subsequently salvaged but was considered beyond repair.

HMS *B.3* was used in early attempts to detect enemy ships and submarines when in 1916 she was fitted with a prototype directional hydrophone.

In the Mediterranean HMS *B.6* and *B.11* had already become inoperable because of a shortage of spares, so during August 1917 these and a further three of the surviving boats were extensively modified to be used as conventional patrol boats. They had their electric motors removed, conning tower cut off and replaced with a wheel house built on a raised deck. The bow was re-profiled and they were armed with a 12-pdr gun. When completed they were allocated the fresh pennant numbers *S.6* to *S.10*.

Eleven B Class were built between 1903 and 1906, and when the war ended

HMS *B.3* was the only boat to remain operational. She had survived primarily because she had been used for various trials and then training.

	Class	B Class	
	Role	Coastal Submarine	
		IMPERIAL	METRIC
Sub Disp – surfaced		287 tons	291.59 tonnes
Sub Disp – submerged		316 tons	321.06 tonnes
Length		142 ft 2.5 in	43.34 m
Beam		12 ft 7 in	3.88 m
Draught		11 ft 2 in	3.4 m
Propulsion		1 × 600 bhp Vickers petrol engine	
		1 × 200 ehp electric motor	
Speed		12 knots surfaced, 6.5 knots submerged	
Range		1,300 nm at 9 knots surfaced, 22.5 nm at 6.5 knots	
		submerged	
Armament		2 × 18 in (457 mm) torpedo tubes (bow)	
		4 torpedoes carried	
Complement (Officers/Men)		15 (2/13)	

Builder	Name	Pennant No.	Class	Launched	Fate	Date
Vickers	HMS *B.1*	I21	B Class	25.10.1904	PO – Scrapped	8.1921
Vickers	HMS *B.2*	I22	B Class	19.8.1905	Sunk – Accident	4.10.1912
Vickers	HMS *B.3*	I23	B Class	31.10.1905	PO – Scrapped	12.1919
Vickers	HMS *B.4*	I24	B Class	14.11.1905	PO – Scrapped	4.1919
Vickers	HMS *B.5*	I25	B Class	14.11.1905	PO – Scrapped	8.1921
Vickers	HMS *B.6*	I26	B Class	30.11.1905	PO – Scrapped	1919
Vickers	HMS *B.7*	I27	B Class	30.11.1905	PO – Scrapped	10.1919
Vickers	HMS *B.8*	I28	B Class	23.1.1906	PO – Scrapped	1919
Vickers	HMS *B.9*	I29	B Class	26.1.1906	PO – Scrapped	1919
Vickers	HMS *B.10*	I20	B Class	28.3.1906	Damaged – PO – Scrapped	9.8.1916
Vickers	HMS *B.11*	I00	B Class	24.2.1906	PO – Scrapped	1919

▲ HMS *B.1* alongside HMS *Victory* in Portsmouth harbour. *(HM Submarine Museum)*

▲ HMS *B.1* with a civilian crew during Vickers' trials off Barrow-in-Furness.
(HM Submarine Museum)

▼ HMS *B.1*. *(HM Submarine Museum)*

▼ HMS *B.4*. *(HM Submarine Museum)*

▶ HMS *B.10* in dry dock at Venice after she had been bombed and sunk by Austrian aircraft in 1916. The damage was considered to be beyond repair, and she was scrapped. *(HM Submarine Museum)*

◀ Damage to HMS *B.10* included the weapons compartment, where wrecked torpedoes can be seen. *(HM Submarine Museum)*

C Class

The C Class were really an extension of the B Class, with little change in the structure or performance initially. However, with a total of 38 boats built between 1905 and 1910, various improvements were incorporated in the light of experience as the new boats were being built. With such a large requirement, it was decided that six of the boats would be built by HM Dockyard at Chatham – the first Royal Navy submarines not built by Vickers.

Safety was beginning to be recognised, and initially four of the boats included specific air locks, together with helmets. The idea was that this would give the crew vital time with air to breathe before escaping through the torpedo hatch. However, petrol engines continued to be used and were now being built by Vickers.

HMS C.11 was the first of the class to be lost, when she was struck by the SS Eddystone off Cromer on the night of 14 July 1909. A total of thirteen of the crew were lost, although three were rescued. HMS C.16 and C.17 also collided in the rush to rescue the survivors. Fortunately, there were no further casualties, although C.17 required towing back to Sheerness.

Once the First World War commenced, the casualties became more frequent. HMS C.31 was considered lost on 4 January 1915 during a patrol off the Belgian Coast. Despite a search, no trace was ever found.

U-boats were attacking and sinking an increasing number of British trawlers in the North Sea, and so a cunning plan was devised. On 23 June 1915, HMS C.24 was joined in the suspected fishing area by a decoy trawler, Taranaki. As the German U-40 moved in to make what she thought was an easy attack, she was caught by surprise and sunk, to become the first victim of the use of decoy ships by the Royal Navy. Another successful ambush was made the following month by HMS C.27, which was being towed submerged by the trawler Princess Louise. This resulted in U-23 being sunk off Aberdeen.

HMS C.33 continued with the plan in August, but having had no success she departed from the trawler Malta at the end of the patrol to head back home. However, C.33 failed to make it back to base. A search was made but no wreckage or survivors were found. Presumably she was the victim of a mine. Also in August, HMS C.29 was being towed submerged by the trawler Ariadne in the North Sea on another decoy patrol, but she struck a mine while submerged and was lost with all hands.

The sea mine had become a real threat to all shipping, but more especially submarines. While on the surface the crew of a stricken ship had the chance to jump overboard and probably find a ship's lifeboat. With submarines, they were often submerged already and so would quickly flood and sink. Even on the surface conditions were so cramped that it would be virtually impossible for all the crew to escape. For those who did, there would be no lifeboat, and the water temperature in the North Sea in winter gave survivors just minutes before they succumbed to the cold.

HMS C.31 was tasked with patrolling off the Belgian Coast in January 1915, and HMS C.33 was on patrol in the North Sea the following August. Both boats failed to return, and it was assumed that they were sunk by mines.

In 1917 the losses of Allied merchant shipping continued to increase at an ever-spiralling rate that was now unsustainable. Various schemes were considered in a desperate need to reduce the losses which would soon strangle the British ability to continue fighting. The U-boats were the primary culprits, and the Admiralty was desperate for them to be checked.

In 1917, HMS C.7 successfully attacked and sank UC-63 and UC-68, and HMS C.15 sank UC-65, while in July HMS C.34 was torpedoed by U-52 off the Shetlands.

However, HMS C.16 was lost during training, following a collision with HMS Melampus on 16 April 1917. In just 16 feet (4.9 m) of water, Lt Anderson attempted to escape through the torpedo tube with a message, but was unable to emerge from the tube. Another plan to escape through the forward hatch was foiled by external damage and resulted in the boat being flooded, with the loss of the whole crew, when it could not be re-sealed. The captain had made a full report and placed it in a bottle which was discovered by his body during the salvage operation. C.16 underwent a refit and was subsequently returned to service.

A number of boats were assigned to the Baltic Flotilla, and operated in various parts of the Baltic to frustrate and attack German shipping movements. In 1917, HMS C.26, C.27, C.32 and C.35 had reached Archangel and were then loaded onto barges and transported to the Baltic using the Siberian Railway and River Dvina. Once in the Baltic, HMS C.32 was badly damaged in October while attacking German warships. As a result she was run aground to allow the crew to escape and then destroyed in the Gulf of Riga.

In April 1918, Germany concluded a peace treaty with Russia which agreed to the surrender of the Baltic Flotilla to Germany. To ensure this did not happen, the crews of HMS C.26, C.27 and C.35, plus four E Class, all destroyed their boats, mainly by scuttling in Helsingfors Bay, before they came ashore and surrendered.

The Germans had a substantial force of U-boats operating out of Bruges which were attacking shipping in the Channel and Western Approaches, as well as into the Atlantic. A daring plan was devised by Rear Admiral Roger Keyes to block access to the German-occupied port, trapping many of the U-boats inside. This plan entailed the use of an old submarine with its bow filled with explosive. Two boats were made available – HMS *C.3*, which was commanded by Lt Richard Douglas Sandford, and HMS *C.1*, coincidentally commanded by Lt Cdr F. H. Sandford – the elder brother of Richard Sandford. *C.3* would carry the explosive and *C.1* would recover the crew and bring them back home. On 23 April 1919, HMS *C.1* and *C.3* quietly slipped their moorings and set course for Zeebrugge on the Belgian coast. Zeebrugge was near the entrance of a canal which was used by the U-boats to access their pens at Bruges. At the mouth of the canal was a viaduct which crossed the river and linked the German defences on the Mole with the shore. The objective was to position *C.3* next to the support girders and detonate the explosives, and the explosion would destroy the viaduct, resulting in an obstruction for the U-boats and the cutting-off supplies for the German defences on the Mole.

The attack was co-ordinated with an assault on the German defences along the Mole. HMS *C.3* made her way in the darkness and laid smoke as she approached the coast. With around a mile and a half left to run, the wind changed direction, leaving her exposed but the German guns seemed to be preoccupied in repelling the assault.

It later transpired that the Germans were fully aware of HMS *C.3* and thought that she was attempting to enter the river to try to reach Bruges, and were setting an ambush for her. Sandford and the crew of *C.3* were very much aware of the danger they were in. An easy option would have been to use the gyro steering and abandon the boat at a safe distance, but while this would have got the boat into the right area, it was vital to the mission for the explosive to be accurately placed. As they approached the viaduct, Sandford ordered the crew onto the casing.

As HMS *C.3* struck the girders at the centre of the viaduct and came to rest in the ideal position, the horrified Germans realised what was happening and opened fire. A skiff was lowered from the boat, the five-minute fuse was lit and the crew abandoned *C.3*. Some of the gunfire was directed straight on the crew in the skiff as they frantically rowed back out to sea, very much aware that they could all be killed by the explosion if they did not get far enough away. Sandford was hit twice by the gunfire, which also injured some other crew members. All of a sudden there was an almighty explosion as the charge detonated, and pieces of wood and metal rained around them. Meanwhile Lt Cdr Sandford aboard HMS *C.1* had launched a picket boat which met the exhausted but jubilant six members of *C.3* and took them back to the escort and then back home. On 23 July 1918, Lt Sandford was awarded the Victoria Cross, each of the four ratings was decorated with the CGM, Lt Howell-Price RN received the DSO.

According to Winston Churchill, 'The raid on Zeebrugge may well rank as the finest feat of arms in the Great War, and certainly as an episode unsurpassed in the history of the Royal Navy.'

HMS *C.14* was damaged in Plymouth Sound when she collided with the dredger *Hopper No. 27* and sank on 10 December 1913, but all the crew were rescued. She was salvaged a few days later and returned to service.

On 6 July 1918, HMS *C.25* was at sea off Harwich when she came under attack from German aircraft. She was badly damaged from the effects of the bombs but managed to struggle back to Harwich. She lost six of her crew in the attack.

In October 1918 HMS *C.12* lost power making her way downstream in the River Humber while departing from Immingham. With no control, she collided with some destroyers that were alongside and was holed. Again, the crew were able to escape before she sank. She was salvaged a few days later, and after some repairs she was returned to service.

All the 38 C Class boats built managed to acquit themselves reasonably well during the First World War. They had sunk four German U-boats for a loss of four of their own to enemy action. Of those that survived the war most were paid off in 1919 and 1920 and scrapped shortly after.

Class	C Class, Group 1	
Role	Coastal Submarine	
	IMPERIAL	METRIC
Sub Disp – surfaced	287 tons	291.59 tonnes
Sub Disp – submerged	316 tons	321.06 tonnes
Length	142 ft	43.28 m
Beam	13 ft 6 in	4.11 m
Draught	11 ft 6 in	3.50 m
Propulsion	1 × 600 bhp Vickers petrol engine	
	1 × 300 ehp electric motor	
Speed	12 knots surfaced, 8 knots submerged	
Range	1,300 nm at 9 knots surfaced, 16 nm at 8 knots submerged	
Armament	2 × 18 in (457 mm) torpedo tubes (bow)	
	4 torpedoes carried	
Complement (Officers/Men)	16 (2/14)	

Builder	Name	Pennant No.	Class	Launched	Fate	Date
Vickers Armstrong	HMS *C.1*	I31	C Class, Group 1	10.7.1906	PO – Scrapped	10.1920
Vickers Armstrong	HMS *C.2*	I32	C Class, Group 1	10.7.1906	PO – Scrapped	10.1920
Vickers Armstrong	HMS *C.3*	I33	C Class, Group 1	3.10.1906	Destroyed	23.4.1918
Vickers Armstrong	HMS *C.4*	I34	C Class, Group 1	18.10.1906	PO – Scrapped	2.1922
Vickers Armstrong	HMS *C.5*	I35	C Class, Group 1	20.8.1906	PO – Scrapped	10.1919
Vickers Armstrong	HMS *C.6*	I36	C Class, Group 1	20.8.1906	PO – Scrapped	11.1919
Vickers Armstrong	HMS *C.7*	I37	C Class, Group 1	15.2.1907	PO – Scrapped	12.1919
Vickers Armstrong	HMS *C.8*	I38	C Class, Group 1	15.2.1907	PO – Scrapped	10.1920
Vickers Armstrong	HMS *C.9*	I39	C Class, Group 1	3.4.1907	PO – Scrapped	7.1922
Vickers Armstrong	HMS *C.10*	I40	C Class, Group 1	15.4.1907	PO – Scrapped	7.1922
Vickers Armstrong	HMS *C.11*	I41	C Class, Group 1	27.5.1907	Sunk – Accident	14.7.1909
Vickers Armstrong	HMS *C.12*	I42	C Class, Group 1	9.9.1907	PO – Scrapped	1920
Vickers Armstrong	HMS *C.13*	I43	C Class, Group 1	9.11.1907	PO – Scrapped	2.1920
Vickers Armstrong	HMS *C.14*	I44	C Class, Group 1	7.12.1907	PO – Scrapped	12.1921
Vickers Armstrong	HMS *C.15*	I45	C Class, Group 1	21.1.1908	PO – Scrapped	2.1922
Vickers Armstrong	HMS *C.16*	I46	C Class, Group 1	19.3.1908	PO – Scrapped	8.1922
HM Dockyard, Chatham	HMS *C.17*	I47	C Class, Group 1	13.8.1908	PO – Scrapped	11.1919
HM Dockyard, Chatham	HMS *C.18*	I48	C Class, Group 1	10.10.1908	PO – Scrapped	5.1921

▲ One of the four C Class boats that were towed to Archangel and then transferred some 400 miles by lighter across lakes and along canals and rivers to Petrograd (St Petersburg). They were then able to assist the Russians in attacking German ships in the Baltic. (*HM Submarine Museum*)

▶ HMS *C.1* in a floating dock with the bow cap and inner door open, exposing one of the 18 in (457 mm) torpedo tubes.

(*HM Submarine Museum*)

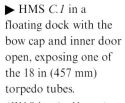

▲ Three C Class boats alongside (HMS *C.2*, *C.1* and *C.4*). *(HM Submarine Museum)*

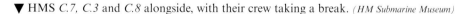

▼ HMS *C.7*, *C.3* and *C.8* alongside, with their crew taking a break. *(HM Submarine Museum)*

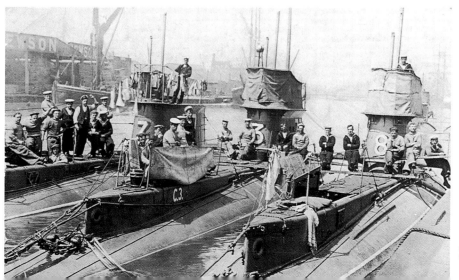

▲ The shattered viaduct linking the Mole off Zeebrugge with the coast. In the middle can be seen the remains of HMS *C.3*. *(HM Submarine Museum)*

▼ HMS *C.11* in the floating dock at Haslar creek, being cleaned. She was subsequently lost in a collision with the SS *Eddystone* in July 1909. *(HM Submarine Museum)*

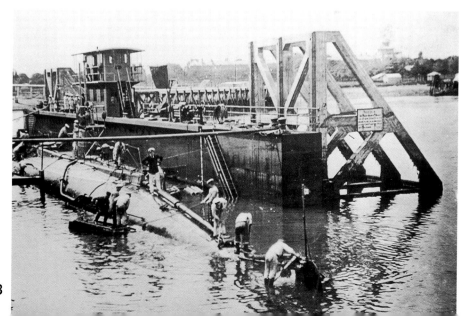

▲ HMS *C.14* in dry dock at Devonport. She is seen here having been salvaged after sinking when she struck the dredger *Hopper No 27* in December 1913. Fortunately, nobody lost their life on this occasion, and after refurbishment she was returned to service. *(HM Submarine Museum)*

▼ HMS *C.14* under way. *(HM Submarine Museum)*

▲ Workers on the bow of HMS *C.14* at Devonport during her refurbishment. *(HM Submarine Museum)*

▼ HMS *C.16* under way. *(HM Submarine Museum)*

Class	C Class, Group 2
Role	Coastal Submarine

	IMPERIAL	METRIC
Sub Disp – surfaced	290 tons	294.64 tonnes
Sub Disp – submerged	320 tons	325.12 tonnes
Length	142 ft 3 in	43.36 m
Beam	13 ft 6 in	4.11 m
Draught	11 ft 6 in	3.50 m
Propulsion	1 × 600 bhp Vickers petrol engine	
	1 × 300 ehp electric motor	
Speed	12 knots surfaced, 6.5 knots submerged	
Range	1,300 nm at 9 knots surfaced, 16 nm at 8 knots submerged	
Armament	2 × 18 in (457 mm) torpedo tubes (bow)	
	4 torpedoes carried	
Complement (Officers/Men)	16 (2/14)	

Builder	Name	Pennant No.	Class	Launched	Fate	Date
HM Dockyard, Chatham	HMS C.19	I49	C Class, Group 2	20.3.1909	PO – Scrapped	2.1920
HM Dockyard, Chatham	HMS C.20	I50	C Class, Group 2	27.11.1909	PO – Scrapped	5.1921
Vickers Armstrong	HMS C.21	I51	C Class, Group 2	26.9.1908	PO – Scrapped	12.1921
Vickers Armstrong	HMS C.22	I52	C Class, Group 2	10.10.1908	PO – Scrapped	2.1920
Vickers Armstrong	HMS C.23	I53	C Class, Group 2	26.11.1908	PO – Scrapped	12.1921
Vickers Armstrong	HMS C.24	I54	C Class, Group 2	26.11.1908	PO – Scrapped	5.1921
Vickers Armstrong	HMS C.25	I55	C Class, Group 2	10.3.1909	PO – Scrapped	1921
Vickers Armstrong	HMS C.26	I56	C Class, Group 2	20.3.1909	Lost – Scuttled	3/4.4.1918
Vickers Armstrong	HMS C.27	I57	C Class, Group 2	22.4.1909	Lost – Scuttled	5.4.1918
Vickers Armstrong	HMS C.28	I58	C Class, Group 2	22.4.1909	PO – Scrapped	1921
Vickers Armstrong	HMS C.29	I59	C Class, Group 2	19.6.1909	Lost – Mine	29.8.1915
Vickers Armstrong	HMS C.30	I60	C Class, Group 2	19.7.1909	PO – Scrapped	8.1921
Vickers Armstrong	HMS C.31	I61	C Class, Group 2	2.9.1909	Lost – Mine?	1.1915
Vickers Armstrong	HMS C.32	I62	C Class, Group 2	29.9.1909	Lost – Scuttled	22.10.1917
HM Dockyard, Chatham	HMS C.33	I63	C Class, Group 2	10.5.1910	Lost – Mine	4.8.1915
HM Dockyard, Chatham	HMS C.34	I64	C Class, Group 2	8.6.1910	Lost – Torpedo	21.7.1917
Vickers Armstrong	HMS C.35	I65	C Class, Group 2	2.11.1909	Lost – Scuttled	5.4.1918
Vickers Armstrong	HMS C.36	I66	C Class, Group 2	30.11.1909	PO – Scrapped	6.1919
Vickers Armstrong	HMS C.37	I67	C Class, Group 2	1.1.1910	PO – Scrapped	6.1919
Vickers Armstrong	HMS C.37	I68	C Class, Group 2	10.2.1910	PO – Scrapped	6.1919

▲ HMS *C.25* under attack from German seaplanes in the North Sea during July 1918. *(HM Submarine Museum)*

▲ HMS *C.25* being fired at and struggling to dive. *(HM Submarine Museum)*

▶ HMS *C.31* under way. *(HM Submarine Museum)*

◀ HMS *C.32* under way. *(HM Submarine Museum)*

▶ HMS *C.34* alongside HMS *Victory* in Portsmouth harbour.

(HM Submarine Museum)

D Class

The first Royal Navy all-diesel-powered submarines were the D Class, and this remained the predominant means of submarine propulsion until the arrival of nuclear power with HMS *Dreadnought*. The dangerous use of petrol engines in the confined space of submarines died out as the surviving boats of the previous classes were paid off. The D Class also introduced the twin screw and the saddle tank arrangements.

Approval to build the D Class was given in 1906, and for the first time the Admiralty produced the basic design. This was a fresh design rather than a further development of the original Holland. It was intended that this new class of boat would be an effective Patrol Submarine. It would encapsulate all the positive features of the earlier boats and eliminate the bad.

Eight D Class boats were built, six by Vickers at Barrow and two at HM Dockyard, Chatham. A further two were ordered – HMS *D.9* and *D.10* – and laid down, but were cancelled and completed as HMS *E.1* and *E.2*.

Surface and submerged speed were still only marginally above those of the previous boats, but these new boats were now capable of undertaking a patrol, because of their greater range, which had now exceeded 2,000 miles (3,200 km). Their manoeuvrability was also improved. The conning tower was further developed to provide better visibility. A new feature of the D boats was the positioning of main water ballast tanks to outside the hull in a saddle tank arrangement, to provide more internal space.

HMS *D.4* became the first Royal Navy submarine to feature a gun, albeit a small 12-pdr. It was mounted in a housing that could be retracted into the conning tower when it was not required. It also became the first boat to have a stern-firing torpedo and a wireless system which enabled them to transmit, as opposed to only receive, as on earlier boats. The pair of bow torpedo tubes were mounted vertically, which enabled a more streamlined shape.

When the First World War commenced, the D boats were positioned along the British east coast, making operations easy in the North Sea and Heligoland. HMS *D.5* was the first boat to fire a torpedo, but it had been set for peacetime training and ran deep without hitting the target.

On 3 November 1914, HMS *D.3, D.5* and *E.10* were despatched to intercept German battleships that were bombarding the coast near Gorston, Norfolk, the first such action of the war. Unfortunately *D.5* struck a mine off Yarmouth and was lost. Later that month HMS *D.2* was lost after being shelled by a German warship. In March 1918 HMS *D.3* was sunk accidentally in the English Channel when she was bombed by a French airship, while HMS *D.6* was attacked and sunk by the German U-boat *UB-73* off Ireland in June 1918.

HMS *D.7* was the only D Class boat to conduct a successful attack, when she sank *U-45* off Malin Head on 12 September 1917.

HMS *D.4, D.7* and *D.8* survived the war and were paid off in July 1919 and scrapped. HMS *D.1* was employed for some trials and then used as a target and sunk just before the end of the war.

Class	D Class	
Role	Overseas Submarine	
	IMPERIAL	**METRIC**
Sub Disp – surfaced	483 tons*	490.73 tonnes
Sub Disp – submerged	595 tons*	604.52 tonnes
Length	164 ft 7 in*	50.16 m
Beam	20 ft 5 in*	6.22 m
Draught	11 ft	3.35 m
Propulsion	2 × 600 bhp Vickers diesel engine 2 × 277 ehp electric motor	
Speed	14 knots surfaced, 9 knots submerged	
Range	2,500 nm at 10 knots surfaced, 45 nm at 5 knots submerged	
Armament	3 × 18 in (457 mm) torpedo tubes (2 bow, 1 stern) 6 torpedoes carried	
Complement (Officers/Men)	25 (2/23)	
Data note	*D.1 and D.2 slightly smaller	

Builder	Name	Pennant No.	Class	Launched	Fate	Date
Vickers	HMS *D.1*	I71	D Class	16.5.1908	PO – Expended as target	23.10.1918
Vickers	HMS *D.2*	I72	D Class	25.5.1910	Lost – Gunfire	25.11.1914
Vickers	HMS *D.3*	I73	D Class	17.10.1910	Lost – Sunk in error	15.3.1918
Vickers	HMS *D.4*	I74	D Class	27.5.1911	PO – Scrapped	19.12.1921
Vickers	HMS *D.5*	I75	D Class	28.8.1911	Lost – Mine	3.11.1914
Vickers	HMS *D.6*	I76	D Class	23.10.1911	Lost – Torpedo	28.6.1918
HM Dockyard, Chatham	HMS *D.7*	I77	D Class	14.1.1911	PO – Scrapped	12.1921
HM Dockyard, Chatham	HMS *D.8*	I78	D Class	23.9.1911	PO – Scrapped	12.1921
HM Dockyard, Chatham	HMS *D.9*		D Class		Cancelled – Built as *E.1*	
HM Dockyard, Chatham	HMS *D.10*		D Class		Cancelled – Built as *E.2*	

▲ HMS *D.2* under way. *(HM Submarine Museum)*

▼ Close-up of the mid-section of HMS *D.2*, showing the conning tower with a canvas screen to give some protection from the elements. *(HM Submarine Museum)*

▲ HMS *D.1* under way. *(HM Submarine Museum)*

▼ HMS *D.2* entering harbour. Her stern cap covering the stern torpedo tube is visible. *(HM Submarine Museum)*

▶ HMS *D.4* and *D.3* alongside. *(HM Submarine Museum)*

◀ HMS *D.1* alongside with HMS *E.29* and *E.54* either side. *(HM Submarine Museum)*

E Class

The E Class was one of the most effective boats in the Royal Navy. The fact that so many of these boats were lost was not through any technical problem, but because of the numbers built. A total of twenty-eight were lost of the fifty-seven built. They were the spearhead of Royal Navy submarine operations and were constantly placed at the front line.

In an attempt to get increased power, larger engines were fitted, but these then required a larger hull to accommodate them. Unfortunately the end result was only a small improvement in performance; however, this did allow an increase in fuel and weapons. One problem with the larger boats was their manoeuvrability. With it necessary to point the boat at the target to fire a torpedo it was then necessary to move forward, and so closer, from an already close firing position to effect an escape. This would make a possible enemy counter-attack more effective. Such were the reservations of this high-risk firing evolution that there was even consideration of omitting bow torpedo tubes. The answer was to be able to fire broadside.

The D Class introduced the torpedo tubes in the beam, but this required a further increase in hull size, to accommodate the torpedo tubes and loading space. The E Class were the first British submarines to have watertight bulkheads, enabling compartments to be sealed in case of emergency. The previous Holland through to the D Class all comprised a single compartment. While this arrangement greatly increased the complexity of pipe and cable runs, the safety benefits were appreciated by all submarine builders and incorporated into their own designs. Crew requirements were now starting to become a consideration with the increased range now making lengthy periods on board routine.

Following the outbreak of war with Germany, the Admiralty convened a hasty meeting with a number of shipbuilders to establish an urgent build programme for the E Class boats. Beardmore was already building two on subcontract to Vickers for the Turkish government. These were immediately taken over and subjected to some design changes before completion and delivery to the Royal Navy. Orders for a further 38 boats were placed on top of the 18 that has been placed before the war. The Group 1 boats were taking in the region of 20–30 months to complete, but with the urgency of war and the experience Vickers had built up, this was reduced dramatically, with HMS *E.19* being completed in just eight months, although most took about a year.

The first Royal Navy submarine war patrol commenced on 5 August, and was conducted by HMS *E.6* and *E.8* from Harwich. They were towed by destroyers out into the North Sea, and then spent two days observing German Navy movements in the Heligoland Bight.

A substantial force of submarines, including seven E boats, were despatched as the British Baltic submarine flotilla in 1914 to assist the Russians. They proved to be very successful in attacking German shipping, especially those carrying Swedish iron ore back to Germany. HMS *E.19* was the first Royal Navy submarine to sink a merchant ship – the *Svionia* – on 3 October 1915 in the Baltic, and it rapidly built up a score of eight sunk, including the light cruiser *Undine*. HMS *E.1* torpedoed *Moltke* in the Gulf of Riga on 19 August 1915. The was the first torpedoing of a German Dreadnought by a Royal Navy submarine, much to the satisfaction of the crew. On 23 October 1915, HMS *E.8* sank the armoured cruiser *Prinz Adalbert*, with only a few survivors. So effective were the boats of this flotilla that the Germans actually withdrew major warships from the Baltic. They didn't have it all their own way, though HMS *E.18* was sunk by SMS *K* in May 1916.

In October 1915 HMS *E.24* and *E.41* were in build when the order was changed for them to be completed as minelayers. In all, six of the E boats were modified to carry mines located in chutes in the saddle tanks. Although this still required the submarine to operate in extremely hostile enemy inshore waters, this was preferable to carrying them internally. This would have used up valuable defensive torpedo-carrying capacity, which was already reduced with the elimination of the beam tubes

On 18 October 1914, HMS *E.3* was attacked by the German U-boat *U-27*, and had the misfortune to become the first Royal Navy submarine to be lost in action. Her wreckage was found near Schiermonnikoog in 1997. HMS *E.10* and *E.37* were considered lost during a patrol in the North Sea during January 1915, when they failed to return home.

Meanwhile, in the latter half of 1915, the war in the Dardanelles and the Sea of Marmara saw considerable action from the Royal Navy, especially from submarines, some of it quite heroic! HMS *E.2* sank a Turkish steamer in Araki Bay on 21 August, and a week later joined HMS *E.11* bombarding a railway yard at Mudania. HMS *E.7* used her gun to fire on and block the railway line near Ismid in July.

HMS *E.11* wreaked havoc wherever she went. During May, in the command of Lt Cdr Martin Eric Nasmith, she passed through the heavily protected Dardanelles. She then attacked and sank no fewer than seven Turkish vessels around the Sea of Marmara, including the *Stambul* in Constantinople, and forced another ashore. As though that was not enough, having cleared the worst of the Turkish defences in the Dardanelles, and returning to periscope depth once clear, it was then that Nasmith spotted a further transport ship, and, determined to complete the task, returned under the minefield to fire yet another torpedo. As the ship sank, Nasmith carefully navigated *E.11* through the strong currents and under the minefield for a final time before setting course for the depot ship.

HMS *E.11* returned in November and sank the Turkish battleship *Barbarousse Heyreddine* on the 8th, followed by the gunboat *Sevket Numa* in the sea of Marmara on 20 November and the Turkish MTB *Yar Hissar* on 3 December.

HMS *E.14* attacked and sank a Turkish transport in the Sea of Marmara on 29 April, followed by the gunboat *Nurelbahr* on 1 May and the Turkish transport *Gul Djemal* on the 10th.

These raids were not without a cost. HMS *E.15* was attempting an attack when she ran aground at Kephez Point on 17 April in range of the Turkish Fort Dardanus. She was soon under fire, and after several hits, one of which killed her captain, the crew, of which seven were killed, had no other alternative but to surrender. With the rest of the crew taken prisoner, HMS *Majestic* and *Triumph* torpedoed *E.15* to ensure that she didn't fall into Turkish hands.

These exploits did not go unrecognised, for on 21 May 1915 Cdr Edward Courney Boyle was awarded the Victoria Cross for conspicuous bravery when in command of HMS *E.14*. He took the boat under enemy minefields and entered the Sea of Marmara on 27 April. Despite the strong currents, which made navigation difficult, and the presence of enemy patrol boats in the narrow waters, he continued with his attack and sank two Turkish gunboats and a large freighter.

On 24 May 1915, Lt Cdr Geoffrey Saxon White was posthumously awarded the Victoria Cross for the role he played in trying the ensure the safety of his crew when they tried to sink the *Goeben*. This German battleship had struck mines during a raid on Mundros, resulting in her running aground in the relative safety of Nargara Point in the Dardanelles to save her. Some 250 Allied air attacks had been flown to bomb her, but without success. Such was the need and opportunity to eliminate this large troublesome enemy warship that HMS *E.14* was again despatched at dusk on 27 January from Imbros to try to torpedo her.

As HMS *E.14* approached the area she became snagged in anti-submarine nets. Eventually she was freed and managed to continue to Nargara Point, only to find that *Goeben* had been refloated and had already left. Disappointed, the only course of action was to return. As the boat passed Chanak, White spotted a large merchant ship and fired a torpedo. For some reason it exploded almost immediately, causing them considerable damage. The crew struggled to contain the leaks, and she continued her escape submerged for a further two hours, but they were fighting a losing battle. Because of the flooding, *E.14* was becoming uncontrollable. She surfaced but was still within range of the forts along the shore, and they sprang into action with accurate fire. *E.14* was hit badly, and so White altered course and headed for the shore to give his crew a chance of reaching safety. White was killed as further rounds hit the boat, which then sank before she reached the shore.

On 24 June 1915, Lt Cdr Martin Eric Nasmith became the third E boat

commander in just over a month to be awarded a Victoria Cross for action in Turkish waters. Like Cdr Boyle, he successfully entered the Sea of Marmara and caused devastation.

The end result of these actions by Royal Navy submarines in 1915 was that the Turks had lost their battleships and half their merchant fleet. They were left with just a few naval vessels that were manned by crews who were now feeling very insecure.

In August, HMS *E.13* suffered a compass failure while trying to join up with the Baltic Flotilla. This resulted in her becoming grounded on a mud bank in the Saltholm Flat between Sweden and Denmark. The Danes, in whose waters she was stuck, were neutral, and under international law gave the captain 24 hours' notice to leave or be interned. When the Germans got wind of her predicament two destroyers soon appeared on the scene and conducted a series of gun and torpedo attacks.

With just a 12-pdr gun to defend themselves, they soon took casualties, and the captain gave the order to abandon ship. Still the Germans continued their attack, with more of the crew being killed while trying to swim away. It wasn't until the intervention of a Danish destroyer, which positioned herself between the survivors and the German destroyers, that they broke off their attack. Sixteen of the crew were rescued and interned.

HMS *E.7* was attempting to enter the Dardanelles in September, but became entangled in anti-submarine nets. Her disturbance attracted some Turkish naval craft, and she was attacked and forced to surface. The crew were captured and taken prisoner, and *E.7* was scuttled.

Communications have always been a problem for submarines, none more so than during the First World War. Rendezvous were frequently prearranged – especially for replenishment or regrouping. Unfortunately, on 6 November 1915, HMS *E.20* fell foul of this procedure when the French submarine *Turquoise* was captured. The French had failed to destroy the secret documents which gave the rendezvous position, and they were found during a search by the Germans. As a result *UB-14* was lying in wait, and then attacked and sank *E.20* as soon as she appeared.

HMS *E.6* was lost on Boxing Day 1915 when she struck a mine in the North Sea off Harwich. HMS *E.17* was lost almost a year after she was launched, when on 6 January she ran aground in the Texel estuary off Denmark and was damaged. Her crew was rescued by the RNN cruiser *Noord Brabant*, and *E.17* sank. The conning tower was later recovered and presented to the Royal Naval Submarine Museum, Gosport, where it is currently displayed.

HMS *E.5* survived an engine room explosion in June 1913 which killed or injured a number of her crew, but was considered lost on 7 March 1916 in the North Sea when she was attacked by the German cruiser *Strassburg* and failed to return to base.

HMS *E.24* was the initial E Class minelayer, and successfully completed placing her first load of mines in the mouth of the Elbe in March 1916. Later that month she disappeared during her next patrol, and was thought to have been a victim of an enemy mine. In 1973 her wreck was found, confirming that she had indeed been destroyed by a mine.

Trials were conducted with HMS *E.22* modified to carry a pair of Sopwith Schneider seaplanes attached to her deck in April 1916. The intention was for the aircraft to be launched in the North Sea to intercept the German Zeppelin airships which were attacking London and other cities. However, the aircraft were too frail to be operated in anything less than calm conditions, and the trials ended. Later that month *E.22* was torpedoed by *UB-18*. Of her crew of 33 just two survived to be rescued.

By coincidence, the following month HMS *E.31* was operating with various other ships when a Zeppelin appeared overhead. She quickly dived to avoid being attacked. After a short period she came up to periscope depth, where it was noticed that the Zeppelin was in difficulties. She was promptly brought to the surface and the 12-pdr gun used to shoot the airship down. Seven of the surviving crew were captured.

Also in May, HMS *E.18* transmitted a radio report to say that she had fired a torpedo at the destroyer *V100*, blowing her bows off. This was the last that was ever heard of *E.18*. Despite the massive damage to *V100*, she managed to limp back to port.

In July a German patrol boat reported that it was following a trail of oil near the Ems, possibly from a submarine. The next day a submarine was spotted and attacked. HMS *E.26* failed to return from a patrol in that area, and so it was assumed to be the same boat.

On 15 August 1916, HMS *E.4* was submerged when she collided with HMS *E.41* near Harwich during a training exercise. Sadly, all the crew of *E.4* were lost; however, seven of *E.41*, which was surfaced at the time, managed to escape. Both boats were salvaged, repaired by the following May and remained in service until they were scrapped in 1922.

In the North Sea a few days later, HMS *E.23* spotted some of the German Fleet off Terschelling. First she attacked with torpedoes the battle cruiser *Seydlitz*, but missed and then fired at the *Westfalen*. This time a torpedo struck home and she was damaged. The battleship managed to limp back to port for repairs, but her threat was confined for a period. About the same time, HMS *E.16* failed to return to base after her patrol off the Scandinavian coast.

HMS *E.54* spotted *UC-10* in the North Sea near the Schouwen Bank light boat. Carefully she manoeuvred into position and then launched her attack, which sank the U-boat.

HMS *E.16* had been successful with sinking the MTB *C188* in July 1915 and U-boat *U-6* the following September, but was lost in August 1916 with all crew during a patrol off the Heligoland Bight. In November, HMS *E.30* also failed to return from a patrol in the North Sea. Both presumably were mine victims. In March 1917 HMS *E.49* was lost after she struck a mine off the Shetlands. The mine was thought to have been laid by *UC-76* only two days previously. In August 1917, HMS *E.47* was lost during a patrol in the North Sea.

In September 1917, HMS *E.9* sank the German cruiser *Hela* and the destroyer *S116* off Heligoland. On returning to base, Lt Max Horton raised the Jolly Roger – a tradition that still continues, to show that the boat has successfully conducted an action against the enemy. It later transpired that the German Navy halted their use of the North Sea for naval exercises following Horton's attacks. Instead they used the Baltic.

On 19 January 1917 HMS *E.43* was en route from Harwich to commence her patrol off Terschelling in foul weather when she struck something. Unable to see anything, she returned to port to check her damage. It was only later, when HMS *E.36* failed to return, that it was discovered what she had actually hit. During October, HMS *E.45* sank *UC-62* and *UC-79* during separate attacks in the North Sea.

In February 1918, HMS *E.50* failed to return from her patrol in the North Sea – she was thought to have struck a mine.

The Russians signed the German–Russian armistice, the Treaty of Brest Litovsk, in December 1917, and a German peace treaty with Finland was agreed four months later. Part of the requirement was that the British Baltic flotilla would be surrendered to the Germans. To ensure that the Germans did not get their hands on any of these valuable boats, the flotilla Commanding Officer ordered that the surviving boats must be scuttled before their crews came ashore. As a result three C Class and four E Class boats were destroyed by their own crews in April 1918.

In April 1918, HMS *E.42* was on patrol when she sighted a number of large wa ships. Wary of getting too close to the powerful ships, torpedoes were fired at a long range but missed. Shortly afterwards, the battle cruiser *Moltke* was spotted struggling on her own with an engine problem. This time *E.42* was perfectly positioned and attacked. The torpedo struck her, and although she did not sink she was put out of action.

HMS *E.34* successfully attacked and sank *UB-16* on 10 May 1918, but failed to return home two months later – probably another victim of a mine. The next day, HMS *E.35* successfully attacked the huge 1,512 ton German *U-154* merchant cruiser submarine.

In 1999 the wreck of a submarine was found in the Sea of Marmara off Turkey. Although HMS *E.20* was lost in this area in November 1915, it is thought that this was *AE.2* of the Royal Australian Navy, which was also lost in this area on 30 April 1915. HMAS *AE.2* was entering the Dardanelles to join the Royal Navy boats already there when she spotted, attacked and sank a Turkish gunboat. However, a few days later in the Sea of Marmara, she encountered the Turkish torpedo boat *Sultan Hisar*. She instigated a dive, but control was lost and she broke surface and dived again. When she broke surface again, *Sultan Hisar* was ready and waiting, and opened fire and holed the hull. With a crippled boat, the captain ordered all hands on deck and then scuttled her. It is hoped that the boat will be raised.

The RAN received two E Class boats, HMAS *AE.1* and *AE.2*, both of which were lost. *AE.1* was on patrol with a mixed RAN/RN crew in the St George's Straits in September 1914 and disappeared without trace.

Of the 58 E Class boats ordered, 29 were lost to various causes and one was cancelled. A total of 29 E Class boats survived the war, and nearly all were scrapped during 1921–3. Two of these had been damaged and sunk but repaired. HMS *E.48* was the last survivor, and was used for training purposes, ending up as a target until she too was scrapped in 1928.

The six minelayers laid almost 2,500 mines, primarily in the North Sea but also some in the Mediterranean. Three of them were sunk, although one was salvaged and returned to operational service.

Class	E Class, Group 1	
Role	Overseas Submarine	

	IMPERIAL	METRIC
Sub Disp – surfaced	655 tons	665.48 tonnes
Sub Disp – submerged	796 tons	808.73 tonnes
Length	176 ft	53.65 m
Beam	22 ft 6 in	6.86 m
Draught	12 ft	3.66 m
Propulsion	2 × 800 bhp Vickers diesel engines	
	2 × 420 ehp electric motors	
Speed	15 knots surface, 9 knots submerged	
Range	3,225 nm at 10 knots surfaced, 85 nm at 5 knots submerged	
Armament	4 × 18 in (457 mm) torpedo tubes (1 bow, 2 beam, 1 stern)	
	8 torpedoes carried	
	1 × gun (various calibres fitted from 1915)	
Complement (Officers/Men)	30 (3/27)	

Builder	Name	Pennant No.	Class	Launched	Fate	Date
HM Dockyard, Chatham	HMS *E.1*	I81	E Class, Group 1	9.11.1912	Lost – Scuttled	3.4.1918
HM Dockyard, Chatham	HMS *E.2*	I82	E Class, Group 1	23.11.1912	PO – Scrapped	3.1921
Vickers	HMS *E.3*	I83	E Class, Group 1	29.10.1912	Lost – Torpedo	18.10.1914
Vickers	HMS *E.4*	I84	E Class, Group 1	5.2.1912	PO – Scrapped	2.1922
Vickers	HMS *E.5*	I85	E Class, Group 1	17.5.1912	Lost – Mine	7.3.1916
Vickers	HMS *E.6*	I86	E Class, Group 1	12.11.1912	Lost – Mine	26.12.1915
HM Dockyard, Chatham	HMS *E.7*	I87	E Class, Group 1	2.10.1913	Lost – Attacked – Scuttled	4.9.1915
HM Dockyard, Chatham	HMS *E 8*	I88	E Class, Group 1	30.10.1913	Lost – Scuttled	3/4.4.1918
Vickers	*AE.1*		E Class, Group 1	22.5.1913	Lost – Unknown	19.9.1914
Vickers	*AE.2*		E Class, Group 1	18.6.1913	Lost – Attacked – Scuttled	30.4.1915

▲ HMS *E.4* was armed with various gun fits. Seen here with what would appear to be a pair of 4 in (101 mm) guns. She was also fitted with four 6-pdr guns early on in the First World War to fire at the Zeppelins as they crossed the North Sea to attack British targets. *(HM Submarine Museum)*

▲ HMS *E.4* and *E.9* alongside with HMS *D.5* outside. *(HM Submarine Museum)*

▶ Radio transmissions from submarines could prove difficult at times, and the Mk.1 carrier pigeon was considered to be easier, as well as being more secure. Here the First Lieutenant prepares to release a bird. *(HM Submarine Museum)*

34

▶ HMS *E.6.* *(HM Submarine Museum)*

▶ HMS *E.7.* *(HM Submarine Museum)*

Class	E Class, Group 2
Role	Overseas Submarine

	IMPERIAL	METRIC
Sub Disp – surfaced	667 tons	677.67 tonnes
Sub Disp – submerged	807 tons	819.91 tonnes
Length	181 ft	55.16 m
Beam	22 ft 6 in	6.86 m
Draught	12 ft 6 in	3.81 m
Propulsion	2 × 800 bhp Vickers diesel engines 2 × 420 ehp electric motors	
Speed	15 knots surfaced, 9 knots submerged	
Range	3,225 nm at 10 knots surfaced, 85 nm at 5 knots submerged	
Armament	5 × 18 in (457 mm) torpedo tubes (2 bow, 2 beam, 1 stern) 10 torpedoes carried 1 × gun (various calibres fitted from 1915)	
Complement (Officers/Men)	30 (3/27)	

Builder	Name	Pennant No.	Class	Launched	Fate	Date
Vickers	HMS E.9	I89	E Class, Group 2	29.11.1913	Lost – Scuttled	3/4.4.1918
Vickers	HMS E.10	I90	E Class, Group 2	29.11.1913	Lost – Unknown	18.1.1915
Vickers	HMS E.11	I91	E Class, Group 2	25.5.1914	PO – Scrapped	1921
HM Dockyard, Chatham	HMS E12	I92	E Class, Group 2	5.9.1914	PO – Scrapped	1921
HM Dockyard, Chatham	HMS E13	I93	E Class, Group 2	22.9.1914	Lost – Salvaged – Scrapped	18.8.1915
Vickers	HMS E.14	I94	E Class, Group 2	7.7.1914	Lost – Gunfire	28.1.1918
Vickers	HMS E.15	I95	E Class, Group 2	23.4.1914	Lost – Scuttled	17.4.1915
Vickers	HMS E 16	I96	E Class, Group 2	23.9.1914	Lost – Mine?	22.8.1916
Vickers	HMS E 17	I97	E Class, Group 2	16.1.1915	Lost – Scuttled	6.1.1916
Vickers	HMS E 18	I98	E Class, Group 2	4.3.1915	Lost – Gunfire	24.5.1916
Vickers	HMS E 19	I99	E Class, Group 2	13.5.1915	Scuttled	3/4.4.1918
Vickers	HMS E 20	I69	E Class, Group 2	12.6.1915	Lost – Torpedo	6.11.1915

▲ A stern view of HMS *E.19* under construction by Vickers at Barrow-in-Furness, with the single stern 18 in (457 mm) torpedo tube and twin-screw arrangement.

(HM Submarine Museum)

▲ HMS *E.9* taking on fresh torpedoes at Reval ready for another patrol in the Baltic. (*HM Submarine Museum*)

▲ HMS *E.18, E.9 and E.19* alongside the depot-ship HMS *Dvina* at Reval on the Russian Baltic coast. (*HM Submarine Museum*)

Class	E Class, Group 3	
Role	Overseas Submarine	

	IMPERIAL	METRIC
Sub Disp – surfaced	664 tons	674.62 tonnes
Sub Disp – submerged	780 tons	792.48 tonnes
Length	181 ft	55.16 m
Beam	22 ft 6 in	6.86 m
Draught	12 ft 6 in	3.81 m
Propulsion	2 × 800 bhp Vickers diesel engines	
	2 × 420 ehp electric motors	
Speed	15 knots surfaced, 9 knots submerged	
Range	3,225 nm at 10 knots surfaced, 85 nm at 5 knots submerged	
Armament	5 × 18 in (457 mm) torpedo tubes (2 bow, 2 beam, 1 stern)	
	10 torpedoes carried	
	1 × 2-pdr gun	
	1 × 12-pdr gun (not fitted to some)	
	Minelayer variants carry 20 mines in place of beam torpedo tubes	
Complement (Officers/Men)	30 (3/27)	

Builder	Name	Pennant No.	Class	Launched	Fate	Date
Vickers	HMS *E.21*	I70	E Class, Group 3	24.7.1915	PO – Scrapped	12.1921
Vickers	HMS *E.22*	I79	E Class, Group 3	27.8.1915	Lost – Torpedo	25.4.1916
Vickers	HMS *E.23*	E23	E Class, Group 3	28.9.1915	PO – Scrapped	9.1922
Vickers	HMS *E.24*	E24	E Class, Group 3	9.12.1915	Lost – Mine	24.3.1916
Beardmore	HMS *E.25*	E25	E Class, Group 3	23.8.1915	PO – Scrapped	12.1921
Beardmore	HMS *E.26*	E26	E Class, Group 3	11.11.1915	Lost – Unknown	3.7.1916
Yarrow	HMS *E.27*	E27	E Class, Group 3	9.6.1917	PO – Scrapped	9.1922
Yarrow	HMS *E.28*	E28	E Class, Group 3		Cancelled	
Armstrong	HMS *E.29*	E29	E Class, Group 3	1.6.1915	PO – Scrapped	9.1922
Armstrong	HMS *E.30*	E30	E Class, Group 3	29.6.1915	Lost – Mine?	22.11.1916
Scott's	HMS *E.31*	E31	E Class, Group 3	23.8.1915	PO – Scrapped	9.1922
J. S. White	HMS *E.32*	E32	E Class, Group 3	16.8.1916	PO – Scrapped	9.1922
Thornycroft	HMS *E.33*	E33	E Class, Group 3	18.4.1916	PO – Scrapped	9.1922
Thornycroft	HMS *E.34*	E34	E Class, Group 3	27.1.1917	Lost – Mine	20.7.1918
J. Brown	HMS *E.35*	E35	E Class, Group 3	20.5.1916	PO – Scrapped	9.1922
J. Brown	HMS *E.36*	E36	E Class, Group 3	16.9.1916	Lost – Accident	19.1.1917
Fairfield	HMS *E.37*	E37	E Class, Group 3	2.9.1915	Lost – Unknown	1.12.1916
Fairfield	HMS *E.38*	E38	E Class, Group 3	13.6.1916	PO – Scrapped	6.9.1922
Palmer's	HMS *E.39*	E39	E Class, Group 3	18.5.1916	PO – Scrapped	10.1921
Palmer's	HMS *E.40*	E40	E Class, Group 3	9.11.1916	PO – Scrapped	12.1921
Cammell Laird	HMS *E.41*	E41	E Class, Group 3	26.7.1915	PO – Scrapped	9.1922
Cammell Laird	HMS *E.42*	E42	E Class, Group 3	23.10.1915	PO – Scrapped	9.1922

Builder	Name	Pennant No.	Class	Launched	Fate	Date
Swan Hunter	HMS *E.43*	E43	E Class, Group 3	10.11.1915	PO – Scrapped	1.1921
Swan Hunter	HMS *E.44*	E44	E Class, Group 3	21.2.1916	PO – Scrapped	10.1921
Cammell Laird	HMS *E.45*	E45	E Class, Group 3	25.1.1916	PO – Scrapped	6.9.1922
Cammell Laird	HMS *E.46*	E46	E Class, Group 3	4.4.1916	PO – Scrapped	9.1922
Fairfield	HMS *E.47*	E47	E Class, Group 3	29.5.1916	Lost – Unknown	20.8.1917
Fairfield	HMS *E.48*	E48	E Class, Group 3	2.8.1916	PO – Scrapped	7.1928
Swan Hunter	HMS *E.49*	E49	E Class, Group 3	18.9.1916	Lost – Mine	12.3.1917
J. Brown	HMS *E.50*	E50	E Class, Group 3	13.11.1916	Lost – Mine	31.1.1918
Scott's	HMS *E.51*	E51	E Class, Group 3	30.11.1916	PO – Scrapped	1921
Denny	HMS *E.52*	E52	E Class, Group 3	25.1.1917	PO – Scrapped	1.1921
Beardmore	HMS *E.53*	E53	E Class, Group 3	1916	PO – Scrapped	9.1922
Beardmore	HMS *E.54*	E54	E Class, Group 3	1916	PO – Scrapped	12.1921
Denny	HMS *E.55*	E55	E Class, Group 3	5.2.1916	PO – Scrapped	9.1922
Denny	HMS *E.56*	E56	E Class, Group 3	19.6.1916	PO – Scrapped	6.1923
Vickers	HMS *E.57*	E57	E Class, Group 3		Cancelled – Built as L.1	
Vickers	HMS *E.58*	E58	E Class, Group 3		Cancelled – Built as L.2	

▼ HMS *E.31* under construction in Scott's yard showing some of the ribbed construction to which the skin plates are riveted, especially on the ballast tanks. *(HM Submarine Museum)*

▶ HMS *E.18* departs for another patrol in May 1916 as part of the British Baltic submarine flotilla based at Reval. This turned out to be her last, as she was not to return. She was sunk by the submarine trapper (Q-boat) SMS *K* off Bornholm on 24 May 1916. *(HM Submarine Museum)*

◀ HMS *E.21* also with a disruptive pattern camouflage. *(HM Submarine Museum)*

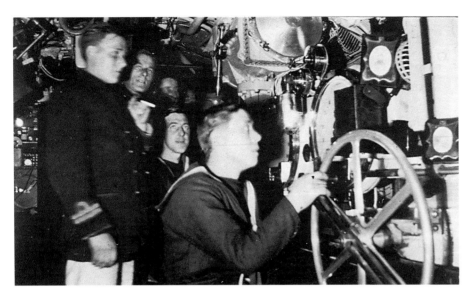

▲ Some of the boat's crew, together with a helmsman, at the after Diving Plane control. *(HM Submarine Museum)*

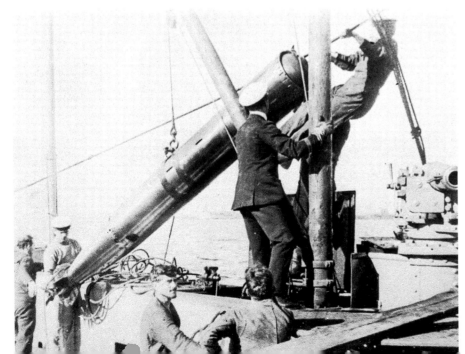

▲ The gun crew of HMS *E.21* in action with their 12-pdr gun. *(HM Submarine Museum)*

◀ Taking in a torpedo aboard HMS *E.54*. Note that the front section of the torpedo is not fitted. *(HM Submarine Museum)*

S Class (Early)

The S Class were an experimental design that were built by Scott's at Greenock at the request of the Admiralty. This was as a result of a visit by Admiralty officers to the Fiat-San Giorgio yard in Spezia, Italy. They inspected a submarine designed by Signor Laurenti for the Italian Navy. As a result, an order for one boat was placed in 1911 to be built under licence, followed by a further order for two in 1913. These boats featured a double hull, as well as ten internal bulkheads, which improved their strength and safety.

The first S Class boat was launched in 1914, and as soon as she was completed she was commissioned into the Royal Navy, and then joined by the second. These two boats were trialled and used operationally from Yarmouth for a short while. They suffered difficulties with the housing hydroplanes and were slow to dive compared to British designs. All three boats were sold to the Italian Navy shortly after she entered the war.

HMS *S.1* suffered the indignity of an engine failure while in the North Sea. With her batteries running low she began to drift. On 24 June, a German trawler was spotted. The captain quickly mustered a boarding party and sent them to capture the trawler, which was then used to tow *S.1* back to Yarmouth.

Class	S Class (Early)	
Role	Experimental Submarine	
	IMPERIAL	**METRIC**
Sub Disp – surfaced	267 tons	271.27 tonnes
Sub Disp – submerged	324 tons	329.18 tonnes
Length	148 ft 6 in	45.26 m
Beam	13 ft 10 in	4.22 m
Draught	10 ft	3.04 m
Propulsion	2 × 325 bhp Scott-Fiat diesel engines	
	2 × 200 ehp electric motors	
Speed	13 knots surfaced, 8.5 knots submerged	
Range	1,600 nm at 8.5 knots surfaced, 75 nm at 5.5 knots submerged	
Armament	2 × 18 in (457 mm) tubes (bow)	
	4 torpedoes carried	
	1 × 12-pdr gun	
Complement (Officers/Men)	18 (2/16)	

Builder	Name	Pennant No.	Class	Launched	Fate	Date
Scott's	HMS *S.1*	I04	S Class (Early)	28.2.1914	PO – Transferred	15.9.1915
Scott's	HMS *S.2*	I0A	S Class (Early)	14.4.1915	PO – Transferred	20.9.1915
Scott's	HMS *S.3*	I1A	S Class (Early)	10.6.1915	Transferred	26.9.1915

◀ Almost complete, HMS *S.1* with her captain-to-be, Lt Cdr Kellett, together with some of Scott's management. (*HM Submarine Museum*)

▲ Signor Laurenti's bow design, with the 18 in (457 mm) torpedo tubes located low on the hull. *(HM Submarine Museum)*

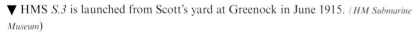

▼ HMS *S.3* is launched from Scott's yard at Greenock in June 1915. *(HM Submarine Museum)*

▲ HMS *S.1* being towed by the German trawler *Ost*. *(HM Submarine Museum)*

▼ HMS *S.1* undergoing contractor's trials in the Clyde in 1914. *(HM Submarine Museum)*

F Class (Early)

The F Class were designed by the Admiralty to the 1912 Submarine Committee specification for comparison purposes with the other experimental boats. They were based on the V Class and had a very similar performance, although the F boats were reputed to be less stable. HMS *F.1* and *F.3* were powered by Vickers diesel engines, and White's installed their licence-built MAN diesel for comparison. The armament of the F boats were an improvement over that of V boats in that they were fitted with an additional stern-mounted torpedo tube.

Three boats were built between 1913 and 1917, and although it had been planned for a further five to be built these were abandoned once war broke out

Once in service, these three boats were used for some local defence patrols, and were later assigned to Portsmouth and Campbeltown for training purposes from 1917 until paid off by July 1919.

▲ HMS *F.2* under construction in the yard of J. S. White on the Isle of Wight, with the ribs in place, together with the underdeck bulkheads. *(HM Submarine Museum)*

▼ HMS *F.3*. *(HM Submarine Museum)*

Class	F Class (Early)	
Role	Overseas Submarine	
	IMPERIAL	METRIC
Sub Disp – surfaced	363 tons	368.8 tonnes
Sub Disp – submerged	441 tons	448.06 tonnes
Length	151 ft	46.02 m
Beam	16 ft	4.88 m
Draught	10 ft 9 in	3.28 m
Propulsion	2 × 450 bhp Vickers diesel engines	
	2 × 200 ehp electric engines	
Speed	14.5 knots surfaced, 8.75 knots submerged	
Range	3,000 nm at 9 knots surfaced, 75 nm at 5 knots submerged	
Armament	3 × 18 in (457 mm) torpedo tubes (2 bow, 1 stern)	
	6 torpedoes carried	
Complement (Officers/Men)	19 (2/17)	

Builder	Name	Pennant No.	Class	Launched	Fate	Date
HM Dockyard, Chatham	HMS *F.1*	IA0	F Class	31.3.1915	PO – Scrapped	1920
J. S. White	HMS *F.2*	IA1	F Class	7.7.1917	PO – Scrapped	1920
Thornycroft	HMS *F.3*	IA2	F Class	19.2.1916	PO – Scrapped	1920

V Class (Early)

Vickers dominated British submarine building, but her position was threatened with the Italian-designed S Class boats being built by Scott's at Greenock and the W Class French boats being built by Armstrong Whitworth at Newcastle-on-Tyne.

As a result, Vickers designed the V Class to compete with these other experimental boats. They were classified as double hulled, although this was only featured around the middle sections. They were fitted with a smaller number of battery cells than was considered normal for that size of boat. However, they met the submerged design speed, but only for a limited range.

Four boats were built, and on completion of trials were accepted by the Royal Navy and commissioned. They remained in service until they were paid off in 1919.

Class	V Class (Early)	
Role	Experimental Submarine	
	IMPERIAL	METRIC
Sub Disp – surfaced	391 tons	397.26 tonnes
Sub Disp – submerged	457 tons	464.31 tonnes
Length	147 ft 6 in	44.95 m
Beam	16 ft 3 in	4.95 m
Draught	11 ft	3.35 m
Propulsion	2 × 450 bhp Vickers diesel engines	
	2 × 190 ehp electric motors	
Speed	14 knots surfaced, 9 knots submerged	
Range	3,000 nm at 9 knots surfaced, 74 nm at 5 knots submerged	
Armament	2 × 18 in (457 mm) torpedo tubes (bow)	
	4 torpedoes carried	
	1 × 12-pdr gun	
Complement (Officers/Men)	20 (2/18)	

Builder	Name	Pennant No.	Class	Launched	Fate	Date
Vickers	HMS *V.1*	I2A	V Class (Early)	23.7.1914	PO – Scrap	11.1921
Vickers	HMS *V.2*	I3A	V Class (Early)	17.2.1915	PO – Scrap	11.1921
Vickers	HMS *V.3*	I4A	V Class (Early)	1.4.1915	PO – Scrap	10.1920
Vickers	HMS *V.4*	I5A	V Class (Early)	25.11.1915	PO – Scrap	10.1920

W Class

The W Class were a design by Monsieur Laubeuf that were then under construction at the Schneider yard near Toulon for the French Navy. It would appear that although the inspecting Admiralty officers found the design of interest they were not convinced of its performance, being too large and slow for Royal Navy requirements. They were also fitted with external torpedoes in frames which they were not happy with. Having been presented with the report, the Admiralty decided against their recommendation and placed an order for two in January 1913 with Armstrong Whitworth at Newcastle-on-Tyne – their first order for a submarine. A further two modified boats were also ordered later that year to honour an agreement to purchase two boats a year from Armstrong Whitworth.

Although HMS *W.1* and *W.2* were unmodified from the original design, it is unclear if the frame-mounted torpedoes were fitted to the British-built W Class. The design of HMS *W.3* and *W.4* was modified by Monsieur Laubeuf to try to improve their performance to meet Royal Navy requirements

Following trials they did not prove popular, and all four boats were sold to the Italian Navy in 1916.

Class	W Class, Group 1
Role	Experimental Submarine

	IMPERIAL	METRIC
Sub Disp – surfaced	333 tons	338.33 tonnes
Sub Disp – submerged	494 tons	501.90 tonnes
Length	171 ft 11 in	52.40 m
Beam	15 ft 5 in	4.70 m
Draught	9 ft	2.74 m
Propulsion	2 × 355 bhp Schneider-Lambert diesel engines 2 × 240 ehp electric motors	
Speed	12 knots surfaced, 8.5 knots submerged	
Range	2,500 nm at 9 knots surfaced, 65 nm at 5 knots submerged	
Armament	4 × 18 in (457 mm) torpedo tubes (2 bow, 2 bow external) 4 torpedoes carried	
Complement (Officers/Men)	18 (2/16)	
Data note	It is unclear if the external drop collars were retained on completion. If so, the total torpedoes carried should be increased by 2	

Builder	Name	Pennant No.	Class	Launched	Fate	Date
Armstrong Whitworth	HMS *W.1*	I6A	W Class, Group 1	19.11.1914	PO – Transferred	23.8.1916
Armstrong Whitworth	HMS *W.2*	I7A	W Class, Group 1	15.2.1915	PO – Transferred	23.8.1916

Class	W Class, Group 2	
Role	Experimental Submarine	
	IMPERIAL	**METRIC**
Sub Disp – surfaced	324 tons	329.18 tonnes
Sub Disp – submerged	495 tons	502.92 tonnes
Length	171 ft 11 in	52.4 m
Beam	15 ft 5 in	4.70 m
Draught	9 ft	2.74 m
Propulsion	2 × 380 bhp Schneider-Lambert diesel engines	
	2 × 240 ehp electric motors	
Speed	12 knots surfaced, 8.5 knots submerged	
Range	2,500 nm at 9 knots surfaced, 65 nm at 5 knots submerged	
Armament	2 × 18 in (457 mm) torpedo tubes (bow)	
	4 torpedoes carried	
Complement (Officers/Men)	18 (2/16)	

Builder	Name	Pennant No.	Class	Launched	Fate	Date
Armstrong Whitworth	HMS *W.3*	I8A	W Class, Group 2	28.7.1915	PO – Transferred	23.8.1916
Armstrong Whitworth	HMS *W.4*	I9A	W Class, Group 2	11.9.1915	PO – Transferred	7.8.1916

▲ HMS *W.2* on the Tyne under way during contractor's trials with Armstrong Whitworth. In the background is HMS *Canada*. *(HM Submarine Museum)*

G Class

Continuing the trend, these G boats were larger than their predecessors and able to provide better accommodation, as well as housing more equipment and weapons. In addition to the pair of 18 in (457 mm) torpedo tubes in the bow and a further pair in the beam, the G Class were the first Royal Navy submarines to be armed with the 21 in (533 mm) torpedo, of which one tube was located in the stern. Various gun arrangements were fitted to these boats, including a 3 in (76 mm) or 12-pdr in front of the conning tower, and some had a 2-pdr added on a raised platform just aft of the conning tower.

The G Class were based on the previous E Class, but incorporated Laurenti's double-hull concept, but performance results showed negligible difference. The Admiralty also wished to widen its source of engines, which had been exclusively Vickers. When orders were placed for boats at other yards they also included alternative engines. Scott's used a Fiat, Armstrong Whitworth planned Nuremberg and Sultzer but ended up using Vickers when their selection became unavailable.

On 16 September 1917, HMS *G.9* was on patrol off the Norwegian coast. She spotted an enemy destroyer and attacked. The torpedo hit the warship but failed to explode. The warship was in fact HMS *Pasley*, and believing that she was under attack from a German U-boat, spotted the submarine, quickly altered course and rammed her. The effect of the collision almost cut *G.9* into two pieces. Only a stoker survived.

On 10 March 1918, HMS *G.13* successfully attacked and sank the German *UC-43* off Muckle Flugga lighthouse. In January and November the following year, HMS *G.7* and *G.8* failed to return from North Sea patrols. *G.7* was the last Royal Navy submarine to be lost in the First World War.

However, although the war was over, the casualties continued. HMS *G.11* ran aground on the Northumberland coast and was wrecked on 22 November, with two of the crew killed.

Between 1914 and 1917 a total of thirteen G Class boats were built of the fourteen ordered. The additional boat was to have been built by White's on the Isle of Wight, but was cancelled in 1915. Four of the surviving ten boats were paid off at the end of the war, and the rest in January 1921.

Class	G Class
Role	Overseas Submarine

	IMPERIAL	METRIC
Sub Disp – surfaced	699 tons	710.18 tonnes
Sub Disp – submerged	967 tons	982.47 tonnes
Length	187 ft 1 in	57.02 m
Beam	22 ft 6 in	6.86 m
Draught	13 ft 6 in	4.11 m
Propulsion	2 × 800 bhp Vickers diesel engines 2 × 420 ehp electric motors	
Speed	15 knots surfaced, 9 knots submerged	
Range	2,400 nm at 12 knots surfaced, 95 nm at 3 knots submerged	
Armament	4 × 18 in (457 mm) torpedo tubes (2 bow, 2 beam) 8 torpedoes carried 1 × 21 in (533 mm) torpedo tube (stern) 2 torpedoes carried 1 × 3 in (76 mm) gun (originally planned for 1 × 12-pdr, 1 × 2-pdr)	
Complement (Officers/Men)	30 (3/27)	
Data note	2 × 800 bhp Scott-Fiat diesel engines fitted to G.14	

Builder	Name	Pennant No.	Class	Launched	Fate	Date
HM Dockyard, Chatham	HMS *G.1*	IA3	G Class	14.8.1915	PO – Scrapped	2.1920
HM Dockyard, Chatham	HMS *G.2*	IA4	G Class	23.12.1915	PO – Scrapped	1.1920
HM Dockyard, Chatham	HMS *G.3*	IA5	G Class	22.1.1916	PO – Scrapped	11.1921
HM Dockyard, Chatham	HMS *G.4*	IA6	G Class	23.10.1915	PO – Scrapped	6.1928
HM Dockyard, Chatham	HMS *G.5*	IA7	G Class	23.11.1915	PO – Scrapped	10.1922
Armstrong Whitworth	HMS *G.6*	IA8	G Class	7.12.1915	PO – Scrapped	11.1921
Armstrong Whitworth	HMS *G.7*	IA9	G Class	14.3.1916	Lost – Unknown	1.11.1918
Vickers	HMS *G.8*	I0C	G Class	1.5.1916	Lost – Unknown	14.1.1918
Vickers	HMS *G.9*	I1C	G Class	15.6.1916	Lost – Sunk in error	16.9.1917
Vickers	HMS *G.10*	I2C	G Class	11.1.1916	PO – Scrapped	1.1923
Vickers	HMS *G.11*	I3C	G Class	22.2.1916	Sunk – Accident	22.11.1918
Vickers	HMS *G.12*	I4C	G Class	24.3.1916	PO – Scrapped	2.1920
Vickers	HMS *G.13*	I5C	G Class	18.7.1916	PO – Scrapped	1.1923
Scott's	HMS *G.14*	I6C	G Class	17.5.1916	PO – Scrapped	3.1921
J. S. White	HMS *G.15*		G Class		Cancelled	

▲ One of the electric motors fitted to the G Class boats. *(HM Submarine Museum)*

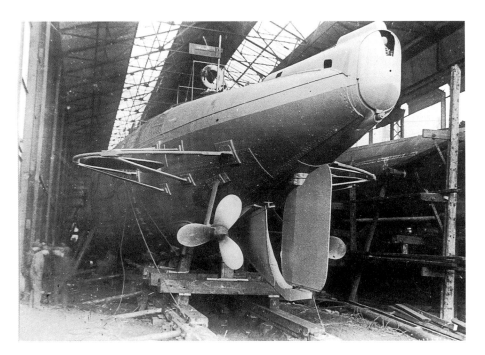

▲ The completed HMS *G.14* at Scott's yard ready for launching.
(HM Submarine Museum)

▼ HMS *G.4* glides down the slipway of HM Dockyard at Chatham in October 1915. Just visible above the wake slightly aft of the conning tower is a small bulge. These double-hull boats were required to have beam torpedo tubes, but without the bulkier ballast tanks of the previous saddle tank arrangements there was insufficient width. To resolve this they had small streamlined bulges either side to provide the necessary width.
(HM Submarine Museum)

▼ HMS *G.8*, armed with 12-pdr and 3-pdr guns, departs from Barrow-in-Furness.
(HM Submarine Museum)

H Class

During the First World War, Great Britain found that she was unable to achieve the numbers of submarines that she required, and so investigated placing offshore orders. In the USA, the Electric Boat Company had proposed its Design 602 for a small, single-hull coastal submarine which could operate well in shallow waters. Twenty were ordered by the Admiralty as the H Class. Initially, these were to be shipped to the UK in a dismantled form, until the US government declared that this breached their neutrality law. As a consequence, it was decided that the first ten were to be built by Canadian Vickers, and production of the balance continued with the Electric Boat Company. It was supposedly intended that these boats would be supplied once the war was over. Some raw materials, components and machinery were shipped to Canada. The first keel was laid on 11 January 1915 and commissioned on the 25 May. However, in early 1916 the US government decided that the ten boats that had been built in the USA still could not be released, and they had to be interned in Boston.

At the same time, legal wrangles arose over a new class of German submarine. The *Deutschland* was claimed by the Germans to be a U-freighter, and being unarmed should be treated as a merchant vessel, and as such could not be attacked without proper warning. With a surface displacement of 1,440 tons and 1,820 tons submerged, and a length of 213 ft (65 m), she was certainly huge for a submarine at that time. The British, on the other hand, deemed that from the fact that the vessel was a submarine it must have had a military purpose, and was therefore a justifiable target.

When *Deutschland* arrived in New York in July 1916, the USA was neutral (USA did not enter the war until 6 April 1917), and the vociferous local German community gave the crew an enthusiastic welcome. The submarine had slipped past the patrolling Royal Navy warships who had orders to intercept and destroy her. At the beginning of the following month, *Deutschland*, loaded with vital raw materials, prepared to return to Germany. The subject of much exaggerated media hype, the Royal Navy warships were waiting outside the American three-mile territorial limit for her to emerge. Luckily for the crew aboard the *Deutschland*, she managed to avoid the warships yet again and returned to Bremen unscathed.

The *Deutschland* was subsequently armed to fulfil a military role in 1917 as *U-155*, and was credited with sinking 42 ships totalling 118,373 tons. A sister ship, the *Bremen*, was later thought to have been sunk while blockade-running after Royal Navy warships reported having hit a large submerged object.

Meanwhile, the legal wrangle resulted in the ten US-built H Class submarines (HMS *H.11* to *H.20*) being released to the Royal Navy. However, six of them were immediately supplied to Chile as compensation for Chilean ships that were being built in British shipyards and had been requisitioned for Royal Navy use. Two of these boats survived with the Chilean Navy into the 1950s. *H.11* and *H.12* served with the Royal Navy, while *H.14* and *H.15* were transferred to the Royal Canadian Navy. All the Canadian-built boats (HMS *H.1* to *H.10*) had already crossed the Atlantic during 1915 and were serving with the Royal Navy.

The initial batch of four Canadian-built boats were fitted with a 6-pdr gun. They made a transatlantic crossing – the first ever attempted by a submarine – escorted by HMS *Calgarian* straight to the Mediterranean. The other six sailed to the UK escorted by a cruiser and accompanied by a couple of freighters, with spares and fuel included in their cargo. Once they arrived, they were fitted with the Sperry gyrocompass and a radio. They proved popular with RN crews with their improved accommodation and facilities, and operated throughout the war.

These boats had a mixture of fortunes. In the Mediterranean *H.4* successfully attacked and sank the German *UB-52* in the Adriatic on 23 May 1918, while HMS *H.3* was lost when she hit a mine while entering the Gulf of Cattaro. She was attempting to enter the Austrian anchorage on the Dalmatian coast. Of the other six, HMS *H.5* was credited with sinking *U-51* by torpedo off the Wesser on 14 July 1916. Sadly, she was incorrectly identified by the crew of the British SS *Rutherglen* at night as a U-boat, and was rammed in the Irish Sea on 2 March 1918, with the loss of all her crew.

HMS *H.6* ran aground off the Dutch coast on 18 January 1918. While eleven of the crew were rescued by a British ship, the rest were interned. *H.6* was salvaged intact, and at the end of the war was bought from the British government and commissioned into the Royal Netherlands Navy as *RNN.08*. She remained in Dutch service until Holland was invaded by the Germans at the beginning of the Second World War, when she was captured and used by the German Navy as *UD-8* for training. She survived almost to the end of the war, only to be scuttled by the Germans.

Only two months after HMS *H.6* ran aground, HMS *H.8* was patrolling in the same area when she snagged the cable of a drifting British mine, causing it to explode. Severely damaged, she rapidly sank in some 80 ft (25.5 m) of water. Although she was leaking badly, her crew fought to get her back to the surface and she limped back home. HMS *H.10* was not so fortunate: she failed to return from another North Sea patrol and was presumed to have been destroyed by a mine around 19 January 1918.

Owing to the success of the H Class, a further order for twelve was placed on Vickers at Barrow, but these were armed with the more powerful 21 in (533 mm) torpedo, which resulted in a longer hull. They were also fitted with a more powerful radio. To speed the construction, most of the components were supplied from the USA. Later in 1917 a further 22 boats were ordered from various British shipbuilders, and most were delivered in 1918/19. However, nine were cancelled when the war ended. The survivors of the original Canadian batch with the smaller 18 in tubes were paid off shortly after the end of the war.

All the British-built H Class boats survived the war, with the exception of HMS *H.41*, which sank while alongside at Blyth following a collision with HMS *Vulcan* on 18 October 1918. Between the wars several accidents resulted in the loss of some of the H boats. March 1922 saw HMS *H.42* taking part in exercises off Gibraltar, when on the 23rd she surfaced to see HMS *Versatile* bearing down on her. The destroyer was just 120 yards away, and despite all efforts the inevitable collision resulted in *H.42* being almost cut in two, and she sank immediately.

On 9 August 1926, HMS *H.29* had completed a refit at Devonport, and was required to undertake a 'trimmed down' dive. For some reason this commenced with the aft hatch open. Unfortunately, a temporary shore connection pipe was passing through it, and despite all efforts the boat sank within a couple of minutes, with the loss of many civilian as well as Naval personnel. In July 1929, HMS *H.47* had been taking part in exercises in the Irish Sea. On the 9th, while returning, she collided with HMS *L.12*, which happened to be training off the Pembrokeshire coast. Unable to avoid the collision, *L.12* rammed *H.47*, and two feet of her bow pierced the hull, causing *H.47* to sink almost immediately. *L.12* was not so badly damaged, and the crew managed to control the leaks and return to port.

By the opening of the Second World War, only nine of the second batch of improved H Class boats remained operational. They continued to serve through the war and beyond, with the survivors relegated to the training role for their latter days.

During October 1940, HMS *H.49* had just commenced a patrol off the Dutch coast when on the 18th she spotted a German anti-submarine flotilla. Unfortunately, she was also spotted, and the five vessels began a full attack on *H.49*. This attack by depth charges lasted some two hours, and despite her having dived straight away to around 60 ft (18.3 m), she was presumed destroyed when oil was seen to rise to the surface. HMS *H.31* was considered lost just before Christmas in 1941 when she did not return to port after a patrol with others boats sent to intercept German battleships, and was thought to have been sunk by a mine in the Bay of Biscay.

An intelligence report was received in December 1941 that the German battleships *Scharnhorst, Gneisenau* and *Prinz Eugen* were being prepared for a breakout from Brest. The Admiralty immediately ordered eight submarines to the area to try to ensure that they did not put to sea. As it turned out, they did not move. HMS *H.31* was one of the boats that left Falmouth on the 19th. On the 24th an attempt was made to contact her, but without success. She failed to return to Falmouth.

On a lighter note, HMS *H.34* was rigged to look like a German U-boat when she took part in the making of the film 'Q Ships' during 1927 off Portland. In October 1945 she was the last of the H Class to be paid off.

Almost identical Electric Boat Company submarines were also built and served with the Italian (8), Russian (11 + 6 ordered but delivered to USN) and Chilean navies, the last ordering an additional boat to the five supplied by the British government. All three countries continued to operate their survivors during the Second World War.

Class	H Class
Role	Coastal Submarine

	IMPERIAL	METRIC
Sub Disp – surfaced	364 tons	369.82 tonnes
Sub Disp – submerged	434 tons	440.94 tonnes
Length	150 ft 3 in	45.79 m
Beam	15 ft 9 in	4.80 m
Draught	12 ft 4 in	3.76 m
Propulsion	2 × 480 bhp Nelseco diesel engines	
	2 × 310 ehp electric motors	
Speed	13 knots surfaced, 10 knots submerged	
Range	1,600 nm at 10 knots surfaced, 130 nm at 2 knots submerged	
Armament	4 × 18 in (457 mm) torpedo tubes (bow)	
	8 torpedoes carried	
Complement (Officers/Men)	22 (3/19)	

▲ HMS *H.11* was built by Fore River in the USA and not delivered until some time after her completion because of the US neutrality restrictions. She is seen here still on contractor's trials. *(Submarine Force Museum)*

Builder	Name	Pennant No.	Class	Launched	Fate	Date
Canadian Vickers	HMS *H.1*	H1	H Class, Group 1	4.1915	PO – Scrapped	3.1921
Canadian Vickers	HMS *H.2*	H2	H Class, Group 1	1915	PO – Scrapped	3.1921
Canadian Vickers	HMS *H.3*	H3	H Class, Group 1	1915	Lost – Mine	15.7.1916
Canadian Vickers	HMS *H.4*	H4	H Class, Group 1	1915	PO – Scrapped	11.1921
Canadian Vickers	HMS *H.5*	H5	H Class, Group 1	1915	Lost – Sunk in error	2.3.1918
Canadian Vickers	HMS *H.6*	H6	H Class, Group 1	1915	Lost – Salvaged – Sold	19.1.1916
Canadian Vickers	HMS *H.7*	H7	H Class, Group 1	1915	PO – Scrapped	11.1921
Canadian Vickers	HMS *H.8*	H8	H Class, Group 1	1915	PO – Scrapped	11.1921
Canadian Vickers	HMS *H.9*	H9	H Class, Group 1	1915	PO – Scrapped	11.1921
Canadian Vickers	HMS *H.10*	H10	H Class, Group 1	1915	Lost – Unknown	19.1.1918
Fore River Shipbuilding Co.	HMS *H.11*	H11	H Class, Group 1	1915	PO – Scrapped	1921
Fore River Shipbuilding Co.	HMS *H.12*	H12	H Class, Group 1	1915	PO – Scrapped	4.1922
Fore River Shipbuilding Co.	HMS *H.13*	H13	H Class, Group 1	1915	Transferred	3.7.1917
Fore River Shipbuilding Co.	HMS *H.14*	H14	H Class, Group 1	1915	Transferred	2.1919
Fore River Shipbuilding Co.	HMS *H.15*	H15	H Class, Group 1	1915	Transferred	2.1919
Fore River Shipbuilding Co.	HMS *H.16*	H16	H Class, Group 1	1915	Transferred	3.7.1917
Fore River Shipbuilding Co.	HMS *H.17*	H17	H Class, Group 1	1915	Transferred	3.7.1917
Fore River Shipbuilding Co.	HMS *H.18*	H18	H Class, Group 1	1915	Transferred	3.7.1917
Fore River Shipbuilding Co.	HMS *H.19*	H19	H Class, Group 1	1915	Transferred	3.7.1917
Fore River Shipbuilding Co.	HMS *H.20*	H20	H Class, Group 1	1915	Transferred	3.7.1917

Class	H Class, Group 2
Role	Coastal Submarine

	IMPERIAL	METRIC
Sub Disp – surfaced	438 tons	445 tonnes
Sub Disp – submerged	504 tons	512.06 tonnes
Length	171 ft 9 in	52.35 m
Beam	15 ft 4 in	4.67 m
Draught	11 ft 3 in	3.42 m
Propulsion	2 × 480 bhp Nelseco diesel engines	
	2 × 310 ehp electric motors	
Speed	13 knots surfaced, 10 knots submerged	
Range	1,600 nm at 10 knots surfaced, 70 nm at 3 knots submerged	
Armament	4 × 21 in (533 mm) torpedo tubes (bow)	
	8 torpedoes carried	
Complement (Officers/Men)	22 (3/19)	
Data note		

Builder	Name	Pennant No.	Class	Launched	Fate	Date
Vickers	HMS *H.21*	H21	H Class, Group 2	20.10.1917	PO – Scrapped	7.1926
Vickers	HMS *H.22*	H22	H Class, Group 2	14.11.1917	PO – Scrapped	2.1929
Vickers	HMS *H.23*	H23	H Class, Group 2	29.1.1918	PO – Scrapped	5.1934
Vickers	HMS *H.24*	H24	H Class, Group 2	14.11.1917	PO – Scrapped	5.1934
Vickers	HMS *H.25*	H25	H Class, Group 2	27.4.1918	PO – Scrapped	2.1929
Vickers	HMS *H.26*	H26	H Class, Group 2	15.11.1917	PO – Scrapped	4.1928
Vickers	HMS *H.27*	H27	H Class, Group 2	25.9.1918	PO – Scrapped	8.1935
Vickers	HMS *H.28*	H28, 28H, 28N, N28	H Class, Group 2	12.3.1918	PO – Scrapped	8.1944
Vickers	HMS *H.29*	H29	H Class, Group 2	8.6.1918	Accident – Scrapped	10.1927
Vickers	HMS *H.30*	H30	H Class, Group 2	9.5.1918	PO – Scrapped	8.1935
Vickers Armstrong	HMS *H.31*	H31, 31H, 31N, N31	H Class, Group 2	16.11.1918	Lost – Unknown	12.1941
Vickers Armstrong	HMS *H.32*	H32, 32H, 32N, N32	H Class, Group 2	19.11.1918	PO – Scrapped	10.1944

Builder	Name	Pennant No.	Class	Launched	Fate	Date
Cammell Laird	HMS *H.33*	H33, 33H, 33N, N33	H Class, Group 2	24.8.1918	PO – Scrapped	10.1944
Cammell Laird	HMS *H.34*	H34, 34H, 34N, N34	H Class, Group 2	5.11.1918	PO – Scrapped	7.1945
Cammell Laird	HMS *H.35*		H Class, Group 2		Cancelled	
Cammell Laird	HMS *H.36*		H Class, Group 2		Cancelled	
Cammell Laird	HMS *H.37*		H Class, Group 2		Cancelled	
Cammell Laird	HMS *H.38*		H Class, Group 2		Cancelled	
Armstrong Whitworth	HMS *H.39*		H Class, Group 2		Cancelled	
Armstrong Whitworth	HMS *H.40*		H Class, Group 2		Cancelled	
Armstrong Whitworth	HMS *H.41*	H41	H Class, Group 2	26.7.1918	Accident – Scrapped	18.10.1919
Armstrong Whitworth	HMS *H.42*	H42	H Class, Group 2	21.10.1918	Sunk – Accident	23.2.1922
Armstrong Whitworth	HMS *H.43*	H43, 43H, 43N, N43	H Class, Group 2	3.2.1919	PO – Scrapped	11.1944
Armstrong Whitworth	HMS *H.44*	H44, 44H, 44N, N44	H Class, Group 2	17.2.1919	PO – Scrapped	2.1945
Armstrong Whitworth	HMS *H.45*		H Class, Group 2		Cancelled	
Armstrong Whitworth	HMS *H.46*		H Class, Group 2		Cancelled	
Beardmore	HMS *H.47*	H47	H Class, Group 2	19.11.1918	Sunk – Accident	9.7.1929
Beardmore	HMS *H.48*	H48, H49	H Class, Group 2	31.3.1919	PO – Scrapped	8.1935
Beardmore	HMS *H.49*	H49, 49H, 49N, N49	H Class, Group 2	15.7.1919	Lost – Depth charge	18.10.1940
Beardmore	HMS *H.50*	H50, 50H, 50N, N50	H Class, Group 2	25.10.1919	PO – Scrapped	7.1945
HM Dockyard, Pembroke	HMS *H.51*	H51	H Class, Group 2	15.11.1918	PO – Scrapped	6.1924
HM Dockyard, Pembroke	HMS *H.52*	H52	H Class, Group 2	31.3.1919	PO – Scrapped	11.1927
HM Dockyard, Devonport	HMS *H.53*		H Class, Group 2		Cancelled	
HM Dockyard, Devonport	HMS *H.54*		H Class, Group 2		Cancelled	

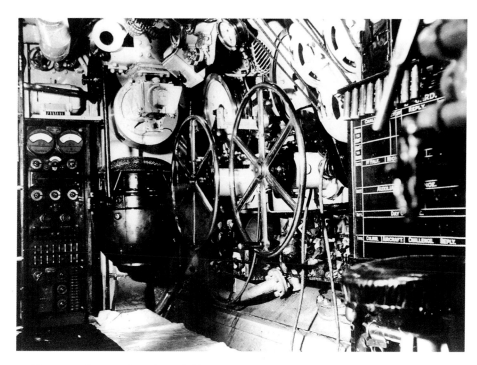

▲ The control room aboard an H Class boat with the hydroplane wheels and the Sperry Gyrocompass which improved navigation while submerged for lengthy periods. *(HM Submarine Museum)*

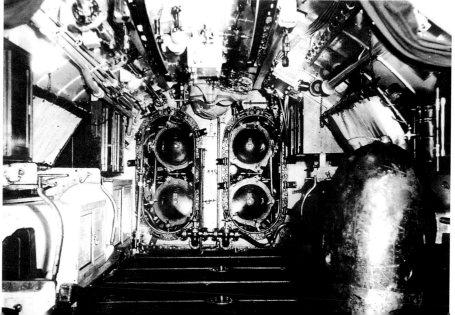

▲ Signalman Newton on HMS *H.28* sends a message to a nearby ship in the time-honoured way on 4 March 1928. *(HM Submarine Museum)*

◀ The weapons compartment of an H Class boat. The British-built boats were fitted with four 21 in (533 mm) torpedo tubes, compared with 18 in (457 mm) in the American- and Canadian-built boats. A torpedo head is stood to the right. *(HM Submarine Museum)*

▲ HMS *H.30* alongside at Great Yarmouth around 1919. *(HM Submarine Museum)*

▼ HMS *H.33*. *(HM Submarine Museum)*

▼ HMS *H.50*. *(HM Submarine Museum)*

J Class

The J Class were built in an attempt to provide the Admiralty Grand Fleet traditionalists with a submarine capable of sailing with the rest of the ships of the fleet. With a speed of fifteen knots being the order of the day for a surfaced submarine, a requirement for 21 knots was going to be ambitious. Initial design proposals included steam power, but the Admiralty wanted diesel-electric. Such was the need to pack extra engine power into the boat that the length increased by well over 50 per cent over the E Class that it was to replace. This was necessary to accommodate an extra shaft, together with a third diesel engine in an attempt to boost the power. But all this did was to create a larger hull with a corresponding increase in weight. The end result was an increase of speed of just four knots.

Nineteen knots was the best that could be made with this design. With the larger K Class also being built, hopes of success were channelled in that direction, and the J Class were reclassified as overseas submarines. A total of eight boats had been ordered in January 1915, but by April two had been cancelled. The hulls were renumbered, *J.7* becoming HMS *J.3* and *J.8* becoming HMS *J.4*, and the following month an additional boat was ordered with a slightly modified design. Although the weight had been reduced slightly there was no appreciable increase in performance.

HMS *J.7* was built with a different layout, the Control Room being positioned between the two engine rooms. This resulted in the conning tower also being positioned further back than the rest of the class. This gave a better access space for the bow torpedo tubes. Although the weight had been reduced a little there was no appreciable increase in performance. All operated from their base at Blyth and were tasked with the Grand Fleet, despite their insufficient performance. As a result they saw little action.

On 5 November 1916 HMS *J.1* attacked four German warships off Horns Reef. She fired a salvo of torpedoes from an estimated 4,000 yards, hitting and seriously damaging the Dreadnoughts *Kronprinz* and *Grosser Kurfurst*.

HMS *J.2* was also in the North Sea on 7 July 1917 when she spotted the U-boat *U-99* and fired her salvo of four torpedoes at a range of two miles. One of the torpedoes was seen to have struck home, sinking the German U-boat.

On 15 October 1918, HMS *J.6* was sunk by the Q-ship *Cymric*. At the Board of Enquiry that was convened to investigate the accident it was accepted that the unusual silhouette of this class of boat had contributed to the confusion that led to the attack. Not recognising the shape, the crew believed she was the German *U-6* and therefore attacked first. Only fifteen of her crew of forty-four were rescued.

Once the war was over, the Royal Navy was keen to dispose of the boats it no longer needed. As a result the surviving six J Class were refurbished and transferred to the Royal Australian Navy, with whom the long range of these boats was considered to be of greater use.

Class	J Class, Group 1	
Role	Overseas Submarine	

	IMPERIAL	METRIC
Sub Disp – surfaced	1,204 tons	1,223.26 tonnes
Sub Disp – submerged	1,820 tons	1,849.12 tonnes
Length	274 ft 9 in	83.74 m
Beam	23 ft 6 in	7.16 m
Draught	14 ft	4.26 m
Propulsion	3 × 1,200 bhp Vickers diesel engines	
	3 × 450 ehp electric engines	
Speed	19 knots surfaced, 9.6 knots submerged	
Range	5,000 nm at 12.5 knots surface, 55nm knots submerged	
Armament	6 × 18 in (457 mm) torpedo tubes (4 bow, 2 beam)	
	12 torpedoes carried	
	1 × 3 in (76 mm) gun (later replaced on some by 4 in (101 mm))	
	1 × 2-pdr gun	
	Depth charges	
Complement (Officers/Men)	44 (5/39)	

Builder	Name	Pennant No.	Class	Launched	Fate	Date
HM Dockyard, Portsmouth	HMS *J.1*	J1	J Class, Group 1	6.11.1915	PO – Transferred	25.3.1919
HM Dockyard, Portsmouth	HMS *J.2*	J2	J Class, Group 1	6.11.1915	PO – Transferred	25.3.1919
HM Dockyard, Pembroke	HMS *J.3*	J3	J Class, Group 1	4.12.1915	Cancelled	
HM Dockyard, Pembroke	HMS *J.3* (ex *J.7*)	J4	J Class, Group 1	4.12.1915	PO – Transferred	25.3.1919
HM Dockyard, Pembroke	HMS *J.4*	J4	J Class, Group 1		Cancelled	
HM Dockyard, Pembroke	HMS *J.4* (ex *J.8*)	J4	J Class, Group 1	2.2.1916	PO – Transferred	25.3.1919
HM Dockyard, Devonport	HMS *J.5*	J5	J Class, Group 1	9.9.1915	PO – Transferred	25.3.1919
HM Dockyard, Devonport	HMS *J.6*	J6	J Class, Group 1	9.9.1915	Lost – Sunk in error	15.10.1918

Class	J Class, Group 2
Role	Overseas Submarine

	IMPERIAL	METRIC
Sub Disp – surfaced	1,210 tons	1,229.36 tonnes
Sub Disp – submerged	1,760 tons	1,788.16 tonnes
Length	274 ft 9 in	83.74 m
Beam	23 ft 6 in	7.16 m
Draught	14 ft	4.26 m
Propulsion	3 × 1,200 bhp Vickers diesel engines	
	3 × 450 ehp electric engines	
Speed	19 knots surfaced, 9.6 knots submerged	
Range	5,000 nm at 12.5 knots surface, 60 nm at 3 knots submerged	
Armament	6 × 18 in (457 mm) torpedo tubes (4 bow, 2 beam)	
	12 torpedoes carried	
	1 × 3 in (76 mm) gun (later replaced on some by	
	4 in (101 mm))	
	1 × 2-pdr gun	
	Depth charges	
Complement (Officers/Men)	44 (5/39)	

Builder	Name	Pennant No.	Class	Launched	Fate	Date
HM Dockyard, Devonport	HMS J.7	J7	J Class, Group 2	21.2.1917	PO – Transferred	25.3.1919

▲ HMS *J.1* departing Portsmouth. *(HM Submarine Museum)*

▼ HMS *J.4* manoeuvring in Blockhouse Creek. *(HM Submarine Museum)*

Swordfish Class

HMS *Swordfish* and HMS *Nautilus* were both designed as an interim between the 670 ton E Class and the 1,980 ton K Class, using the latest technology. The Admiralty intended that these would be the fleet submarine that they continued to hanker after. This required them to be able to keep station with the Grand Fleet at 21 knots.

While HMS *Nautilus* was frustrated with the power of her diesel engines, HMS *Swordfish* was the first Royal Navy submarine to be powered by steam. However, while this provided some improvements in safety, the heat made her highly uncomfortable. She featured a mount that enabled the gun to be stowed when not required. During trials it was determined that an exposed gun created less resistance than had been thought, and so this development ceased.

In the end, neither HMS *Swordfish* nor *Nautilus* had the power to keep up with the Grand Fleet when they were on the surface, and they had even less when they submerged. This, combined with the restricted vision from a submarine at periscope depth, never mind when submerged, and the poor manoeuvrability of these larger boats, meant that they were hazardous in the company of other ships. Submarines had already suffered considerable losses through collisions without increasing the odds, but this was not to be the end of this saga.

In the end HMS *Swordfish* was converted to a surface patrol boat and was fitted with two 12-pdr guns.

Class	Swordfish Class	
Role	Experimental Submarine	
	IMPERIAL	METRIC
Sub Disp – surfaced	932 tons	946.91 tonnes
Sub Disp – submerged	1,470 tons	1,493.52 tonnes
Length	231 ft 3 in	70.48 m
Beam	22 ft 9 in	6.93 m
Draught	13 ft 6 in	4.11 m
Propulsion	2 × 2,000 shp Parsons geared impulse reactor steam turbines with Yarrow boiler	
	2 × 1,400 ehp electric motors	
Speed	18 knots surfaced, 10 knots submerged	
Range	3,000 nm at 8.5 knots surface	
Armament	2 × 21 in (533 mm) tubes (bow)	
	4 torpedoes carried	
	4 × 18 in (457 mm) tubes (beam)	
	8 torpedoes carried	
	2 × 3 in guns	
Complement (Officers/Men)	42 (4/38)	

Builder	Name	Pennant No.	Class	Launched	Fate	Date
Scott's	HMS *Swordfish* (ex Swordfish, *S.1*)	ICA, 30	Swordfish Class (Early)	18.3.1916	PO – Scrapped	7.1922

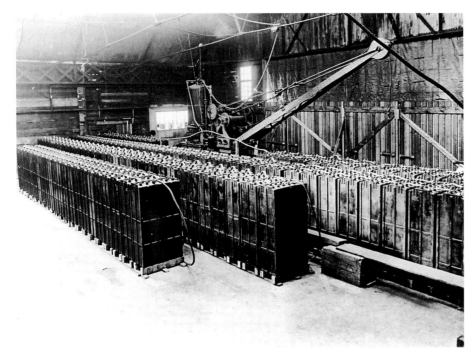

▲ Batteries provide the power for submerged operation. As the boats grew in size and required a greater performance, so the volume of batteries expanded. HMS *Swordfish* had a total of 224 cells, which weighed 97 tons (98.5 tonnes). They provided 220 V when connected in series, or 110 V in parallel. *(HM Submarine Museum)*

▼ HMS *Swordfish* alongside at Scott's, still being fitted out. *(HM Submarine Museum)*

Nautilus Class

The Nautilus Class was a proposal for an overseas type designed to meet the 1912 Submarine Committee requirement. A one-off order for HMS *Nautilus* was placed with Vickers in 1913. She was designed to be constructed with a double hull and have an increased patrol duration. Her substantially increased length improved her sea-keeping qualities, especially in bad weather. The Admiralty was not enthused with her 17 knot design performance and requested improvement. Engine technology at that time was already being stretched from 800 bhp engines to 1,850 bhp, and this could only lead to unknown difficulties. The Admiralty removed her priority status, and as a result she took until October 1917 to be completed. Although operated by the First Flotilla at Portsmouth she was never used operationally and was plagued with teething troubles, as was to be expected.

HMS *Nautilus* was the first Royal Navy submarine to be officially given a name, but in June 1917 she was renamed HMS *N.1* and became relegated to a battery-charging vessel. She was paid off in July 1919 and finally scrapped in 1922.

Class	Nautilus Class	
Role	Experimental Submarine	
	IMPERIAL	METRIC
Sub Disp – surfaced	1,441 tons	1,464.06 tonnes
Sub Disp – submerged	2,026 tons	2,058.42 tonnes
Length	258 ft 4 in	78.73 m
Beam	26 ft	7.92 m
Draught	16 ft	4.87 m
Propulsion	2 × 1,850 bhp Vickers diesel engines	
	2 × 500 ehp electric motors	
Speed	17 knots surfaced, 9 knots submerged	
Range	4,400 nm at 11 knots surfaced, 72 nm at 6 knots submerged	
Armament	8 × 18 in (457 mm) torpedo tubes (2 bow, 4 beam, 2 stern)	
	16 torpedoes carried	
	1 × 3 in (76 mm) gun	
Complement (Officers/Men)	42 (5/37)	
Data note		

Builder	Name	Pennant No.	Class	Launched	Fate	Date
Vickers	HMS *Nautilus*	IAC, N1	Nautilus Class	16.12.1914	PO – Scrapped	6.1922

◄ HMS *Nautilus* departs Barrow-in-Furness on completion by Vickers. Although the engines failed to produce the required leap in power needed, the size of this boat represented a considerable advance. (*HM Submarine Museum*)

K Class

The steam-driven K boat was a class that submariners would have preferred never to have received. The Admiralty ordered them to satisfy the Grand Fleet traditionalists' obsession with a fleet submarine. For this they were designed to have the capability of 24 knots. This was also a knee jerk reaction to an unsubstantiated report in 1914 that the Germans had developed a submarine capable of 22 knots. The requirement had originated with the Grand Fleet but then became a priority to match the Germans.

The size of the K Class was largely dictated by the size of power-plant selected. Petrol and diesel engines were just not capable of developing sufficient power at that time, and so they used steam. At the time, they were the largest and fastest submarines in the world. They were armed with six torpedo tubes in the bow plus a further four beam tubes, plus three guns. It was soon found that two of the bow torpedo tubes, which had been added to the original design, had to be removed to increase stability. One of the guns was also subsequently removed.

Their speed was about that of a destroyer; however, the turning circle was more akin to a battleship and the control from the bridge was reputed to be about that of a picket boat. Considering the speeds of submarines at that time, it was no mean achievement for them to be within half a knot of their design speed. At 339 ft (103.32 m) long, they certainly looked impressive on the surface, as did most of the major warships of the Grand Fleet. Unfortunately, this did not guarantee their effectiveness. Because of their size they were slow to dive and proved unwieldy when submerged

For a submarine of this class it is surprising that they were fitted with 18 in (457 mm) tubes rather than the much more effective 21 in (533 mm) that had been tested on HMS *Swordfish*. This was indicative of the lack of understanding of submarine warfare on the part of the decision makers.

During a gunnery trial in October 1912 against the obsolete Holland 4, it was concluded that a submarine fifteen feet (4.5 m) deep would suffer negligible damage from a 6 in (152 mm) lyddite shell, despite the fact that the second shot fired sank the Holland. If caught on the surface it was deemed to be no more vulnerable than any other vessel: after all it did have three guns! These were later reduced to one 4 in (101 mm) and one 3 in (76 mm). The problem with the guns, which were slow to bring into action, was that they had poor gunnery control and the ammunition was stored either in the bow or the stern, thus requiring excessive manhandling.

With the surface difficulties described, the Ks continued to struggle as soon as any attempt was made to dive. With a length-to-beam ratio of 12.8:1 this was always going to be interesting. She had twenty external ballast tanks plus a further eight located internally. A new control system was devised to control the forty vent valves, but it was a fraught job to ensure a correct dive and not nosedive or have a list.

Diving was a lengthy operation lasting three to five minutes, because of the number of hatches, vents and other openings requiring closing before the ballast tanks could be vented. The boiler room had four domes that were three feet in diameter and weighed 8 cwt (406.4 kg) each. HMS *K.13* sank in Gare Loch when it dived during trials and had left the domes unsealed. The pair of funnels required stowing and twin door sealing took approximately 30 seconds to complete – about the time for an H Class to complete her dive. After manoeuvring with the fleet at speed it was frequently found that the tubes were fouled. This was because the bow shutters were unable to withstand the high water pressure. Confidence did not improve later on when a redesigned bulbous bow needed to be fitted, especially when crews were already becoming sceptical as to the seaworthiness of these boats.

Such was its status within the Royal Navy that the captain of a K Class was initially considered to be a prestigious command; however, this was short lived. There soon followed sixteen major accidents and eight disasters. On only one occasion were torpedoes fired at the enemy – the German submarine *U-95* – and then the salvo failed to do any damage!

The incident with HMS *K.13* on 29 January 1917 in Gare Loch was to be the final trial before the boat was handed over to the Admiralty. The builder was Fairfield, who had only previously built four submarines and they had now secured an order for two of these huge 339 ft (103.32 m) boats. The atmosphere was somewhat excited as the 53-strong naval crew was joined by 29 civilians, including company directors and employees, plus a further two RN observers. Once she had arrived at the diving area in Gare Loch she proceeded to make a shallow dive, but to the consternation of the captain she continued down, despite emptying the ballast tanks of water, until she hit the bottom at 50 ft (15.24 m). With water pouring through the dome seals, the boiler space was becoming flooded. With no alternative because of the emergency, the watertight door to the aft of the boat had to be closed and locked. While this meant 31 men behind the door would be drowned within minutes, it would provide a chance for those 53 forward of the door – a terrible decision to have to make instantly.

A hurried calculation discovered that there was at least eight hours' air left in the hull, but it took about an hour for K.13's escort to raise the alarm of possible trouble. More valuable time was lost while suitable vessels were prepared and arrived. It took nearly eight hours to get in position to lower a diver, but he was almost drowned when it was discovered that the only diving suit aboard had perished. The next vessel to arrive did not have a suit. Eventually a Fairfield diver arrived and was lowered. He managed to make contact by tapping Morse code on the hull.

Time continued to pass and was now past critical when the captain, Lt Cdr Herbert, decided that a desperate plan had to be implemented. One of the naval observers would be released from the conning tower and should rise to the surface in the air bubble. Such was the risk that Herbert decided that he would enter the double trap-door of the conning tower to assist the officer and to seal it back up after he had gone. With them both in position the tap was opened to allow water to gradually flood the chamber. As the water rose the air compressed and the officer started to release the outer trap-door. All of a sudden the door burst open and both men were sucked out. The officer struck his head on the bridge, was knocked out and drowned. Herbert was more fortunate and broke the surface a moment or two later. He was hurriedly plucked from the water by the boat crew.

Herbert was anxious to provide vital detailed information about the state of his boat in order to assist in the rescue of the personnel trapped below. Inexplicably this resulted in further arguments as to the best course of action and wasted more valuable time. Eventually, divers were sent down with high-pressure air hoses, but they were unable to find any means of attaching them. After hours of wrangling and frantic messages from the trapped crew, a means of attaching the hoses was devised. Once an ice blockage was cleared, the vital fresh air began to be pumped aboard.

This was just the first hurdle, and arguments continued as to how the crew were to be freed. Eventually a cable was used to raise the bow until it gradually emerged out of the water. Herbert decided that it would be easiest to get the crew out through the torpedo tubes, but before this could commence K.13 slipped back to just below the surface. Herbert then proposed that oxy-acetylene should be used to cut through the hull, and yet more time was wasted arguing round alternatives before work began. Despite some further difficulties, a rescue was effected and 46 survivors were released. Some weeks later K.13 was raised, and it was found that the cause of the accident was that the boiler room ventilators had been left open. She was refurbished by Fairfield and commissioned as HMS K.22.

This was to be the last time that the number 13 would be applied to a Royal Navy submarine, but the number had already tainted the K Class. Or was it just that they were too big and unwieldy and steam-turbine powered?

HMS K.7 had the misfortune to be misidentified as a U-boat in the Channel by two destroyers who commenced depth-charging her. She managed to escape the attack, surfaced and signalled to the warships, eventually convincing them that she was not the enemy. A few hours later, HMS K.7 spotted a surfaced U-boat and fired a torpedo, which missed. A second attack was made against the unsuspecting German submarine with a salvo of four torpedoes. This time one of them struck the enemy vessel on the beam but it failed to detonate. K.7 surfaced while the U-boat submerged for cover, and both vessels beat a hasty retreat. This was the only attack on the enemy by a K Class boat.

Around the same time, HMS K.1 was on patrol when she ran aground near Bow Rock, and although damage was minor her captain was court-martialled with a charge of hazarding his ship. Without batting an eyelid, the captain gave the reason as being that rats had eaten the chart. The court accepted his reason and the charge was dropped.

On 16 November 1917, the Twelfth Flotilla was tasked with the Grand Fleet on an offensive sweep. They headed out following HMS Blonde towards Denmark. When she changed heading, the lumbering K boats gradually altered course and bunched. Unfortunately, HMS K.4 was a little slower to react than the others and struck HMS K.1 on the stern. Quick reactions in sealing watertight doors saved the boat without loss of life, and Blonde took the disabled K.1 in tow after the crew had been taken off. However, the weather deteriorated, and despite all efforts K.1 had to be cut loose while still off the Danish coast and sunk by gunfire from Blonde to avoid her falling into enemy hands.

On 31 January 1918, the Twelfth and Thirteenth Submarine flotilla (four and five boats respectively) were ordered to leave Rosyth with the Fleet. Each led by a light cruiser, they were to depart from the harbour in darkness with the battle cruisers to follow and rendezvous with the rest of the Grand Fleet

Fleet manoeuvres at speed can be interesting at the best of times, but mixed ships in close formation and at night could be extremely hazardous without adequate training. While the surface fleet had routinely perfected its training, the Ks had only recently moved to Rosyth and had little opportunity to undertake the appropriate training.

The Fleet departed in sequence, and eventually some forty warships were heading out to sea in a twenty-mile line. The plan required the flagship, HMS Courageous, who was leading the formation, to increase speed to 20 knots when she passed May Island. She was then to alter heading for the rendezvous.

A group of armed trawlers were in the area searching for a reported U-boat. Unfortunately, they had not been informed of the transiting darkened fleet, which was operating with radio silence.

HMS Courageous manoeuvred according to the plan. The light cruiser, HMS Ithuriel, leading the Thirteenth Submarine Flotilla, had lost sight of the dimmed blue stern light of the flagship in the mist and made her manoeuvre at a calculated position. As the submarines followed, two of the armed trawlers crossed in front of HMS K.14, requiring the captain to take avoiding action. It was at this inappropriate time that the helm jammed and chaos then ensued. It commenced with HMS K.22 ramming K.14, and HMS Inflexible ramming K.22 in turn.

The captain of HMS *Ithuriel*, now with just three submarines, received garbled, inaccurate coded messages when the radio silence was broken and decided to return to the position to attempt a rescue. To avoid one warship still heading out to sea the three Ks were inadvertently led across the path of HMS *Fearless*, which was leading the Twelfth Submarine Flotilla. HMS *Fearless* collided with HMS *K.17*, and she sank shortly after. HMS *K.4* was following HMS *Fearless* and managed to veer off and stopped. HMS *K.6* was next-but-one in line, and despite going full astern rammed *K.4* near her conning tower. Sadly, this was enough to sink her, and she nearly pulled *K.6* with her before they separated. HMS *K.7* was last in the line and passed right over the sinking *K.4*.

All the crew of HMS *K.17* managed to escape, but while survivors were being rescued, some of the escorting destroyers, which were unaware of the chaos, passed straight through at speed over the spot where she had sunk. This was where many of her survivors were swimming, and 47 were killed. In all, 103 officers and men lost their lives that night, two boats were lost and three damaged.

The First Lord of the Admiralty put the accident down to the standard of efficiency, and failed to recognise any of the shortcomings of the K Class. This tragic loss of life became known as the Battle of May Island.

HMS *K.16* suffered a similar, frightening experience to HMS *K.12* during her diving trials in Gare Loch, when she failed to respond to the controls and settled on the bottom. Fortunately, she surfaced under her own power when all the ballast tanks were blown.

HMS *K.15* had only been completed at the end of April 1918 when the following month she was at sea, and while surfaced, large waves hit her on the beam. This resulted in water entering the funnels and flooding the boilers. At the last moment, the captain saw this happening and immediately ordered, 'Shut off for diving'. All hatches were immediately closed, but the weight of the water was enough to weigh the stern down to the bottom, while the bow stuck out of the water. The unexpected order and quick reaction of the crew had prevented the situation from being far worse, although all was not well. The valves had jammed and were preventing the ballast tanks from being emptied. Fortunately, after a worrying eight hours of trying to resolve the problem, *K.15* returned to her more natural angle.

It is interesting to note that the cause of this accident was that the funnel ports were designed to open both ways, which allowed water to accidentally enter. This oversight had been detected and rectified on all the K Class with the exception of HMS *K.15*, which had apparently been overlooked!

HMS *K.3* suffered the 'diving-out-of-control syndrome' in the Pentland Firth, which was considered to be shallow water. Somehow, *K.3* had managed to select a slight hollow and hit the bottom at 266 ft (81 m). Despite her only being designed for diving to 200 ft (61 m), her crew struggled to bring her back to the surface, but she required substantial repairs. In Stokes Bay she nosed down and buried her bows in the mud during a Royal visit with Prince George aboard. Eventually she managed to surface under her own power after a twenty-minute struggle. On another occasion she nosed down while the funnels were still open. This extinguished the boilers and flooded the boiler room.

Similar diving problems were encountered by HMS *K.9* and *K.22* at different times. But on 20 January 1921, HMS *K.5* was participating in an exercise when she failed to surface. Oil and pieces of wood were found floating in the area, and she was assumed to have broken up. She had on a previous occasion been involved in a collision with a destroyer in Milford Haven. Whether this had caused an undetected weakness or whether the reason was the K Class 'syndrome' we shall never know. What is fact is that her whole crew of 57 officers and men were lost.

In June 1921 HMS *K.15* was moored alongside HMS *Canterbury* in Portsmouth harbour. All of a sudden the watch keeper became aware that she was gradually settling lower in the water. He alerted the few crew on board, and all managed to scrambled off before she sank. The conclusion of the investigation, once she had been salvaged, was that the hydraulic fluid had expanded in the excessive heat, and this had caused a loss of pressure when it cooled. This had allowed the vents to open and the ballast tanks to fill with water.

Of the 27 K Class boats ordered, seventeen were built from 1915 to 1917 (HMS *K.1–K.17*). A further four (HMS *K.18–K.21*) were redesigned and built as M Class (HMS *M.1–M.4*), although the last was cancelled before being completed. The M Class also suffered from the K curse, with *M.1* and *M.2* being lost in accidents. HMS *K.13,* which sank in Gare Loch during trials in 1917 was salvaged, refurbished and recommissioned as HMS *K.22*. HMS *K.23–K.25*, *K.27* and *K.28* were cancelled.

An improved boat in the form of HMS *K.26* was built by Vickers at Barrow, with 21 in (533 mm) torpedo tubes and an improved diving performance, although speed was slightly lower. She was finished at HM Dockyard, Chatham, in 1923. It had been planned that she would be the first of a new class, but fortunately, as many must have said at the time, it did not happen. Compared to the rest of her Class, *K.26* was reasonably successful and survived until she was paid off in April 1931.

	IMPERIAL	METRIC
Class	K Class, Group 1	
Role	Fleet Submarine	
Sub Disp – surfaced	1,980 tons	2,011.68 tonnes
Sub Disp – submerged	2,560 tons	2,600.96 tonnes
Length	339 ft	103.32 m
Beam	26 ft 6 in	8.07 m
Draught	20 ft 11 in	6.37 m
Propulsion	2 × 5,250 bhp Parsons/Brown Curtis steam turbine + 1 × 600 bhp diesel engine	
	4 × 720 ehp electric motors	
Speed	24 knots surfaced, 9 knots submerged	
Range	3,000 nm at 13.5 knots surfaced, 30 nm at 5 knots submerged	
Armament	10 × 18 in (457 mm) torpedo tubes (4 bow, 4 beam, 2 casing) (2 casing later removed)	
	18 torpedoes carried	
	2 × 4 in (101 mm) gun	
	1 × 3 in (76 mm) AA gun	
	Depth charges	
Complement (Officers/Men)	59 (5/54)	

Builder	Name	Class	Launched	Fate	Date
HM Dockyard, Portsmouth	HMS *K.1*	K Class, Group 1	14.11.1916	Lost – Accident	18.11.1917
HM Dockyard, Portsmouth	HMS *K.2*	K Class, Group 1	14.10.1916	PO – Scrapped	7.1926
Vickers	HMS *K.3*	K Class, Group 1	20.5.1916	PO – Scrapped	10.1921
Vickers	HMS *K.4*	K Class, Group 1	15.7.1916	Lost – Accident	31.1.1918
HM Dockyard, Portsmouth	HMS *K.5*	K Class, Group 1	16.12.1916	Sunk – Accident	20.1.1921
HM Dockyard, Devonport	HMS *K.6*	K Class, Group 1	31.5.1916	PO – Scrapped	7.1926
HM Dockyard, Devonport	HMS *K.7*	K Class, Group 1	31.5.1916	PO – Scrapped	9.1921
Vickers	HMS *K.8*	K Class, Group 1	10.10.1916	PO – Scrapped	10.1923
Vickers	HMS *K.9*	K Class, Group 1	8.11.1916	PO – Scrapped	7.1926
Vickers	HMS *K.10*	K Class, Group 1	27.12.1916	PO – Scrapped	11.1921
Armstrong Whitworth	HMS *K.11*	K Class, Group 1	16.8.1916	PO – Scrapped	11.1921
Armstrong Whitworth	HMS *K.12*	K Class, Group 1	23.1.1917	PO – Scrapped	7.1926
Fairfield	HMS *K.13* renumbered *K22*	K Class, Group 1	11.11.1916	Accident – Renumbered	12.1926
Fairfield	HMS *K.14*	K Class, Group 1	8.2.1917	PO – Scrapped	12.1926
Scott's	HMS *K.15*	K Class, Group 1	31.10.1917	PO – Scrapped	8.1924
Beardmore	HMS *K.16*	K Class, Group 1	5.11.1917	PO – Scrapped	8.1924
Vickers	HMS *K.17*	K Class, Group 1	10.4.1917	Lost – Accident	31.1.1918
Vickers	HMS *K.18*	K Class, Group 1		Cancelled	
Vickers	HMS *K.19*	K Class, Group 1		Cancelled	
Armstrong Whitworth	HMS *K.20*	K Class, Group 1		Cancelled	
Armstrong Whitworth	HMS *K.21*	K Class, Group 1		Cancelled	
Fairfield	HMS *K.22* (ex *K.13*)	K Class, Group 1		PO – Scrapped	12.1926

▲ HMS *K.14* in her original layout. Her funnels can be seen roughly mid-ships on the raised structure aft of the mast. *(HM Submarine Museum)*

▲ HMS *K.6* modified with the enlarged bow to improve her diving and surfacing responses. *(HM Submarine Museum)*

▲ The K Class were subjected to a high rate of accidents. HMS *K.4* is seen here grounded on a sandbank at Walney Island during her trials. Later she was lost with all her crew following a collision with HMS *K.6* in the 'Battle of May Island' in 1918.
(HM Submarine Museum)

▲ HMS *K.15* makes smoke from a single funnel after her refit by Scott's in 1918.
(HM Submarine Museum)

▼ HMS *K.16* alongside at Beardmore's during her fitting out. *(HM Submarine Museum)*

▼ HMS *K.22* puts on a turn of speed. They were required to operate with the Grand Fleet, and were designed to make 24 knots, but the turning circle was appalling.
(HM Submarine Museum)

		IMPERIAL	METRIC
Class		K Class, Group 2	
Role		Fleet Submarine	
Sub Disp – surfaced		1,955 tons	1,986.28 tonnes
Sub Disp – submerged		2,110 tons	2,143.76 tonnes
Length		351 ft	106.98 m
Beam		28 ft	8.53 m
Draught		16 ft 10 in	5.13 m
Propulsion		2 × 5,250 bhp Parsons/Brown Curtis steam turbine + 1 × 600 shp diesel engine	
		4 × 720 ehp electric motors	
Speed		24 knots surfaced, 9 knots submerged	
Range		3,000 nm at 13.5 knots surfaced, 30 nm at 5 knots submerged	
Armament		10 × 21 in (533 mm) torpedo tubes (6 bow, 4 beam, 2 casing) (2 casing later removed)	
		20 torpedoes carried	
		3 × 4 in (101 mm) guns	
		Depth charges	
Complement (Officers/Men)		59 (5/54)	

Builder	Name	Class	Launched	Fate	Date
Armstrong Whitworth	HMS *K.23*	K Class, Group 2		Cancelled	
Armstrong Whitworth	HMS *K.24*	K Class, Group 2		Cancelled	
Armstrong Whitworth	HMS *K.25*	K Class, Group 2		Cancelled	
Vickers	HMS *K.26*	K Class, Group 2	26.8.1919	PO – Scrapped	3.1931
Vickers	HMS *K.27*	K Class, Group 2		Cancelled	
Vickers	HMS *K.28*	K Class, Group 2		Cancelled	

▲ HMS *K.26* was an improved K Class boat, but was the only one built of six planned. (*HM Submarine Museum*)

L Class

The L Class was developed from the successful E Class, with increased speed and range, as well as an improved armament. The first two boats were initially laid down as E boats named HMS *E.57* and *E.58*, with a revised longer hull. However, such were the improvements that they were reclassified L Class and renamed HMS *L.1* and *L.2*.

The initial batch of eight boats (HMS *L.1–L.8*) were armed with six 18 in (457 mm) torpedoes, four forward and two beam firing. Twenty-six of the second batch were ordered (HMS *L.9–L.36* omitting *L.13*), the eighteen that were built were armed with four 21 in (533 mm) torpedoes in the bow, which required a slight increase in length. Six were modified to enable them to be used as minelayers. These omitted the beam torpedo tubes and carried sixteen mines in vertical chutes located in the saddle tanks (only fourteen on HMS *L.24* and *L.25*). A final batch of twenty-five were ordered (HMS *L.50–L.74*), but only the first seven were delivered to the Royal Navy. These had increased the number of bow tubes to six 21 in (533 mm), and omitted the beam tubes. A total of 25 of the second and third batches were cancelled, including a number that were in various states of construction. Two that were virtually complete (*L.67* and *L.68*) were subsequently completed and sold to the Turkish Navy in 1927.

Nearly all this class were fitted with one 4 in (101 mm) gun (3 in (76 mm) in some early boats), and the last batch were fitted with an additional rearward-firing gun located in an enlarged conning tower. The gun fitted to HMS *L.26* was removed for a while while she was engaged in boom obstruction trials.

On 3 October 1918, HMS *L.10* attacked and hit the German destroyer *S33* off Texel with torpedoes. Unfortunately, she was spotted by other enemy destroyers, which attacked and sank her.

HMS *L.12* was luckier, She fired a salvo of four torpedoes at the German U-boat *UB-90* during a an encounter in the Skagerrak between Norway and Denmark. On this occasion *L.12* was the victor.

When the Armistice was signed, a number of the L Class were cancelled, although six were close to completion and managed to survive with extended delivery dates. They were towed from the builders' yards for finishing in various HM Dockyards.

On 4 June 1919, HMS *L.55* had been attacked and sunk by Russian destroyers in the Baltic. In 1928 she was raised by the Russians, and a request was made by the British government for the return of the bodies. They were brought back to the UK and buried at the Royal Naval Cemetery at Haslar. After repairs and refurbishment, the Russians put her into service as the *L.55*, and she was reported to have been used for training up to the Second World War.

HMS *L.9* foundered while moored at Hong Kong during a typhoon in January 1923. She was salvaged shortly after and returned to service following repairs.

A year later, HMS *L.24* was taking part in an exercise with several warships. It was believed that she was manoeuvring while submerged to make a mock attack, when HMS *Resolution* arrived to participate. As they approached the exercise area, one of the lookouts noticed movement in the water immediately in front of the battleship, followed by a slight bump. Shortly afterwards it was discovered that *L.24* was missing and a rescue was mounted, but with rapidly worsening weather conditions this was restricted to a surface search. A couple of days later, with no hope for any survivors, the search was called off.

During May 1926 HMS *L.12* was one of several submarines that were used as electricity generators during the General Strike where they were located at the Royal Victoria and Albert Docks. In October 1929 she collided with HMS *H.47* in the Irish Sea and managed to limp to Milford Haven. Three of her crew were killed in the accident.

HMS *L.8* could be classed as the boat that would not sink. Her crew must have thought her to have a charmed life as she had already survived two collisions in 1918. One was with HMS *Dove*, followed by another two months later with HMS *P.12*. What must have finally convinced them was that in October 1929, after she had been paid off, she was used as a target for trials with new 4.7 in (119 mm) ammunition. Despite a number of direct hits, she remained afloat and was eventually towed to Portsmouth for examination before being scrapped.

By 1939 only three of the L Class remained in service when war broke out, and by then they were already considered obsolete. Although they initially served operationally, they were soon relegated to the training role. In 1944 they were transferred to Canada, where they were used to give anti-submarine training for convoy escort vessels. In October 1945, HMS *L.23* was the last of the L boats to be paid off, but she did not make it to the breakers as she foundered off Nova Scotia while being towed to be scrapped in 1946.

Class	L Class, Group 1					
Role	Overseas Submarine					

	IMPERIAL	METRIC
Sub Disp – surfaced	891 tons	905.26 tonnes
Sub Disp – submerged	1,074 tons	1,091.18 tonnes
Length	231 ft 1 in	70.43 m
Beam	23 ft 5.5 in	7.15 m
Draught	13 ft 6 in	4.11 m
Propulsion	2 × 1,200 bhp Vickers diesel engines	
	4 × 400 ehp electric motors	
Speed	16.5 knots surfaced, 10 knots submerged	
Range	3,800 nm at 10 knots surfaced, 65 nm at 5 knots submerged	
Armament	6 × 18 in (457 mm) torpedo tubes (4 bow, 4 beam)	
	10 torpedoes carried	
	1 × 3 in (76 mm) gun (later replaced with 4 in (101 mm) Mk. 7 gun)	
Complement (Officers/Men)	35 (4/31)	
Data note		

Builder	Name	Pennant No.	Class	Launched	Fate	Date
Vickers	HMS *L.1* (ex *E.57*)	(57E) L1, 1L	L Class, Group 1	10.5.1917	PO – Scrapped	3.1930
Vickers	HMS *L.2* (ex *E.58*)	(58E) L2, 2L	L Class, Group 1	6.7.1917	PO – Scrapped	3.1930
Vickers	HMS *L.3*	L3, 3L	L Class, Group 1	1.9.1917	PO – Scrapped	2.1931
Vickers	HMS *L.4*	L4, 4L	L Class, Group 1	17.11.1917	PO – Scrapped	2.1934
Swan Hunter	HMS *L.5*	L5, 5L	L Class, Group 1	26.1.1918	PO – Scrapped	1931
Beardmore	HMS *L.6*	L6, 6L	L Class, Group 1	14.1.1918	PO – Scrapped	1.1935
Cammell Laird	HMS *L.7*	L7, 7L	L Class, Group 1	24.4.1917	PO – Scrapped	2.1930
Cammell Laird	HMS *L.8*	L8, 8L	L Class, Group 1	7.7.1917	PO – Scrapped	10.1930

▲ HMS *L.3* almost complete in Vickers' yard at Barrow-in-Furness. *(HM Submarine Museum)*

▼ One of the L Class boats in the dry dock at Harwich for maintenance, along with the smaller E Class boat which they replaced. *(HM Submarine Museum)*

▲ HMS *L.6* under way in 1918. *(HM Submarine Museum)*

▲ HMS *L.4* manoeuvres slowly as she comes alongside in Hong Kong in 1926/7. Note, besides the temporary shade erected for protection from the sun, the fairing around the conning tower has been extended to give some protection to the gun crew.

(HM Submarine Museum)

▶ HMS *L.5* shown with identification marking in the form of a white stripe fore and aft of the conning tower. Initially, the 3 in (76 mm) gun was located on the casing with a mount that could be retracted. *(HM Submarine Museum)*

				IMPERIAL	METRIC
Class		L Class, Group 2			
Role		Overseas & Minelayer Submarine			

	IMPERIAL	METRIC
Sub Disp – surfaced	920 tons	934.72 tonnes
Sub Disp – submerged	1,090 tons	1,107.44 tonnes
Length	238 ft 7 in	72.72 m
Beam	23 ft 6 in	7.16 m
Draught	13 ft 6 in	4.11 m
Propulsion	2 × 1,200 bhp Vickers diesel engines	
	4 × 400 ehp electric motors	
Speed	16.5 knots surfaced, 10 knots submerged	
Range	3,800 nm at 10 kt surfaced, 65 nm at 5 kt submerged	
Armament	4 × 21 in (533 mm) torpedo tubes (bow)	
	8 torpedoes carried	
	2 × 18 in (457 mm) torpedo tubes (beam)	
	2 torpedoes carried	
	1 × 4 in (101 mm) Mk. 4 gun (not fitted to all)	
	16 mines for minelayers but no beam torpedoes (L.24 & L.25 only 14 mines)	
Complement (Officers/Men)	39 (4/35)	

Builder	Name	Pennant No.	Class	Launched	Fate	Date
Denny	HMS *L.9*	L9, 9L	L Class, Group 2	29.1.1918	PO – Scrapped	6.1927
Denny	HMS *L.10*	L10, 10L	L Class, Group 2	24.1.1918	Lost – Gunfire	3.10.1918
Vickers	HMS *L.11*	L11, 11L	L Class, Group 2	26.2.1918	PO – Scrapped	2.1932
Vickers	HMS *L.12*	L12, 12L	L Class, Group 2	16.3.1918	PO – Scrapped	2.1932
Vickers	HMS *L.14*	L14, 14L	L Class, Group 2	10.6.1918	PO – Scrapped	5.1934
Fairfield	HMS *L.15*	L15, 15L	L Class, Group 2	16.1.1918	PO – Scrapped	2.1932
Fairfield	HMS *L.16*	L16, 16L	L Class, Group 2	9.4.1918	PO – Scrapped	2.1932
Vickers Armstrong	HMS *L.17*	L17, 17L	L Class, Group 2	13.5.1918	PO – Scrapped	2.1934
Vickers Armstrong	HMS *L.18*	L18, 18L	L Class, Group 2	21.11.1918	PO – Scrapped	10.1936
Vickers Armstrong	HMS *L.19*	L19, 19L	L Class, Group 2	4.2.1919	PO – Scrapped	4.1937
Vickers Armstrong	HMS *L.20*	L20, 20L	L Class, Group 2	23.9.1918	PO – Scrapped	1.1935
Vickers	HMS *L.21*	L21, 21L	L Class, Group 2	11.10.1919	PO – Scrapped	2.1939
Vickers	HMS *L.22*	L22, 22L	L Class, Group 2	25.10.1919	PO – Scrapped	8.1935
Vickers Armstrong	HMS *L.23*	L23, 23L, 23N, N23	L Class, Group 2	1.7.1919	PO – Foundered	5.1946
Vickers	HMS *L.24*	L24, 24L	L Class, Group 2	19.2.1919	Lost – Accident	10.1.1924
Vickers	HMS *L.25*	L25, 25L	L Class, Group 2	13.2.1919	PO – Scrapped	1935
Vickers Armstrong	HMS *L.26*	L26, 26L, 26N, N26	L Class, Group 2	19.5.1919	PO – Expended as target	4.1945

Builder	Name	Pennant No.	Class	Launched	Fate	Date
Vickers Armstrong	HMS *L.27*	L27, 27L, 27N, N27	L Class, Group 2	14.6.1919	PO – Scrapped	1946
Vickers	HMS *L.28*		L Class, Group 2		Cancelled	
Vickers	HMS *L.29*		L Class, Group 2		Cancelled	
Vickers	HMS *L.30*		L Class, Group 2		Cancelled	
Vickers	HMS *L.31*		L Class, Group 2		Cancelled	
Vickers	HMS *L.32*		L Class, Group 2	23.8.1919	Cancelled – Scrapped	1920
Swan Hunter	HMS *L.33, 33L*		L Class, Group 2	29.5.1919	PO – Scrapped	2.1932
HM Dockyard, Pembroke	HMS *L.34*		L Class, Group 2		Cancelled	
HM Dockyard, Pembroke	HMS *L.35*		L Class, Group 2		Cancelled	
Fairfield	HMS *L.36*		L Class, Group 2		Cancelled	

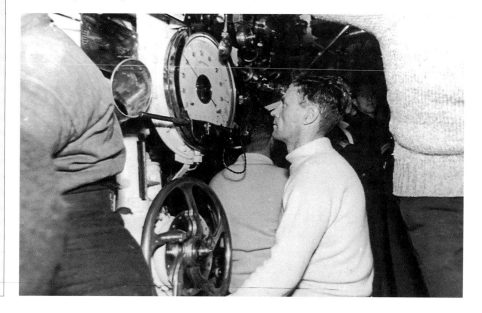

▼ The coxswain mans the forward planes and maintains the boat at 30 feet (9.14 m) while the periscope is being used. *(HM Submarine Museum)*

▲ HMS *L.14*. *(HM Submarine Museum)*

▼ HMS *L.15*. *(HM Submarine Museum)*

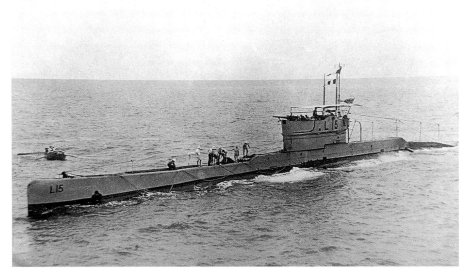

▲ An officer keeps a lookout through the periscope, not only for potential targets but to avoid a collision. *(HM Submarine Museum)*

▲ HMS *L.9* being salvaged in Hong Kong after having foundered during a typhoon in January 1923. Following a refurbishment she was returned to service and not paid off until April 1926. *(HM Submarine Museum)*

▲ HMS *L.15* returns to Wei-Hai-Wei with some of her crew at harbour stations and a torpedo displayed on deck. *(HM Submarine Museum)*

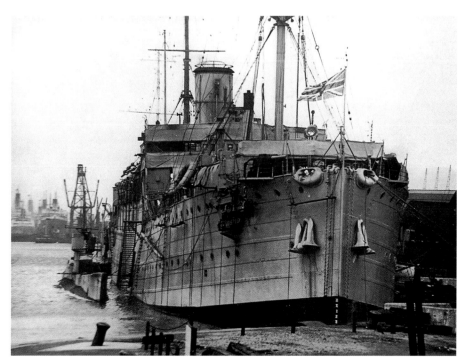

▲ HMS *L.22*. *(HM Submarine Museum)*

◄ Dwarfed by HMS *Titania*, HMS *L.21* and three other boats were located to the Victoria and Albert Docks in London to provide electricity during the General Strike. *(HM Submarine Museum)*

71

◀ HMS *L.33* taking in a torpedo.
(HM Submarine Museum)

▲ HMS *L.20* lies beached at
Newport in 1935, having been sold
to Cashmore for breaking up.
(HM Submarine Museum)

▼ The guncrew of HMS *L.27* continue to train, even when alongside at Fort Blockhouse.
This photo was taken about 1940 with barrage balloons over Gosport.
(HM Submarine Museum)

▶ HMS *L.23* undergoing a refit at
Chatham in 1924. *(HM Submarine
Museum)*

Class	L Class, Group 3
Role	Overseas Submarine

	IMPERIAL	METRIC
Sub Disp – surfaced	960 tons	975.36 tonnes
Sub Disp – submerged	1,150 tons	1,168.40 tonnes
Length	235 ft 6 in	71.78 m
Beam	23 ft 6 in	7.16 m
Draught	13 ft 6 in	4.11 m
Propulsion	2 × 1,200 bhp Vickers diesel engines	
	4 × 400 ehp electric motors	
Speed	16.5 knots surfaced, 10 knots submerged	
Range	3,800 nm at 10 knots surfaced, 65 nm at 5 knots submerged	
Armament	6 × 21 in (533 mm) bow torpedo tubes	
	12 torpedoes carried	
	2 × 4 in (101 mm) Mk. 12 gun (removed from some)	
Complement (Officers/Men)	40 (4/36)	

Builder	Name	Pennant No.	Class	Launched	Fate	Date
Cammell Laird	HMS *L.50*		L Class, Group 3		Cancelled – Scrapped	
Cammell Laird	HMS *L.51*		L Class, Group 3		Cancelled	
Armstrong Whitworth	HMS *L.52*	L52, 52L	L Class, Group 3	18.12.1918	PO – Foundered	9.1935
Armstrong Whitworth	HMS *L.53*	L53, 53L	L Class, Group 3	12.8.1919	PO – Scrapped	1938
Denny	HMS *L.54*	L54, 54L	L Class, Group 3	20.8.1919	Struck off	5.1939
Fairfield	HMS *L.55*	L55, 55L	L Class, Group 3	21.9.1918	Lost – Enemy action	4.6.1919
Fairfield	HMS *L.56*	L56, 56L	L Class, Group 3	29.5.1919	PO – Scrapped	3.1938
Fairfield	HMS *L.57*		L Class, Group 3		Cancelled – Scrapped	
Fairfield	HMS *L.58*		L Class, Group 3		Cancelled – Scrapped	
Beardmore	HMS *L.59*		L Class, Group 3		Cancelled	
Cammell Laird	HMS *L.60*		L Class, Group 3		Cancelled	
Cammell Laird	HMS *L.61*		L Class, Group 3		Cancelled	
Fairfield	HMS L.62		L Class, Group 3		Cancelled	
Scott's	HMS *L.63*		L Class, Group 3		Cancelled	
Scott's	HMS *L.64*		L Class, Group 3		Cancelled	
Swan Hunter	HMS *L.65*		L Class, Group 3		Cancelled – Scrapped	
Swan Hunter	HMS *L.66*		L Class, Group 3		Cancelled	
Armstrong	HMS *L.67*		L Class, Group 3		Cancelled – Sold	
Armstrong	HMS *L.68*		L Class, Group 3		Cancelled – Sold	
Beardmore	HMS *L.69*	L69, 69L	L Class, Group 3	6.12.1923	PO – Scrapped	2.1939
Beardmore	HMS *L.70*		L Class, Group 3		Cancelled – Scrapped	
Scott's	HMS *L.71*	L71, 71L	L Class, Group 3	17.5.1919	PO – Scrapped	3.1938
Scott's	HMS *L.72*		L Class, Group 3		Cancelled – Scrapped	
Denny	HMS *L.73*		L Class, Group 3		Cancelled	
Denny	HMS *L.74*		L Class, Group 3		Cancelled	

▲ HMS *L.71* at Malta in the mid-20s. *(HM Submarine Museum)*

M Class

In August 1915, Admiral Sir John Arbuthnot Fisher, who had instigated the Dreadnought Class of battleships, proposed to the Admiralty the idea of a 'Dreadnought submarine'. These submarine monitors were to be fitted with a 12 in (305 mm) gun mounted forward of the conning tower, as he considered that the torpedoes then in service were incapable of stopping, never-mind sinking, a warship at sea.

Red tape in the Admiralty meant that it was six months before any action began to surface. Vickers had already laid the keel of HMS *K.18* before the decision was made to change the order to use it as the base of HMS *M.1*. The same happened with a further three, which were completed using HMS *K.19, K.20* and *K.21*.

A difficulty the Admiralty had with the M Class was that if the Royal Navy were seen operating such a boat the Germans would follow suit, probably inflicting more damage to Allied shipping than would be done to German shipping.

The 12 in (305 mm) Mk IX gun that was fitted to the M Class was similar to those that were fitted to the Majestic battleships, and was immediately available. They were subsequently exchanged with the Mk VIII when the guns needed to be replaced. A smaller, high-angle 3 in (76 mm) gun was also fitted specifically to use against aircraft, which were by that time starting to become a threat.

The Mk IX gun weighed a total of 122 tons (123.95 tonnes) including the mount. Forty rounds were stowed, and these weighed a further 29 tons (29.5 tonnes). The gun crew comprised eleven specialist gunnery ratings, plus sixteen for the ammunition party for the main gun, plus a further six for the anti-aircraft gun. However, this weight made the boat very stable.

The 12 in (305 mm) gun had a limited amount of travel, twenty degrees of elevation and ten degrees depressed, with ten degrees either side of the centreline. The gun mount was protected by a non-watertight fairing, while the machinery for loading the shell and charge were inside a watertight tower. This meant that to fire the gun the boat would need to surface to load, and although the gun had a 32,700 yard (29,900 m) range, because of the movement of the boat and absence of a separate spotter, accuracy would be approximate. Later, in 1923, Max Horton, who was Captain of the K and M Squadron, reported that the operation of such a squadron that was able to approach a coastline unseen until about to open fire was an important factor. This effectiveness was at a maximum at 21,000 yards (19,200 m) when aided with spotters.

When in attack mode, the boat would 'dipchick' up and down from periscope depth to approach close to the target. Once the order to break surface was given, it was possible for the boat to surface, gun to be loaded and fired in 30 to 40 seconds. Within another 50 to 55 seconds the boat could dive back down to periscope depth. But it then was required to surface once again to reload. This break in continuity meant that it was impossible to use the previous shot to provide the necessary adjustment to precisely place a shell on a target.

HMS *M.1* went to sea in 1919 and was not joined by HMS *M.2* until 1920. None of the M Class were to fire their formidable guns in anger, but they were to be subjected to some interesting times. The powerful 12 in (305 mm) gun was waterproofed with an effective tampion at the barrel end, but for some reason was not made watertight at the breech end. The effect of any water in the barrel when firing was disastrous, and the barrel burst on at least four occasions. On another occasion off Portland, the director-layer failed to notice that the tampion had not been opened, a safety interlock also failed and when the gun was fired, the tampion was shot off. As if this was not bad enough, the heavy tampion remained attached to a strand of the wire bound barrel. As a result the boat became anchored by a piece of its own gun and took many hours to be released.

HMS *M.1* continued to operate with her gun after the war. On 12 November 1925, during an exercise to simulate the passage of a troop convoy with minesweepers representing destroyers, *M.1* dived and was never seen again. This baffled many experts for a number of days. It wasn't until the report of the missing boat was read in a newspaper by the captain of the Swedish SS *Vidar* when she arrived in Germany that the pieces began to fall into place. The captain had seen the exercise taking place during his passage when suddenly there was a noise and the boat juddered. The captain put this down to some explosive being used in the exercise. After a check for any leaks, satisfied that there was no damage done to his ship, he continued on his way. As soon as he read the report, the captain reported the incident on the 19th. Despite a month-long search by divers and survey ships she was never located. An inspection of the SS *Vidar* confirmed that she had been involved in a collision, and there was proof that it was *M.1* when some paint was found. On 18 June 1999 a group of divers managed to locate HMS *M.1* some 55 miles (88.6 km) south-east of Plymouth.

The Washington Disarmament Treaty of 1920 stated that no submarine could have a gun larger than 8 in (203 mm), and as a result HMS *M.2* and HMS *M.3* had their guns removed. *M.2* then became the subject of a conversion into an aircraft carrier. She retained the 3 in (76 mm) gun, as well as the four 18 in (457 mm) torpedoes, and a hangar was constructed forward of the conning tower where the original 12 in gun was located. This hangar was to accommodate a single Parnell Peto, which had been specially designed and built for the project. *M.2* was recommissioned towards the end of 1927 and began a series of trials.

Although HMS *M.2* was not the first submarine to carry an aircraft – HMS

E.22 had already done that back in 1916 – she was certainly the first to have a watertight hangar which could remain sealed while submerged. In a slick routine in ideal weather conditions, she was able to surface and catapult the Peto in around twelve minutes, and recovery would be a little quicker. However, this could take significantly longer in less good weather. The Peto was supposed to be restricted to a maximum of Force 2 conditions.

Sadly, on 26 January 1932 one of the hatch doors was left open and she sank off Portland Bill. On this occasion, the boat was located. When divers approached her, they found the hatch leading into the hangar and the hangar door were both open, possible in error whilst trying to improve the launching time. With the hangar floor usually awash, the effect of a large wave or loss of stability of the boat could have caused sufficient water to enter the boat and control to be lost. Quite possibly, a mechanical fault manifested itself at a critical point or orders were misunderstood – we shall never know. What was known was that yet again, another M Class had claimed the lives of her whole crew.

The Royal Navy never built another aircraft carrier submarine, although examples were built by France, Germany, Italy and USA, and in substantial numbers by the Japanese Navy.

In June 1927 HMS *M.3* arrived at Chatham, where she underwent a different transformation, this time to a minelayer. She was fitted with a storage and delivery system mounted outside the pressure hull that was protected by a new casing. One hundred mines could be carried, and a conveyor transported them to the stern of the boat, where they were released. Trials were conducted and the system proved satisfactory, but the volume of water contained in the new casing resulted in significant control difficulties and lack of response.

HMS *M.3* was classed as an experimental boat, and owing to her questionable handling capabilities she was scrapped in 1932. The information gained on minelaying technology for submarines proved invaluable for the Porpoise Class boats, but these did not approach the capability of the *M.3*. She might have been extremely useful in the Second World War had she not been so vulnerable. However, the experience gained was used in the design of the Porpoise Class minelayers.

HMS *M.4* was to be the last of the M Class, but it was cancelled before completion in October 1919. The hull remained at the High Walker Yard of Armstrong Whitworth as a fender until she was finally scrapped in 1921.

Of the four M Class boats that were ordered, only three were to be completed. Of these, two were lost in accidents.

Class	M Class
Role	Monitor Submarine

	IMPERIAL	METRIC
Sub Disp – surfaced	1,610 tons	1,635.76 tonnes
Sub Disp – submerged	1,946 tons	1,977.13 tonnes
Length	295 ft 9 in*	90.14 m
Beam	24 ft 7 in	7.49 m
Draught	15 ft 9 in	4.80 m
Propulsion	2 × 1,200 bhp Vickers diesel engines	
	4 × 800 ehp electric motors	
Speed	15 knots on surface, 9 knots submerged	
Range	2,500 nm at 16 knots surfaced, 10 nm at 10 knots submerged	
Armament	4 × 21 in (533 mm) torpedo tubes (bow) (18 in)	
	(457 mm) on *M.1* & *M.2*)	
	10 torpedoes carried	
	1 × 12 in (305 mm) Mk IX gun (later replaced by Mk VIII)	
	1 × 3 in (76 mm) AA gun	
	When converted *M.3* could carry 100 mines (but only 8 torpedoes)	
Complement (Officers/Men)	64 (6/58)	
Data note	*303 ft on *M.3* and *M.4*	

Builder	Name	Class	Launched	Fate	Date
Vickers	HMS *M.1*	M Class	9.7.1917	Lost – Accident	12.11.1925
Vickers	HMS *M.2*	M Class	15.4.1919	Sunk – Accident	26.1.1932
Armstrong Whitworth	HMS *M.1*	M Class	19.10.1918	PO – Scrapped	2.1932
Armstrong Whitworth	HMS *M.4*	M Class	20.7.1919	Cancelled	10.1919

▲ HMS *M.1* armed with her 12 in (305 mm) gun and camouflaged to break up her shape. *(HM Submarine Museum)*

▲ HMS *M.3* undergoes maintenance in a dry dock at Gibraltar. *(HM Submarine Museum)*

▼ Water in the gun barrel has a disastrous consequence when fired, as captured by the bosun of nearby HMS *Conquest* when the barrel on HMS *M.1* exploded off Gibraltar in 1923. This happened on a number of occasions. *(HM Submarine Museum)*

▼ HMS *M.2* with her Parnell Peto being prepared for flight. *(HM Submarine Museum)*

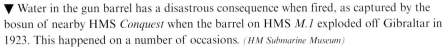

▲ The Parnell Peto is catapulted off HMS *M.2*. *(HM Submarine Museum)*

▼ With flying stations over, HMS *M.2* returns beneath the waves. *(HM Submarine Museum)*

▼ HMS *M.3* had her gun removed and was converted to a minelayer with a capacity of 100 mines in an enlarged casing. *(HM Submarine Museum)*

R Class (Early)

The R Class were designed as anti-submarine submarines, and entered service in 1917. Today they would be classed as Hunter Killers. For this role they were designed to have a greater submerged speed than surfaced, plus six 18 in (457 mm) torpedo tubes in the bow. The design only allowed for one reload, but in practice six were usually carried during active service by making use of accommodation space.

The design of the superstructure of the R boats was made as light as possible. A 4 in (101 mm) gun was originally planned to be fitted, but this was omitted to keep the weight down. Ballast tanks were fitted internally, all to keep the shape as streamlined as possible. They were fitted with a pair of powerful 1,200 bhp electric motors which enabled them to reach a speed of 15 knots when submerged – a speed that was not to be beaten until the later stages of the Second World War. Their surface speed was far less spectacular, with only 9.5 knots attained because of the small 240 bhp diesel engine, which was found to be insufficient to recharge the 220 batteries. Not only that, but when on the surface it proved difficult to steer because of this lack of power.

Apart from the periscope, to assist in the detection of enemy submarines, the R boats were fitted with five fairly primitive hydrophones. The R Class boats entered service shortly before the war ended, and only mounted one actual attack on a German U-boat, and even then the torpedo failed to explode.

Without having proved themselves in action, the R Class failed to get the support that they should have done. Of the twelve that had been ordered only ten were built in 1918/19, the other two being cancelled before being launched. All had been paid off by 1925.

Class	R Class (Early)
Role	Anti-submarine Submarine

	IMPERIAL	METRIC
Sub Disp – surfaced	415 tons	421.64 tonnes
Sub Disp – submerged	505 tons	513.08 tonnes
Length	163 ft 9 in	49.91 m
Beam	15 ft 1.5 in	4.61 m
Draught	11 ft 7 in	3.53 m
Propulsion	1 × 240 bhp American diesel engine	
	2 × 1,200 bhp electric motors	
Speed	10 knots on surface, 15 knots submerged	
Range	2,000 nm at 9 knots surfaced, 150 nm at 1.5 knots submerged	
Armament	6 × 18 in (457 mm) torpedo tubes (bow)	
	12 torpedoes carried	
Complement (Officers/Men)	22 (3/19)	

Builder	Name	Class	Launched	Fate	Date
HM Dockyard, Chatham	HMS R.1	R Class (Early)	25.4.1918	PO – Scrapped	1.1923
HM Dockyard, Chatham	HMS R.2	R Class (Early)	25.4.1918	PO – Scrapped	2.1923
HM Dockyard, Chatham	HMS R.3	R Class (Early)	8.6.1918	PO – Scrapped	2.1923
HM Dockyard, Chatham	HMS R.4	R Class (Early)	8.6.1918	PO – Scrapped	5.1934
HM Dockyard, Pembroke	HMS R.5	R Class (Early)		Cancelled – Scrapped	
HM Dockyard, Pembroke	HMS R.6	R Class (Early)		Cancelled – Scrapped	
Vickers	HMS R.7	R Class (Early)	14.5.1918	PO – Scrapped	2.1923
Vickers	HMS R.8	R Class (Early)	28.6.1918	PO – Scrapped	2.1923
Armstrong Whitworth	HMS R.9	R Class (Early)	12.8.1918	PO – Scrapped	2.1923
Armstrong Whitworth	HMS R.10	R Class (Early)	15.10.1918	PO – Scrapped	2.1929
Cammell Laird	HMS R.11	R Class (Early)	16.3.1918	PO – Scrapped	2.1923
Cammell Laird	HMS R.12	R Class (Early)	9.4.1918	PO – Scrapped	2.1923

▶ The control room of HMS *R.8* with (*l* to *r*) the Sperry gyrocompass, hydroplane control and helm. *(HM Submarine Museum)*

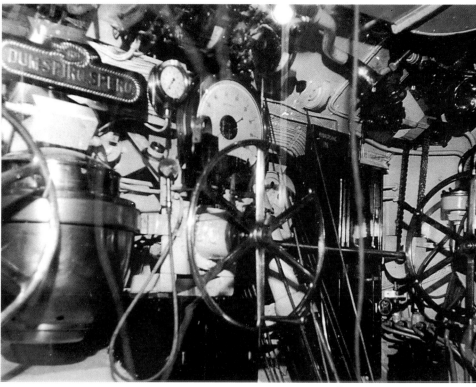

◀ HMS *R.3*. *(HM Submarine Museum)*

X1 Class

The sole X1 Class was originally conceived in the spring of 1915 by the Royal Navy Submarine Committee. While the mainstream Navy plans were for submarines to operate as part of the Grand Fleet, most submariners saw the submarine operating as an independent boat. The X1 Class was planned to be a cruiser submarine with heavy armament in the form of guns, as well as torpedoes. She would inevitably be a large boat, needing to be fast and capable of operating at extended ranges. In fact when she was completed she was the largest submarine in the world. Not only that, at 2,780 tons, she was the largest submarine built for the Royal Navy until the nuclear boats.

The idea for the cruiser submarine was not allowed to progress with build capacity needed for the Grand Fleet. Once the war was over and an opportunity to examine captured submarines had been completed, including the German cruisers *U-151* to *U-157*, the idea surfaced once more. By 1921, the plans were well advanced, with funding included in the Naval Estimates for 1921/22, and HMS *X.1* was laid down in Chatham Dockyard that November – the first new boat to be built since the First World War.

It was about this time that the Washington Conference of the five major naval powers was trying to limit fleet sizes, including that of submarines. The British government wished to eliminate submarines altogether, but its arguments were rejected. The treaty eventually resulted in restricting development of the submarine for military purposes only and not to be used against merchant shipping. This was signed by four of the five, with France refusing to ratify that part of the treaty. Germany had already been banned from building submarines.

HMS *X.1* was completed on 23 September 1925, and accepted the following April. She was the largest submarine at sea in the world. She undertook a passage to Gibraltar and back which highlighted a problem that was to persist with her MAN engines, and she was returned to the dockyard for rectification. In January she passed a full-power demonstration and was despatched to join the Mediterranean Fleet. Within a year *X.1* was laid up in Malta after major engine problems which were to occur again only a couple of months after being repaired. Various other troubles dogged her, but according to her officers most of the operating troubles were because of crew errors – basically she handled well when she was running properly.

HMS *X.1* was laid up in reserve in Fareham Creek in May 1933 and taken off the Active List three years later and scrapped. She was the only Royal Navy submarine that had been built after the First World War that did not survive until the Second.

Class	X1 Class
Role	Experimental Cruiser Submarine

	IMPERIAL	METRIC
Sub Disp – surfaced	2,780 tons	2,824.48 tonnes
Sub Disp – submerged	3,600 tons	3,657.6 tonnes
Length	350 ft	106.68 m
Beam	29 ft 9 in	9.07 m
Draught	15 ft 9 in	4.8 m
Propulsion	2 × 3,000 bhp MAN diesel engines	
	2 × 1,300 ehp electric motors + 1,200 bhp diesel generators	
Speed	19 knots surfaced, 9 knots submerged	
Range	16,200 nm at 10 knots or 5,300 nm at 18 knots surfaced, 18 nm at 4 knots submerged	
Armament	6 × 21 in (533 mm) torpedo tubes (bow)	
	12 torpedoes carried	
	2 × twin 5.2 in (132 mm) guns	
Complement (Officers/Men)	109 (8/101)	

Builder	Name	Pennant No.	Class	Launched	Fate	Date
HM Dockyard, Chatham	HMS *X.1*	X1	X1 Class	16.6.1923	PO – Scrapped	12.1936

▲ HMS *X.1*. *(HM Submarine Museum)*

▼ Plagued with problems, HMS *X.1* was undergoing maintenance in dry-dock at Portsmouth in June 1931 when the shoring timbers collapsed, causing her to topple over. *(HM Submarine Museum)*

Oberon, Oxley and Odin Class (O Class)

The O Class came into being owing to an increase in uneasiness following the failure to renew the Anglo-Japanese Alliance in 1922. The Admiralty produced various designs for warships capable of operations in Far East waters. One was a proposal for a much improved L Class ocean-going submarine, which became the O Class. An order was placed for HMS *O.1*, which was subsequently named HMS *Oberon*.

Some 40 ft (12 m) longer than the L Class, their maximum speed was 2 knots slower, but they could carry double the number of torpedoes and had nearly double the range. The improvements also included an increase in wireless range as well as diving depth. The O Class design development continued as production ensued. A 4 in (101 mm) gun was mounted on the front of the conning tower. Later modifications included fitting the gun in a revolving mount and some additional fuel being stored in the upper section of the saddle tanks, but this resulted in incurable leaks. Later-built boats had a sloping ram bow. HMS *Oberon* became the first British submarine to be fitted with Asdic (Allied Submarine Detection Investigation Committee), which later developed as Sonar.

The good overall performance specification of the O Class led the Australian Navy to order a pair of these submarines. However, subsequent economic problems in Australia led to these being supplied to the Royal Navy as HMS *Otway* (ex RAN *A0.1*) and *Oxley* (ex RAN *A0.2*) in 1931. Although built at the same time as Oberon, they featured the ram-shaped bow of the later-built O Class. A further identification of these two boats was the net cutter fitted to the bow. A further three similar examples were built for, and delivered to, the Chilean Navy

HMS *Oberon* and *Otway* both saw operational service in the Second World War, but were later transferred to the training role. HMS *Oxley* became the first Royal Navy submarine to be lost in the war, when she was torpedoed in error by another submarine, HMS *Triton*, on 10 September 1939 off the Norwegian coast. Two survivors were recovered and then the unfortunate error was discovered.

HMS *Triton* had in fact originally thought this boat was HMS *Oxley*. They had both been in contact during the patrol to block the top exit from the North Sea, and she was known to be in the area, although they should not have been close to each other. The crew of *Triton* sent some recognition signals, but with no response could only assume that HMS *Oxley* was an enemy U-boat, and she was attacked with torpedoes. In fact HMS *Oxley* had been signalling, but with a faulty lamp.

Owing to the sensitivity of the time the true facts did not emerge until the 1950s.

The story that was released was that she had suffered an accidental explosion. When a similar occurrence between HMS *Sturgeon* and *Swordfish* also happened off Norway a few days later, the Admiralty decided to increase the spacing of these boat patrols from four to sixteen miles.

The second O Class batch comprised six boats that looked similar to those built for Australia with the ram bow, but they were not fitted with the net cutter. A more powerful diesel engine was fitted that gave a higher surface speed. The forward hydroplanes were relocated from the bottom of the pressure hull to the top, and were hinged to allow the planes to be turned in when not in use. Although this increased the diving time, as the boat now required to be partially submerged before that came into effect, it made them less prone to damage which was difficult to repair when constantly submerged.

During a patrol to the Gulf of Taranto late on 13 June 1940, HMS *Odin* was spotted on the surface by the Italian destroyer *Strale*. She immediately launched an attack by firing her guns and then attempted to ram *Odin*, which was desperately trying to dive. As she slipped through the waves with the destroyer bearing down on her, she fired a torpedo from her stern tube. *Strale* replied by firing a number of depth charges, but as nothing else was seen in the darkness, she resumed her patrol. A couple of hours later HMS *Odin* was again spotted on the surface and attacked by the torpedo boat *Balento*, which again tried to ram her and made several passes firing depth charges as she escaped below the waves. No more was heard, and later, in daylight, an Italian Air Force aircraft reported two separate oil slicks resulting in the Italians claiming to have destroyed two submarines. When *Odin* failed to return from her patrol, it was thought that what probably happened was that she was damaged during the first attack and was withdrawing when she was attacked for the second time, and this time she was fatally damaged.

A few days later, HMS *Orpheus* was reported missing after she failed to return home from her patrol off the Libyan coast.

On 1 August 1940, HMS *Oswald* was on patrol near Sicily when an escorted convoy was spotted passing through the Straits of Messina. She moved in but was unsuccessful in her attack, but as a result the Italians sent out destroyers to hunt down the submarine that was threatening their ships. *Oswald* was caught on the surface and was rammed by the Italian destroyer *Ugolino Vivaldi*. The crew immediately abandoned ship, and all but three of them were picked up by the Italians.

HMS *Odin* was the first of three of these larger boats that were lost in just four days!

HMS *Olympus* had spent most her time in either the Far East or Mediterranean. On 8 May 1942 she was leaving Malta heading for Gibraltar with the surviving and injured crew of various boats that had been bombed by enemy aircraft when she struck a German mine. While there were a number of survivors, a total of 89 were lost.

Malta was a vital position for the Royal Navy during the Second World War. It was frequently subjected to German air attacks and mining of her coast, even to the point of blockading her. Supply convoys were attacked and suffered horrendous losses. The larger submarines were utilised as a less visible transport, carrying vital materials such as ammunition, aviation fuel and torpedoes. Various boats were used for this vital role.

Class	Oberon/O Class prototype	
Role	Patrol Submarine Prototype	
	IMPERIAL	**METRIC**
Sub Disp – surfaced	1,490 tons	1,513.84 tonnes
Sub Disp – submerged	1,892 tons	1,922.27 tonnes
Length	269 ft 8 in	82.19 m
Beam	28 ft	8.53 m
Draught	15 ft 6 in	4.72 m
Propulsion	2 × 1,350 bhp Admiralty diesel engines	
	2 × 650 ehp electric motors	
Speed	13.5 knots surfaced, 7.5 knots submerged	
Range	6,500 nm at 10 knots surfaced, 60 nm at 4 knots submerged	
Armament	8 × 21 in (533 mm) torpedo tubes (6 bow, 2 stern)	
	16 torpedoes carried	
	1 × 4 in (101 mm) gun	
Complement (Officers/Men)	53 (6/47)	

Builder	Name	Pennant No.	Class	Launched	Fate	Date
HM Dockyard, Chatham	HMS *Oberon* (ex *O.1*)	21P, 21N, N21	Oberon Class prototype	24.9.1926	PO – Scrapped	8.1945

▼ HMS *Oberon*. (*HM Submarine Museum*)

	IMPERIAL	METRIC
Class	Oxley/O Class, Group 1	
Role	Patrol Submarine	
Sub Disp – surfaced	1,540 tons	1,564.64 tonnes
Sub Disp – submerged	1,860 tons	1,889.76 tonnes
Length	270 ft 6 in	82.45 m
Beam	27 ft 6 in	8.38 m
Draught	15 ft 6 in	4.72 m
Propulsion	2 × 1,500 bhp Admiralty diesel engines	
	2 × 660 ehp electric motors	
Speed	15 knots surfaced, 8.5 knots submerged	
Range	7,000 nm at 10 knots surfaced, 60 nm at 4 knots submerged	
Armament	8 × 21 in (533 mm) torpedo tubes (6 bow, 2 stern)	
	16 torpedoes carried	
	1 × 4 in (101 mm) gun	
Complement (Officers/Men)	53 (5/48)	

Builder	Name	Pennant No.	Class	Launched	Fate	Date
Vickers Armstrong	HMS *Otway* (ex *AO.2*)	51P, 51N, N51	Oxley Class	7.9.1926	PO – Scrapped	8.1945
Vickers Armstrong	HMS *Oxley* (ex *AO.1*)	55P	Oxley Class	29.6.1926	Lost – Sunk in error	10.9.1945

▲ HMS *Oxley* alongside at Fort Blockhouse in 1937, with HMS *L.23* and *L.26* outside her. *(HM Submarine Museum)*

Class	Odin/O Class, Group 2
Role	Patrol Submarine

	IMPERIAL	METRIC
Sub Disp – surfaced	1,743 tons	1,770.89 tonnes
Sub Disp – submerged	2,029 tons	2,061.46 tonnes
Length	283 ft 6 in	86.41 m
Beam	29 ft 10 in	9.09 m
Draught	16 ft 1 in	4.90 m
Propulsion	2 × 2,200 bhp Admiralty diesel engines	
	2 × 660 ehp electric motors	
Speed	17.5 knots surfaced, 8.5 knots submerged	
Range	9,700 nm at 8 knots surfaced, 52 nm at 4 knots submerged	
Armament	8 × 21 in (533 mm) torpedo tubes (6 bow, 2 stern)	
	14 torpedoes carried	
	1 × 4 in (101 mm) gun	
Complement (Officers/Men)	53 (5/48)	

Builder	Name	Pennant No.	Class	Launched	Fate	Date
HM Dockyard, Chatham	HMS *Odin*	84P, 84N, N84	Odin Class	5.2.1928	Lost – Enemy action	14.6.1940
Beardmore	HMS *Olympus*	35P, 35N, N35	Odin Class	11.12.1928	Lost – Mine	8.5.1942
Beardmore	HMS *Orpheus*	46P, 46N, N46	Odin Class	26.2.1929	Lost – Unknown	6.1940
Vickers Armstrong	HMS *Osiris*	67P, 67N, N67	Odin Class	19.5.1928	PO – Scrapped	9.1946
Vickers Armstrong	HMS *Oswald*	58P, 58N, N58	Odin Class	19.6.1928	Lost – Rammed	1.8.1940
Vickers Armstrong	HMS *Otus*	92P, 92N, N92	Odin Class	31.8.1928	PO – Scuttled	9.1946

▲ HMS *Olympus*. *(HM Submarine Museum)*

▼ HMS *Osiris* being launched by Vickers at Barrow-in-Furness in May 1928. *(HM Submarine Museum)*

Parthian Class

The Parthian Class were very similar to the O Class but with a raked bow and a fitted shield for the 4 in (101 mm) gun. As with the O Class, these boats carried some of their fuel in the saddle tanks. However, in common with other similarly configured boats, the effect of pressures on riveted tanks when submerged caused fuel to leak, which always left a tell-tale trace on the surface.

On 9 June 1931, HMS *Poseidon* was lost after a collision with the Chinese coaster *Yuta* off Wei-Hai-Wei in the Yellow Sea. Thirty-five of the 57 crew escaped in what was the first real use of the Davis Submarine Escape Apparatus.

During 1941/2, HMS *Pandora* and *Parthian*, along with the O Class *Otus* and R Class *Regent*, were utilised as supply boats to Malta. For these operations one section of batteries were removed and no spare torpedoes carried, to enable dry stores to be carried. Petrol and other fuels were carried and fresh water was stored in the ballast tanks.

In July 1940 HMS *Phoenix* failed to return to Malta after a patrol off Sicily. She had sent a signal on the night of 14 July, and the Italian torpedo boat *Albatross* reported counter-attacking with depth charges a submarine that was attacking their tanker *Dora* on the 16th. This may have been her fate.

HMS *Perseus* was certainly a mine victim. On 6 December 1941 she was operating in the Ionian Sea when she struck an Italian mine. Leading Stoker Capes and four other crew members were trapped at a depth of 170 ft (52 m) in the sunken vessel. They decided that their only chance of escape was the Davis Submarine Escape Apparatus. They drank a bottle of rum for Dutch courage and attempted the escape. Only Capes made it to the surface. By his own single-minded effort he struggled some five or six miles to the island of Cephalonia, where he was later found by some locals, and eventually made it back home after some eighteen months through the assistance of a number of other locals and the Resistance, who had risked their lives in doing so. Leading Stoker John Capes was awarded the British Empire Medal. So remarkable was this escape that many found it difficult to believe, but in 1998 the wreck of HMS *Perseus* was found providing the evidence, including the rum bottle. Unfortunately, John Capes, who had become a CPO before he retired, had died ten years earlier. But what a remarkable feat of endurance.

HMS *Pandora* saw considerable action, sinking a French Colonial sloop off Algiers in July 1940 and a further three transport ships over the next year. She survived a depth charge attack in September 1940, but her luck ran out when she was one of a number of boats that were caught up in the German bombing raids on the docks at Valetta, Malta, on 1 April 1942 during supply runs from Gibraltar. She was moved the following year and was finally broken up after the war

HMS *Parthian* also had success, with the sinking of the Italian submarine *Diamante* off Tobruk on 20 June 1940. Six months later she sank the merchant ship *Carlo Martinolich*. During 1941 she sank three transport ships and, on 25 June, the Vichy French submarine *Souffleur*. She underwent a refit at the beginning of 1942 in the USA before returning to the Mediterranean, where she was heavily utilised in carrying vital war supplies of aviation fuel and ammunition to Malta. In July 1943 she was on patrol in the Southern Adriatic, but failed to return to her base at Beirut in August. She was assumed to be yet another probable mine victim.

HMS *Proteus* was probably the most successful of the Parthian Class. Having spent her peacetime years in the Far East, she was tasked to the Mediterranean. Like many of the larger submarines, she transported vital war supplies to Malta. But more importantly, by the time she was redeployed to the UK in 1943 she had attacked and damaged or sunk eleven Italian transport ships.

	Class	Parthian Class
	Role	Overseas-patrol Submarine

	IMPERIAL	METRIC
Sub Disp – surfaced	1,768 tons	1,796.29 tonnes
Sub Disp – submerged	2,035 tons	2,067.56 tonnes
Length	289 ft 2 in	88.13 m
Beam	29 ft 11 in	9.12 m
Draught	13 ft 9 in	4.19 m
Propulsion	2 × 2,320 bhp Admiralty diesel engines	
	2 × 660 ehp electric motors	
Speed	18 knots surfaced, 8.5 knots submerged	
Range	8,400 nm at 10 knots, 60 nm at 4 knots submerged	
Armament	8 × 21 in (533 mm) torpedo tubes (6 bow, 2 stern)	
	14 torpedoes carried	
	1 × 4 in (101 mm) gun	
Complement (Officers/Men)	53 (5/48)	

Builder	Name	Pennant No.	Class	Launched	Reason	
Vickers Armstrong	HMS *Pandora* (ex *Python*)	42P, 42N, N42	Parthian Class	22.8.1929	Lost – Salvaged – Scrapped	1.4.1942
HM Dockyard, Chatham	HMS *Parthian*	75P, 75N, N75	Parthian Class	22.6.1929	Lost – Unknown	8.1943

Builder	Name	Pennant No.	Class	Launched	Fate	Date
Vickers Armstrong	HMS *Perseus*	36P, 36N, N36	Parthian Class	22.5.1929	Lost – Mine	6.12.1941
Cammell Laird	HMS *Phoenix*	96P, 96N, N96	Parthian Class	3.10.1929	Lost – Depth charge	16.7.1940
Vickers Armstrong	HMS *Poseidon*	99P	Parthian Class	21.6.1929	Accident	9.6.1931
Vickers Armstrong	HMS *Proteus*	29P, 29N N29	Parthian Class	23.7.1929	PO – Scrapped	2.1946

▲ HMS *Parthian*. *(HM Submarine Museum)*

▼ HMS *Parthian* seen attacking the Axis resin refinery in Camnavitsa Bay in 1943. The small craft on fire were loaded with turpentine and resin. *(HM Submarine Museum)*

▼ HMS *Poseidon*. *(HM Submarine Museum)*

Rainbow Class

The Rainbow Class were another development of the successful O Class and subsequent Parthian Class, but two feet (.06 m) shorter. On these boats the gun was mounted lower and without the shield. As with the previous classes, these boats were intended primarily for Far East use. In an attempt to improve conditions, they were fitted with a galley, and even had a shower that was built into the conning tower. Although otherwise well equipped, the large boats suffered badly when used in the shallower coastal waters.

HMS *Rainbow* spent much time in the Mediterranean. She had been modified to run vital supplies to Malta by having half her batteries removed to carry aviation fuel. More fuel oil, as well as fresh water, was carried in her ballast tanks.

In October 1940, HMS *Rainbow* failed to return to Alexandria from a patrol off Taranto. It is probable that on 4 October she attacked the SS *Antonetta Costa* in the Straits of Messina off Calabria and was out-manoeuvred and rammed by the merchant ship, which resulted in her being sunk. It is also possible that she was involved with the Italian submarine *Enrico Toti* which was involved in a gun battle with an unidentified British submarine which she sank near Colonne on the night of 14/15 October. HMS *Triad* also failed to return about the same time, and without further evidence the discussion continues as to who attacked whom.

HMS *Regulus* also failed to return from her patrol. She was to have operated in the Adriatic and returned to Alexandria on 6 December. The Italians claimed to have attacked a submarine off Taranto on 26 November, and this may have been *Regulus*.

In April 1943, HMS *Regent* left Malta for a patrol off Sicily and Taranto. She had previously successfully attacked and sunk four transport ships, but on the 18th she unsuccessfully attacked a merchant ship. Later that day a large explosion was heard, and as she failed to return to her base at Malta it was concluded that the sound was probably her hitting a mine.

HMS *Rover* was the only example to survive the Second World War. She had been badly damaged by enemy aircraft off Crete in 1942 and repaired. After that she was only used for training duties, and was scrapped in 1946.

Class	Rainbow Class
Role	Patrol Submarine

	IMPERIAL	METRIC
Sub Disp – surfaced	1,750 tons	1,778 tonnes
Sub Disp – submerged	2,007 tons	2,039.11 tonnes
Length	287 ft 2 in	87.52 m
Beam	29 ft 11 in	9.13 m
Draught	13 ft 9 in	4.19 m
Propulsion	2 × 2,320 bhp Admiralty diesel engines	
	2 × 660 ehp electric motors	
Speed	18 knots surfaced, 8.5 knots submerged	
Range	9,700 nm at 8 knots surfaced, 60 nm at 4 knots submerged	
Armament	8 × 21 in (533 mm) torpedo tubes (6 bow, 2 stern)	
	16 torpedoes carried	
	1 × 4.7 in (119 mm) gun	
Complement (Officers/Men)	53 (5/48)	

Builder	Name	Pennant No.	Class	Launched	Fate	Date
HM Dockyard, Chatham	HMS *Rainbow*	16R, 16N, N16	Rainbow Class	14.5.1930	Lost – Rammed?	10.1940
Vickers Armstrong	HMS *Regent*	41R, 41N, N41	Rainbow Class	11.6.1930	Lost – Mine	18.4.1943
Vickers Armstrong	HMS *Regulus*	88R, 88N, N88	Rainbow Class	11.6.1940	Lost – Unknown	12.1940
Vickers Armstrong	HMS *Rover*	62R, 62N, N62	Rainbow Class	11.6.1930	PO – Scrapped	7.1946
Beardmore	HMS *Royalist*		Rainbow Class		Cancelled – Scrapped	
Cammell Laird	HMS *Rupert*		Rainbow Class		Cancelled	

▼ During the 1930s HMS *Rover* had been operating in Far East waters. The code prominently painted on the conning tower was to identify her to the Japanese Navy, which aggressively operated in those waters. HMS *Rover* was badly damaged in 1941 but was the only Rainbow Class boat to survive the war. *(HM Submarine Museum)*

▲ HMS *Rainbow* was modified to carry desperately needed supplies to the beleaguered island of Malta with half her batteries removed. This enabled her to carry extra aviation fuel. Her ballast tanks were also used. She failed to return to Alexandria in October 1940. With two boats disappearing in the same area at about the same time, her actual fate has never been conclusively proved. *(HM Submarine Museum)*

Thames Class

The Thames Class were a further attempt by the Admiralty to produce a fleet submarine to escort the Grand Fleet. This was despite the fact that experience with the previous K Class had shown that the principle did not work. Because of the space available within a submarine for engines, it was just not possible to produce enough power to continuously keep up with surface warships, apart from the difficulty of communications. The London Treaty limited any new submarines to a maximum of 2,000 tons, thereby ruling out any thoughts of using an additional engine.

The performance of the Thames Class made some progress by using newer, more powerful diesel engines which were fitted with turbochargers. This enabled speed in excess of 21 knots, but these were fitted at the expense of the stern torpedo tubes. Despite this progress, the speed gap had not changed much, as technology advances had also given the Grand Fleet a greater speed.

Construction commenced in 1929 with a plan to build up to twenty of this new class. HMS *Thames* was laid down in January 1931, to be followed by HMS *Severn*. *Thames* was effectively used as a prototype, and so work on *Severn* did not commence until after *Thames* had been completed. Once construction of HMS *Clyde* was under way, it became time to order the rest of the batch. Despite the boats exceeding their designed performance, Admiralty policy towards the fleet submarine had finally cooled to the extent that the planned orders did not materialise.

Once it was eventually decided that the idea of a fleet submarine was not practical, the three Thames Class were operated as ocean-going boats, for which their speed and long range was ideal. HMS *Clyde* attempted a gun battle with the German auxiliary cruiser *Widder* in May 1940 without success. However, she located, attacked and sank the German battle-cruiser *Gneisenau* with torpedoes off Trondheim on 20 July 1940. The following month HMS *Thames* was lost while also patrolling off Norway, but she took the German torpedo boat *Luchs* with her.

HMS *Clyde* and *Severn* were deployed to the Mediterranean in 1941. *Clyde* underwent a refit in the USA in 1943 before operating out of Holy Loch for a few months with the Third Flotilla. HMS *Severn*, which had already sunk one ship off Norway in June 1940, sank a further two, plus the Italian submarine *Michele Bianchi*, during 1941. Both boats were then transferred to the Far East, but later

Severn was broken up in Bombay as spares for *Clyde*.

HMS *Clyde* was eventually broken up in South Africa, where some of her machinery survived to be used in local industry.

Class	Thames Class		
Role	Fleet Submarine		
		IMPERIAL	METRIC
Sub Disp – surfaced		2,155 tons	2,189.48 tonnes
Sub Disp – submerged		2,640 tons	2,682.24 tonnes
Length		345 ft	105.15 m
Beam		28 ft 1 in	8.56 m
Draught		15 ft 9 in	4.80 m
Propulsion		2 × 5,000 bhp Admiralty diesel engines	
		2 × 1,250 ehp electric motors	
Speed		21.5 knots surfaced, 10 knots submerged	
Range		12,000 nm at 8 knots surfaced, 10 nm at 10 knots submerged	
Armament		6 × 21 in (533 mm) torpedo tubes (all bow)	
		12 torpedoes carried	
		1 × 4.7 in (119 mm) gun (later replaced by 4 in (101 mm))	
Complement (Officers/Men)		61 (5/56)	

Builder	Name	Pennant No.	Class	Launched	Fate	Date
Vickers Armstrong	HMS *Clyde*	12F, 12N, N12	Thames Class	15.3.1934	PO – Scrapped	7.1946
Vickers Armstrong	HMS *Severn*	57F, 57N, N57	Thames Class	16.1.1934	PO – Scrapped	1946
Vickers Armstrong	HMS *Thames*	71F, 71N, N71	Thames Class	26.1.1932	Lost – Mine?	7.1940

▲ HMS *Severn*. *(HM Submarine Museum)*

▲ HMS *Severn* was one of the three Thames Class boats capable of over 21 knots.
(HM Submarine Museum)

▼ HMS *Thames* being launched by Vickers at Barrow-in-Furness in January 1932.
(HM Submarine Museum)

▼ HMS *Thames*. *(HM Submarine Museum)*

91

S Class

The S Class of sea-going submarines were designed to replace the H Class. They were intended for use in most theatres, and although larger than the H boats they were smaller than the O, P and R Classes, which were primarily designed for the longer-range Far East operations. The new size of these boats gave what was planned to be an optimum of range and weapon carriage with a capability to operate the shallower, more confined waters. They also had an improved underwater capability, not only in speed but also in range and depth to reduce their vulnerability to the increasing menace of German anti-submarine operations. They were reputed to be fast divers, capable of submerging in just 30 seconds!

A new feature of the S Class boat was the inclusion of an escape hatch located in the fore compartment, with another in the aft. This valuable feature, that was incorporated in all subsequent boats, would save the lives of many submariners who worked in difficult conditions in an often very hostile environment.

Once in service, the S Class boats proved to be extremely capable, and as a result they were built in substantial numbers over some fifteen years. During this period several variants reflected the fine tuning of the design.

The initial batch of four boats entered service in 1932/3. These were built with a 3 in (76 mm) gun located in a forward extension to the conning tower with a mounting that was hinged, enabling it to be stowed before diving.

In the second batch of eight boats the gun was mounted on the casing deck, which allowed the conning tower to be reduced in height. A small extension to the front of the conning tower contained an ammunition store. The first batch were later modified to have a similar arrangement. The last of this batch were launched in 1937.

In March 1939, four submarines were ordered by the Turkish Navy. These were basically built to the S Class design, but only had four torpedo tubes in the bow and one fitted in the stern. When war broke out they were still being completed, and were quickly requisitioned by the Admiralty for use by the Royal Navy.

The third and largest batch commenced production at the outbreak of the Second World War, and continued throughout the conflict. Within this batch there were several sub-variants with different features. Welding of hulls was still being developed, and about half were still partially riveted. As in most wars technologies accelerated faster than normal, and as a result subsequent hulls had an all-welded construction. P.231 onwards featured an external stern torpedo tube, as well as replacing the .303 in machine-gun with a 20 mm gun for anti-aircraft defence. An air-warning RDF (Radio Direction Finder) was introduced. These features were modified onto some of the previous batch, and later still on to the first batch during their refits. Seventeen of the later build featured a 4 in (101 mm)

gun which was mounted as the first batch. These were specifically for operations in the Far East.

The initial orders for the third batch were allocated pennant numbers in the range P.61 to P.89. With wartime production expanding rapidly, they were renumbered in a higher range before they were launched to avoid duplication. Although most had unofficial names, these were not officially adopted until 1943. HMS Sirdar was originally allocated P.76, which was changed to P.226 in July 1941. However, in February 1943 this was changed again, so that she became the first to be launched with a name. In the table below for Group 3 vessels, the name is followed in most cases by a bracket. Where there is a bracket within the bracket this in an attempt to reflect the name allocated but changed before she was launched.

Although the Batch 3 boats were supposed to have seven torpedo tubes, including one external at the stern, the stern tube was not fitted to them all. Some later boats had a higher freeboard extending forward.

Those S Class boats that were to operate in the Far East had some of their ballast tanks converted to carry an additional 50 tons of fuel. Eventually this was increased to a total of some 91 tons of fuel to extend their range. As gunnery was a major feature in this region, most boats would depart with extra ammunition stowed in all sorts of unlikely places, even though this was potentially dangerous and against regulations.

Developments in detection raced ahead during the Second World War, and these boats were fitted with various forms of hydrophone and Asdic (an early form of Sonar), as well as air-warning RDF.

With the outbreak of war, the S Class were soon in the thick of it. In September, HMS Spearfish had been on patrol in the North Sea when she was attacked. Although badly damaged, she managed to survive the attack, and a rescue force of warships and the carrier HMS Ark Royal were despatched to bring her back home, and she was repaired.

A patrol line had been established from the Shetlands to Norway to try to ensure that German warships were bottled up in the North Sea. Further patrols were also mounted off the German coast. Unfortunately, the submarine action was not always targeted at the enemy during these early days of the war, when everyone was understandably twitchy. HMS Oxley had just been sunk by HMS Triton when a few days later HMS Swordfish was attacked by Sturgeon. This fortunately failed, but a week later HMS Seahorse narrowly survived being attacked by an RAF Anson. After these home goal attacks, the Admiralty decided to widen the gaps between the patrolling submarines from four miles to sixteen.

Meanwhile, destroying the enemy ships was proving a problem for many boats.

HMS *Sea Wolf* attempted an attack on the torpedo boat *Falke* using her torpedoes, but failed to manage a hit. HMS *Sealion* had a similar result after she expended six torpedoes at *U-21*. HMS *Sterlet* attacked a convoy, while HMS *Shark* unleashed five torpedoes at her German convoy, but again with no success. The problem was not unique to the British boats. In Germany the commander of the German submarine force, Karl Dönitz, wrote in his war diary that 30 per cent of their torpedoes did not work.

HMS *Sturgeon* sank the anti-submarine trawler *V209* off Heligoland on 20 November 1939, which was the first successful Royal Navy submarine attack of the war. HMS *Sea Wolf* and *Sealion* improved their accuracy later with two and five ships respectively. HMS *Sterlet* damaged one a week later but was lost during a counter-attack. HMS *Shark* was sunk three months after her attempted attack.

HMS *Salmon* was much more successful, with an attack on the U-boat *U-36*, which she sank on 4 December 1939. This was the first U-boat to be sunk by a Royal Navy submarine. Her attack on the troop carrier *Bremen* on 12 December was foiled by a German Dornier patrol aircraft. However, on the next day she spotted a formation of German warships and fired a salvo of torpedoes. These hit the light cruisers *Leipzig* and *Nürnberg*. HMS *Ursula* shortly appeared on the scene and made her attack, hitting the *F9*.

HMS *Seahorse* left Rosyth on Boxing Day 1939 for a patrol off the Danish and German coast in the area of the Heligoland Bight, but didn't return. What actually happened to her is uncertain, although German reports of a depth charge attack on an unidentified submarine on 7 January does provide a probable answer.

A couple of days later, HMS *Starfish* was attacking a German warship. Her first attempt failed, and as she upped periscope for a second time she was struck by a series of depth charges from the minesweeper *M7*. Damaged, she sank but later managed a controlled return to the surface, where she was abandoned and scuttled. The whole crew were rescued and became prisoners of war. Along with HMS *Undine*, this was the third boat to have been lost in this area within less than a week. The Admiralty then decided that being so close to German naval ports was proving too costly for a patrol to be maintained, and subsequent patrols were made further out into the North Sea.

During the German invasion of Norway in April, HMS *Spearfish* was charging her batteries when the pocket battleship *Lützow* was spotted. As she approached within striking distance, *Spearfish* fired a salvo of torpedoes. One hit the German warship, disabling her propellers and rudder, and rendering her helpless. Expecting a substantial escort to be in the area, *Spearfish* , now with her batteries almost depleted, withdrew. *Lützow* summoned assistance and was towed to Kiel, but it took around twelve months before she was fit to sail again. The U-boat *U-54* was not so lucky when she was attacked by HMS *Salmon* on 12 April and sunk, as was the *Hamm* by HMS *Sea Wolf*. Later, HMS *Salmon* was declared

missing from her patrol off Norway after she failed to make a report on 15 July. HMS *Sea Wolf* was used to put an agent ashore in Norway, and was subsequently used for a number of similar clandestine operations.

In July 1940, HMS *Shark* was caught on the surface by a seaplane. Bombs were dropped as she dived, which damaged the steering gear and forced her back to the surface to be greeted with more bombs. She began to sink uncontrollably, but managed to vent her ballast tanks to regain control, and struggled back to the surface. Here more aircraft were circling and continued with the attack. Unable to manoeuvre, her captain had little option but to surrender. The crew were taken prisoner and *Shark* was taken in tow but sank before she reached a harbour.

In August, HMS *Spearfish* was caught on the surface by the German U-boat *U-34* during a patrol off the Norwegian coast, and was sunk by a torpedo.

HMS *Swordfish* departed Portsmouth on 7 November 1940 for a patrol in the North Sea and to relieve HMS *Usk*. She was due to signal her position a week later, but nothing was heard and she was posted as missing. In 1983 her wreck was discovered off the Isle of Wight, where she must have struck a mine just after leaving port.

The cause of the loss of HMS *Snapper* in February 1941 is uncertain. She departed the Clyde to take up her patrol in the Bay of Biscay, and was due to be escorted back on the 10th but failed to appear. A German minesweeper signalled that it had attacked a submarine in the area on the 11th. She should have already left the area by then, so this was probably not *Snapper* . Whether she and her crew of 42 had been the victims of a mine will probably never be known.

In August HMS *Saracen* had been on patrol in the Iceland Gap when she was signalled about a pair of approaching U-boats. On full alert at periscope depth, the crew spotted *U-335* on the 3rd. As they closed in, a total of six torpedoes were fired at short intervals, and *U-335* was destroyed with a large explosion. When they surfaced to look for survivors they could only find two, of whom one refused to be rescued and drowned.

HMS *Seraph* was used in October 1942 to land General Clark in Algeria to try to persuade the Vichy French to support the planned North Africa landings by the Allies. A month later she helped in the rescue of General Giraud. He had escaped from a German prison but insisted that he would only be rescued by a US boat. With none available, HMS *Seraph* became 'USS *Seraph*' under the nominal command of a US Naval officer. General Giraud, together with his son and some officers, were taken to a rendezvous with a Catalina flying boat for their onward journey. The following day a further seven of his staff were also rescued by HMS *Sibyl*.

HMS *Sea Wolf* sank the *Bressheim* while operating from Ployarnoe, but luck for HMS *P.222* had run out. On 30 November 1942, she departed Gibraltar for a patrol off Naples. Apart from signals on the 7th she was not heard of again. The

Italian destroyer *Fortnale* claimed to have depth-charged and sunk a submarine on the 12th in the approximate area, and the conclusion was that this was *P.222*.

HMS *Splendid* departed Malta to commence a patrol off Naples and Corsica in mid-April. She was detected by the German destroyer *Hermes* on the 21st and damaged during a depth-charge attack, giving her no option but to surface. With *Hermes* waiting, the crew were ordered to abandon ship, and *Splendid* was scuttled to avoid capture. Eighteen of the crew were lost and thirty became prisoners of war. Credited with ten enemy ships sunk, HMS *Splendid* had certainly played her part in the battle to defeat the enemy.

Meanwhile, HMS *Sahib* had attacked and sunk the Italian merchant ship *Galileo* off Capa Milazzo on 16 April. As she started to surface she was attacked by an aircraft which attempted to bomb her. Shortly after, the Italian torpedo boat *Climene* located her and commenced a depth-charge attack. *Sahib* was damaged and forced to surface. Again the order to abandon ship was given, and she was scuttled off northern Sicily.

In August 1942, HMS *Saracen* had successfully sunk the U-boat *U-335*, and the Italian submarine *Granito* the following December, but in August 1943 she was not so lucky. She was spotted by a couple of Italian corvettes off Corsica. Before she could manoeuvre to make her attack, the corvettes attacked with depth charges. Damaged, she struggled to the surface, where they abandoned ship and quickly scuttled *Saracen* to ensure she was not captured.

After repairs following an accidental ramming of a U-boat the previous December, HMS *Seraph* resumed her clandestine role. This would later be made into a film – 'The Man Who Never Was'. The Allies were planning for the invasion of Sicily. In an attempt to mislead the Germans as to their real intentions, a body was dressed in Royal Navy officer clothing. He was carrying fake documents with details of a planned invasion of Corsica. The body was carefully placed on the Spanish coast near Huelva, where he was found and the information believed.

Later, the Captain of HMS *Seraph,* Lt Jewell, was awarded the American Legion of Merit for assisting US forces landing on Sicily, as well as, for her previous covert activities.

During 1943, HMS *Sickle* steadily built up her list of victims. In May she sank the tanker *Herour* off the coast of Monte Carlo, followed by the U-boat *U-303* a week later. In July she sank a tug and a schooner, and in November she sank the *Giovanni Boccacio*. The following June she sank the German merchant ship *Reamur*, but then failed to return from that patrol in the Aegean.

HMS *Sturgeon* was transferred to the Royal Netherlands Navy as *Zeehond* in 1943, and was returned in 1945.

Various boats had been used to provide intelligence about possible landing beaches prior to the invasion of Sicily. On 10 July 1943 HMS *Seraph* acted as a beacon for the fleet of ships, providing them with a marker to help ensure that they landed at the right place at the right time.

HMS *Shakespeare* successfully attacked and sank the Italian submarine *Velella* in the Gulf of Salerno on 7 September 1943.

HMS *Simoom*, which had sunk the Italian destroyer *Vincenzo Gioberti* near La Spezia on 9 August, vanished without trace in the Aegean during November 1943. The Germans reported the destruction of a submarine on the 15th, and although they claimed to have rescued some crew, a link has never been proved.

HMS *Stonehenge* was operating in the Far East in February 1944 and was to patrol the Malacca Straits off Sumatra. She was due to arrive at Ceylon on 20 March but failed to arrive. Meanwhile, off Norway HMS *Stubborn* was remarkably lucky. She had unsuccessfully attacked a German convoy and was subjected to a counter-attack. The hydroplanes jammed and she dived down to 400 ft (120 m). She managed to surface, but was still close to the escorting warships. She attempted to make another dive, but, unable to control it properly, she descended to 500 ft (150 m) before she stabilised. Above her the depth charges could be heard exploding, but they would not have expected her to be that deep. A few hours later she resurfaced with difficulty, breaking the surface at a steep angle.

HMS *Stubborn* had survived the deep dive, but, already damaged, the dive had caused further malfunctions. Despite this she managed to limp back to base on the surface without being spotted. She was eventually used as a target and sunk off Malta in 1946. (Considering the diving trials by HMS *Stoic* in 1948 described below, the crew of HMS *Stubborn* had a very lucky escape.)

In March, HMS *Syrtis* was on patrol off Norway and was signalled to proceed north to near Bodø. After a couple of days she spotted and sank the *Narvik* on the 22nd. But when signalled to return to her base at Lerwick on the 28th she failed to acknowledge and was not heard of again. German shore batteries claim to have sunk a submarine about this time and this may have led to her loss.

HMS *Sickle* was on patrol in the Aegean during June 1944 when she was involved in a gun battle with a number of boats in Mitylene Harbour. *Sickle* managed to escape undamaged, although one of her crew was washed overboard and later rescued to become a prisoner of war. A week later she signalled that she was following a convoy. Reports were made that some depth charges were dropped on a suspected submarine. Whether they were successful or not is unknown but *Sickle* failed to return. HMS *Satyr* sank U-boat *U-987* on the 15th.

Arrangements had been made for HMS *Sunfish* to be transferred to the Soviet Navy. In July she commenced her passage from Dundee to Murmansk as the *V1*, with a Soviet Navy crew, together with a British liaison team. On 27 July 1944 she was spotted well off route by an RAF Liberator patrol aircraft. Rather than firing identification flares as briefed, she dived. The RAF crew then believed this to be an enemy boat and attacked. She was lost with all on board.

HMS *Stratagem* was on patrol from Ceylon in November 1944 when she spotted and sank the Japanese merchant ship *Nichinan Maru* near Malacca. Three days later she was spotted and attacked by depth charges from a Japanese patrol boat. Some of the crew managed to escape from the stricken boat, and eight were picked up by the Japanese. Three of the survivors were transferred as prisoners of war to Japan, but a mystery surrounds what happened to the other five. Circumstances are unclear, but a theory being investigated is that they were executed for some reason by the Japanese Navy.

HMS *Sickle* had the misfortune to be the 45th and last submarine to be lost in the Mediterranean. Like many before her, her fate is unknown. The last signal was heard from her on 12 June 1944. She was supposed to be undertaking a patrol in the Aegean, and was probably destroyed by a mine – a weapon that caused so many boats to disappear unknown to anybody while on their lonely patrols.

The patrols continued, and in January 1945, HMS *Shakespeare* was making a surface attack on a merchant ship. She was damaged by return fire and unable to dive. While heading for Trincomalee she was spotted by Japanese aircraft and attacked. Two of her crew were killed and fourteen injured in the brave attempt to beat off the attackers. She eventually made it back to Ceylon. Repairs commenced but the victory over Japan came before they were completed, and she was scrapped.

In May 1945 HMS *Statesman* and *Subtle* were in the Malacca Straits when the Japanese cruiser *Haguro* and destroyer *Kamikaze* passed through. A signal was sent to Trincomalee, from where a task force was despatched, sinking the *Haguro*. In July HMS *Spark* and *Stygian* towed HMS *XE.1* and HMS *XE.3* from Brunei to Singapore to attack Japanese targets. And in August, HMS *Selene* and *Spearhead* assisted in the prelude to Operation *Zipper* by towing HMS *XE.5* and *XE.4* to positions off Hong Kong, where they cut vital telephone cables.

Once the war ended, British military forces were contracting. While much was scrapped, some equipment was supplied to various re-emerging defence forces around the world. HMS *Spearhead* was sold to the Portuguese and served with their Navy as *Neptuno*, and HMS *Spur* became *Narval*. HMS *Sportsman* was loaned to the French Navy in 1951 and was renamed *Sibylle*. The loan period was to have been four years, but in September 1952 she was lost off Toulon. HMS *Spiteful* was also loaned to the French Navy, as was HMS *Statesman*, which had sunk some thirty ships in the Far East. They were renamed *Sirene* and *Sultane* respectively, and were returned in 1958.

In 1958 HMS *Springer* was sold to Israel, who renamed her *Tanin* when in service with her navy.

With further surplus boats, a number were also used for some 'What if' trials.

HMS *Stoic* was taken to a point off Kyle in 1948 and lowered until it was detected that she had become flooded owing to structural damage. This did not happen until she reached a depth 200 ft (60 m) below her maximum safe diving depth of 300 ft (90 m).

On 16 June 1951, HMS *Sidon* was alongside HMS *Maidstone*. She was preparing to participate in a live firing exercise with a hydrogen-peroxide-powered torpedo and about to cast off when a large explosion rocked her. The order to abandon ship was given, and smoke was seen to billow out of her conning tower. Shortly afterwards she sank. Despite the efforts of divers, no sign of life could be found of the missing thirteen crew who had failed to escape from the stricken boat. A week later *Sidon* was salvaged and the bodies recovered. In 1957 she was towed out of the harbour, and still remains where she was sunk, having been used for many years as a target in about 100 ft (30 m) of water.

During an exercise in 1957 off Northern Ireland, HMS *Springer* was under simulated attack from an anti-submarine helicopter. The helicopter was hovering and dunking its Sonar. With his options running short, the captain decided to ram the Sonar that was tracking him. It produced the result the captain was after but he only just avoided a court martial. It was possible that the wire could have become snagged, and that would have pulled the helicopter down into the water, possibly even crashing onto the submarine, with an ensuing loss of life. The action did trigger some thoughts, as eventually HMS *Aeneas* undertook trials with the Blowpipe surface-to-air missile for self-defence.

After the war HMS *Scotsman* underwent a refit which entailed significant modifications. Much of the casing between the bow and conning tower was removed, as was the gun, giving her a more streamlined shape. Her engines were removed and replaced with a 1,250 bhp motor from an A Class and an 824 hp electric motor (from U Class). This enabled her to undertake high-speed runs which were useful in the training of the submarine hunter-killer crews, although the batteries had to charged for a day after each run. She was also used for trials, including research for a quieter propeller. In 1960 she was laid up, and a few years later was sunk off the Isle of Bute for some lifting exercises before being sold for scrap.

HMS *Sea Devil* was the last of the S Class boats to remain operational, being sold for scrap in 1965. Some parts of HMS *Seraph* were removed while awaiting scrapping in 1963 for inclusion in a war memorial to Anglo-American co-operation at the Military College of South Carolina. The spirit of HMS *Seraph* continues not only with the memorial, but in two books – 'The Ship with Two Captains' and 'The Man Who Never Was', which was also made into a film.

Class	Swordfish/S Class, Group 1
Role	Medium Patrol Submarine

	IMPERIAL	METRIC
Sub Disp – surfaced	640 tons	650.24 tonnes
Sub Disp – submerged	927 tons	941.83 tonnes
Length	202 ft 6 in	61.72 m
Beam	24 ft	7.31 m
Draught	11 ft 11 in	3.63 m
Propulsion	2 × 775 bhp Admiralty diesel engines	
	1 × 650 ehp electric motor	
Speed	13.5 knots surfaced, 10 knots submerged	
Range	3,700 nm at 10 knots surfaced, 106 nm at 10 knots submerged	
Armament	6 × 21 in (533 mm) torpedo tubes	
	12 torpedoes carried	
	1 × 3 in (76 mm) gun (removed on some)	
Complement (Officers/Men)	38 (4/34)	

Builder	Name	Pennant No.	Class	Launched	Fate	Date
HM Dockyard, Chatham	HMS Seahorse	98S	Swordfish Class	15.11.1932	Lost – Unknown	12.1939
HM Dockyard, Chatham	HMS Starfish	19S	Swordfish Class	14.3.1933	Lost – Attacked – Scuttled	9.1.1940
HM Dockyard, Chatham	HMS Sturgeon	73S, 73N, N73	Swordfish Class	8.1.1932	PO – Scrapped	1.1947
HM Dockyard, Chatham	HMS Swordfish	61S, 61N, N61	Swordfish Class	10.11.1931	Lost – Mine	7.11.1940

▲ HMS *Sturgeon* departing Blyth in September 1940. *(HM Submarine Museum)*

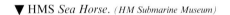

▼ HMS *Sea Horse*. *(HM Submarine Museum)*

Class	Shark/S Class, Group 2
Role	Medium Patrol Submarine

	IMPERIAL	METRIC
Sub Disp – surfaced	670 tons	680.72 tonnes
Sub Disp – submerged	960 tons	975.36 tonnes
Length	208 ft 8 in	63.56 m
Beam	24 ft	7.31 m
Draught	11 ft 10 in	3.6 m
Propulsion	2 × 775 bhp Admiralty diesel engines	
	1 × 650 ehp electric motor	
Speed	13.75 knots surfaced, 10 knots submerged	
Range	3,800 nm at 10 knots surfaced, 106 nm at 4 knots submerged	
Armament	6 × 21 in (533 mm) torpedo tubes (bow)	
	12 torpedoes carried	
	1 × 20 mm anti-aircraft gun	
Complement (Officers/Men)	40 (5/35)	

Builder	Name	Pennant No.	Class	Launched	Fate	Date
Cammell Laird	HMS *Salmon*	65S	Shark Class, Group 2	30.4.1934	Lost – Mine	7.1940
Cammell Laird	HMS *Sealion*	72S, 72N, N72	Shark Class, Group 2	16.3.1934	PO – Sunk – Target	3.3.1945
Scott's	HMS *Seawolf*	47S, 47N, N47	Shark Class, Group 2	28.11.1935	PO – Scrap	11.1945
HM Dockyard, Chatham	HMS *Shark*	54S	Shark Class, Group 2	31.5.1934	Lost – Attacked – Scuttled	6.7.1940
HM Dockyard, Chatham	HMS *Snapper*	39S, 39N, N39	Shark Class, Group 2	25.10.1934	Lost – Depth charge	11.2.1941
Cammell Laird	HMS *Spearfish*	69S	Shark Class, Group 2	21.4.1936	Lost – Torpedo	2.8.1940
HM Dockyard, Chatham	HMS *Sterlet*	22S	Shark Class, Group 2	22.9.1937	Lost – Depth charge	18.4.1940
HM Dockyard, Chatham	HMS *Sunfish*	81S, 81N, N81	Shark Class, Group 2	30.9.1936	PO – Transferred	27.7.1944

▶ Loading a torpedo through the forward hatch on HMS *Snapper*.

(HM Submarine Museum)

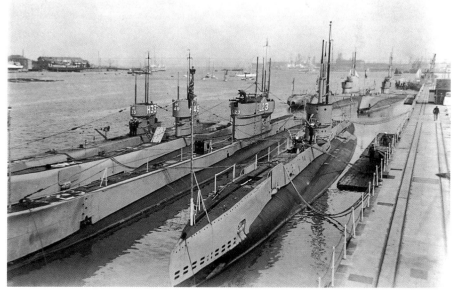

▶ HMS *Sunfish* alongside at Fort Blockhouse, together with a pair of H Class boats and HMS *L.23*. In the background are an O and a Unity Class boat. *(HM Submarine Museum)*

▲ HMS *Snapper* under way with low visibility identification markings on her conning tower. It is thought that she may have been heading for the waters off Spain, where she would be protecting passing British shipping that was being harassed during the Spanish Civil War.

(*HM Submarine Museum*)

◄ On 12 April 1940 HMS *Snapper* intercepted the German petrol tanker SS *Moodsund* off Norway. A single shell from her 3 in (76 mm) gun caused her to explode, and she sank shortly afterwards.

(*HM Submarine Museum*)

Class	Shark/S Class, Group 3	
Role	Medium Patrol Submarine	

	IMPERIAL	METRIC
Sub Disp – surfaced	854 tons*	867.66 tonnes
Sub Disp – submerged	990 tons*	1,005.84 tonnes
Length	217 ft	66.14 m
Beam	23 ft 9 in	7.24 m
Draught	13 ft 6 in	4.11 m
Propulsion	2 × 950 bhp Admiralty diesel engines	
	2 × 650 ehp electric motors	
Speed	14.75 knots surfaced, 10 knots submerged	
Range	6,000 nm at 10 knots surfaced, 106 nm at 4 knots submerged	
Armament	7 × 21 in (533 mm) torpedo tubes (6 bow, 1 stern)	
	(6 on some)	
	13 torpedoes carried	
	1 × 3 in (76 mm) gun (4 in (101 mm) gun on some)	
	1 × 20 mm anti-aircraft gun	
Complement (Officers/Men)	48 (5/43)	
Data note	*Varied over build period – values given cover majority	

Builder	Name	Pennant No.	Class	Launched	Fate	Date
Cammell Laird	HMS *Safari* (ex (*P.61*), *P.211*)	P211	Shark Class, Group 3	18.11.1941	PO – Foundered	1.1946
Cammell Laird	HMS *Saga*	P257	Shark Class, Group 3	14.3.1945	PO – Sold	11.10.1948
Cammell Laird	HMS *Sahib* (ex (*P.62*), *P.212*)	P212	Shark Class, Group 3	19.1.1942	Lost – Depth charge	24.4.1943
Cammell Laird	HMS *Sanguine*	P266, S66	Shark Class, Group 3	15.2.1945	PO – Sold	10.1958
Cammell Laird	HMS *Saracen* (ex (*P.63*), *P.213*, *P.247*)	P215 P247	Shark Class, Group 3	16.2.1942	Lost – Attacked	14.8.1943
Scott's	HMS *Satyr* (ex (*P.64*), *P.214*)	P214	Shark Class, Group 3	28.9.1942	PO – Scrapped	4.1962
Scott's	HMS *Sceptre* (ex (*P.65*), *P.215*)	P215	Shark Class, Group 3	9.1.1943	Accident – Scrapped	9.1949
Cammell Laird	HMS *Scorcher*	P258, S58	Shark Class, Group 3	18.12.1944	PO – Scrapped	9.1962
Scott's	HMS *Scotsman* (ex *243*)	P243, S143	Shark Class, Group 3	18.8.1944	PO – Scrapped	11.1964
Scott's	HMS *Scythian* (ex *P.237*)	P237, S137	Shark Class, Group 3	14.4.1944	PO – Scrapped	8.1960
Scott's	HMS *Sea Devil* (ex *P.244*)	P244, S244	Shark Class, Group 3	30.1.1945	PO – Scrapped	12.1965
Cammell Laird	HMS *Sea Dog* (ex (*P.66*), *P.216*)	P216	Shark Class, Group 3	11.6.1942	PO – Scrapped	8.1948
Cammell Laird	HMS *Sea Nymph* (ex (*P.73*), *P.223*)	P223	Shark Class, Group 3	29.7.1942	PO – Scrapped	8.1948
Cammell Laird	HMS *Sea Robin*	P267	Shark Class, Group 3		Cancelled	

Builder	Name	Pennant No.	Class	Launched	Fate	Date
Scott's	HMS Sea Rover (ex (P.68), P.218)	P218	Shark Class, Group 3	25.2.1943	PO – Scrapped	10.1949
Cammell Laird	HMS Sea Scout (ex (P.253)	P253, S153	Shark Class, Group 3	24.3.1944	PO – Scrapped	12.1965
Cammell Laird	HMS Selene (ex (P.254)	P254, S154	Shark Class, Group 3	24.4.1944	PO – Scrapped	6.1961
Scott's	HMS Seneschal (ex (P.255)	P255, S75	Shark Class, Group 3	23.4.1945	PO – Scrapped	8.1960
Scott's	HMS Sentinel (ex (P.256)	P256	Shark Class, Group 3	27.7.1945	PO – Scrapped	2.1962
Vickers Armstrong	HMS Seraph (ex (P.69), P.219)	P219, S89	Shark Class, Group 3	25.10.1941	PO – Scrapped	12.1965
Vickers Armstrong	HMS Shakespeare (ex (P.71), P.221)	P221	Shark Class, Group 3	8.12.1941	Damaged – Scrapped	14.7.1946
HM Dockyard, Chatham	HMS Shalimar (ex (P.242)	P242	Shark Class, Group 3	22.4.1943	PO – Scrapped	7.1950
Cammell Laird	HMS Sybil (ex (P.67), P.217)	P217	Shark Class, Group 3	29.4.1942	PO – Scrapped	3.1948
Cammell Laird	HMS Sickle (ex (P.74), P.224)	P224	Shark Class, Group 3	27.8.1942	Lost – Mine?	6.1944
Cammell Laird	HMS Sidon	P259, S59	Shark Class, Group 3	4.9.1944	Accident – Exp as target	14.6.1957
Cammell Laird	HMS Simoom (ex (P.75), P.225)	P225	Shark Class, Group 3	12.10.1942	Lost – Mine?	11.1943
Scott's	HMS Sirdar (ex (P.76), P.226)	P226, S76	Shark Class, Group 3	26.3.1943	PO – Scrapped	5.1965
Cammell Laird	HMS Sleuth	P261, S61	Shark Class, Group 3	6.7.1944	PO – Scrapped	9.1958
Cammell Laird	HMS Solent	P262, S62	Shark Class, Group 3	8.6.1944	PO – Scrapped	8.1962
Scott's	HMS Spark (ex (P.23)	P236	Shark Class, Group 3	28.12.1943	PO – Scrapped	10.1949
Cammell Laird	HMS Spearhead	P263	Shark Class, Group 3	2.10.1944	PO – Sold	8.1948
Cammell Laird	HMS Spirit (ex (P.245)	P245	Shark Class, Group 3	20.7.1943	PO – Scrapped	7.1950
Scott's	HMS Spiteful (ex (P.77), P.277)	P227	Shark Class, Group 3	5.6.1943	PO – Scrapped	7.1963
HM Dockyard, Chatham	HMS Splendid (ex (P.78), P.228)	P228	Shark Class, Group 3	19.1.1942	Lost – Attacked – Scuttled	21.4.1943
HM Dockyard, Chatham	HMS Sportsman (ex (P.79), P.229)	P229	Shark Class, Group 3	17.4.1942	PO – Loan – Sank	1951
Cammell Laird	HMS Sprightly	P268	Shark Class, Group 3		Cancelled	
Cammell Laird	HMS Springer	P264, S64	Shark Class, Group 3	14.5.1945	PO – Sold	9.10.1958

Builder	Name	Pennant No.	Class	Launched	Fate	Date
Cammell Laird	HMS Spur	P265	Shark Class, Group 3	17.11.1944	PO – Sold	11.1948
Cammell Laird	HMS Statesman (ex (P.246)	P246	Shark Class, Group 3	14.9.1943	PO – Scrapped	3.1.1961
Cammell Laird	HMS Stoic (ex (P.231)	P231	Shark Class, Group 3	9.4.1943	PO – Trial – Scrap	7.1950
Cammell Laird	HMS Stonehenge (ex (P.232)	P232	Shark Class, Group 3	23.3.1943	Lost – Unknown	3.1944
Cammell Laird	HMS Storm (ex (P.233)	P233	Shark Class, Group 3	18.5.1943	PO – Scrapped	9.1949
Cammell Laird	HMS Stratagem (ex (P.234)	P234	Shark Class, Group 3	21.6.1943	Lost – Depth charge	22.11.1944
Scott's	HMS Strongbow (ex (P.235)	P235	Shark Class, Group 3	30.8.1943	PO – Scrapped	4.1946
Cammell Laird	HMS Stubborn (ex (P.88), P.238)	P238	Shark Class, Group 3	11.11.1942	PO – Expended as target	30.4.1946
Cammell Laird	HMS Sturdy (ex (P.248)	P248, S48	Shark Class, Group 3	30.9.1943	PO – Scrapped	5.1958
Cammell Laird	HMS Stygian (ex (P.249)	P249	Shark Class, Group 3	30.11.1943	PO – Scrapped	10.1949
Cammell Laird	HMS Subtle (ex (P.251)	P251, S51	Shark Class, Group 3	27.1.1944	PO – Scrapped	6.1959
Cammell Laird	HMS Supreme (ex (P.252)	P252	Shark Class, Group 3	24.2.1944	PO – Scrapped	7.1950
Cammell Laird	HMS Surf (ex (P.89), P.239)	P239	Shark Class, Group 3	10.12.1942	PO – Scrapped	10.1949
Cammell Laird	HMS Surface	P269	Shark Class, Group 3		Cancelled	
Cammell Laird	HMS Surge	P271	Shark Class, Group 3		Cancelled	
Cammell Laird	HMS Syrtis (ex (P.241)	P241	Shark Class, Group 3	4.2.1943	Lost – Unknown	3.1944
Vickers Armstrong	HMS P.222 (ex (P.72)	P222	Shark Class, Group 3	20.9.1941	Lost – Depth charge	12.12.1942
	HMS P.81	P81	Shark Class, Group 3		Cancelled	
	HMS P.82	P82	Shark Class, Group 3		Cancelled	
	HMS P.83	P83	Shark Class, Group 3		Cancelled	
	HMS P.84	P84	Shark Class, Group 3		Cancelled	
	HMS P.85	P85	Shark Class, Group 3		Cancelled	
	HMS P.86	P86	Shark Class, Group 3		Cancelled	
	HMS P.87	P87	Shark Class, Group 3		Cancelled	

◄ HMS *Spur* leaving Cammell Laird at Birkenhead during her acceptance trial. The small cylindrical shape at the aft end of the casing is the Type 138 Asdic. *(HM Submarine Museum)*

► The modified HMS *Springer* joins HMS *Scorcher* alongside at Gibraltar. Both have had their stern torpedo tubes removed, as well as the gun. *(HM Submarine Museum)*

Porpoise Class

The Porpoise Class were designed specifically as submarine minelayers. Their design resulted from experience gained during trials with HMS *M.3*. They featured a chain conveyor and rail system located on top of the pressurised hull that would accommodate 50 of the standard Mk.XVI mines. This was covered by a high casing that extending for most of the length of the boat, with the exception of HMS *Porpoise*. The mechanics of the system were basically similar to that of surface minelayer ships.

During 1941/2 the Porpoise Class were widely used to transport vital supplies to Malta using their substantial storage capacity, which was normally used for the mines. Vital items carried ranged from ammunition and fuel to food

When a specially designed submarine mine was developed that could be launched from the 21 in (533 mm) torpedo tubes, the last three of the Porpoise Class were cancelled. Despite this, no other Royal Navy submarines were used for minelaying on the scale carried out by these boats.

The effectiveness of mines can be seen by the number of Royal Navy boats whose fate is detailed as lost to mines throughout this book. HMS *Rorqual* laid a substantial number, not only around the North Sea, but also in the Mediterranean. A new minefield often caught a few ships before its precise location was actually mapped. She laid a number to the east of Sicily on 25 March 1941. Within a few days two Italian merchant ships and a torpedo boat had been sunk. Her success was not restricted to mines, as while on the same patrol she spotted, attacked and sank the Italian submarine *Pier Capponi* on 31 March off Sicily. A similar mining success was achieved with a pair of torpedo boats sunk in the Gulf of Athens later that October.

Owing to the nature of their work, the Porpoise Class were vulnerable boats in that they would often have to operate in restricted enemy coastal waters to lay the minefields. As a result, four boats were lost and HMS *Seal* was captured, Only HMS *Rorqual* survived until the end of the war.

HMS *Seal* had been tasked with minelaying in the Kattegat. She was spotted by a German aircraft, which made an immediate attack. The pilot raised the alarm and anti-submarine boats were sent to the scene. Before they could find her, *Seal* struck a mine, sank and became stuck in mud. She was eventually able to release herself, but when she appeared on the surface aircraft immediately attacked once again. Now incapable of diving, she had no alternative but to surrender.

HMS *Seal* had commenced an operation at the end of April which would take her to the Kattegat, between Denmark and Sweden, where she was to lay her load of fifty mines. These were to create a minefield to trap German ships sailing to and from Norway. On the evening of 4 May she was spotted by a German Heinkel He 115 aircraft. The pilot raised the alarm before he made his attack. Only slightly damaged, she managed to continue with the operation and lay the mines as planned. While on the return journey she struck a mine and was further damaged, causing the aft compartment to be flooded. Already alerted by the He 115, surface ships were trying to locate her, so she had to remain submerged until the following day. The captain decided that the best course of action was to try to limp to Sweden. They surfaced only to find that their rudder had also been damaged, resulting in them simply turning in circles. While they were trying to sort this out, a German Arado Ar 196 reconnaissance plane spotted them and attacked with bombs. The small floatplane was joined by another, and during these attacks several of the crew were injured, and finally the Lewis anti-aircraft gun jammed.

Now totally disabled, HMS *Seal* had few options but to surrender. When the German trawler *UJ-128* arrived the next morning they attempted to scuttle the boat, but for some reason she did not sink and was captured and towed ashore. The Germans decided to make good propaganda with this boat. Eventually she was refurbished at Kiel and commissioned as *UB* in November 1940. Besides the publicity, *UB* was only used for training – she was never used operationally. However, intelligence gathered from the torpedoes found on board led to the Germans improving the reliability of their own by copying the detonation mechanism. She was eventually scuttled in May 1945. She was later found and raised and then scrapped. Four German ships were subsequently sunk by the mines laid by HMS *Seal*.

On 10 June 1940, Italy entered the war as part of the Axis powers. HMS *Grampus* was operating from Malta and was tasked with laying mines by the entrance to the port of Agusta. Three days after she left Malta she sent a signal to confirm she had completed her mission, but she never returned. On 16 June the Italian torpedo boats *Circe* and *Clio* reported spotting a periscope, and together with *Polluce* fired a number of depth charges. Wreckage was eventually spotted, but no survivors. It was assumed that this was how HMS *Grampus* met her demise.

HMS *Narwhal* also disappeared during July during a patrol from Blyth in the North Sea. This time the Germans reported one of their aircraft attacking a submarine, although they are reported as having claimed it to have been HMS *Porpoise*. However, as she survived until 1945 they must have been mistaken.

On 20 August 1940 HMS *Cachalot* was returning from a patrol in the Bay of Biscay when she spotted *U-51* limping back to Lorient after being attacked by an RAF Sunderland ASW aircraft. *Cachalot* closed in and torpedoed the U-boat, with the loss of all hands.

In July 1941 HMS *Cachalot* was tasked with shipping vital stores to Malta from

Alexandria. On the return with some passengers, she was instructed to keep watch for an Italian tanker. On the 30th she spotted the Italian torpedo boat *General Achille Papa*, which caused her to dive. On resurfacing, she found the torpedo boat was waiting for her and already heading for her with guns firing. *Cachalot* returned to diving stations but her upper hatch jammed and she remained on the surface. Her captain, realising the impending doom, ordered abandon ship. At the last moment, the Italian captain realised what was happening but was too late to stop the collision. As a result of the collision and the crew opening the main vents, *Cachalot* quickly sank. The Italians managed to pick up all but one of the crew, who then became Prisoners of War.

HMS *Pandora* was one of several boats that were lost to German bombing in Malta in March and April 1942.

HMS *Porpoise* had been busy laying mines off the Libyan coast in 1942, and these were successful in sinking at least one Italian torpedo boat. She was bombed in January 1945, this time it was by the Japanese near Penang. *Porpoise* had just completed laying mines when she was spotted. She was not destroyed in the bomb attack but was damaged and was leaving a a tell-tale trail of oil as she tried to head back to base. The oil on the surface made it easy for a Japanese anti-submarine vessel to locate her. As *Porpoise* never made it back to the Fleet HQ at Trincomalee it is assumed that they must have caught up with her.

A total of nine Porpoise Class boats were ordered. It had been planned to place a further order, but the development of the torpedo-tube-launched mine halted that and resulted in the last three boats that had been ordered being cancelled.

By the end of the war the six Porpoise Class minelayers had laid over 2,500 mines with HMS *Rorqual* laying some 1,300 of them. Apart from HMS *Seal*, which had been captured by the Germans, only *Rorqual* survived to the end of the war.

Class	Porpoise Class prototype
Role	Minelayer Submarine

	IMPERIAL	METRIC
Sub Disp – surfaced	1,764 tons	1,792.22 tonnes
Sub Disp – submerged	2,036 tons	2,068.58 tonnes
Length	288 ft	87.78 m
Beam	29 ft 11 in	9.12 m
Draught	13 ft 9 in	4.19 m
Propulsion	2 × 1,650 bhp Admiralty diesel engines	
	2 × 815 ehp electric motors	
Speed	15 knots surfaced, 8 knots submerged	
Range	11,265 nm at 8.8 knots surfaced, 66 nm at 4 knots submerged	
Armament	6 × 21 in (533 mm) torpedo tubes (6 bow)	
	12 torpedoes carried	
	50 mines (later additional mines could replace torpedoes)	
	1 × 4 in (101 mm) gun	
Complement (Officers/Men)	59 (5/54)	

Builder	Name	Pennant No.	Class	Launched	Fate	Date
Vickers Armstrong	HMS *Porpoise*	14M, 14N, N14	Porpoise Class, prototype	30.8.1932	Lost – Enemy action	19.1.1945

▶ HMS *Porpoise* was the prototype of the first purpose-built minelaying submarines for the Royal Navy. (*HM Submarine Museum*)

	IMPERIAL	METRIC
Class	Porpoise Class	
Role	Minelayer Submarine	
Sub Disp – surfaced	1,750 tons	1,778 tonnes
Sub Disp – submerged	2,138 tons	2,172.2 tonnes
Length	293 ft	89.30 m
Beam	25 ft 4.75 in	7.74 m
Draught	17 ft	5.18 m
Propulsion	2 × 1,650 bhp Admiralty diesel engines	
	2 × 815 ehp electric motors	
Speed	15 knots surfaced, 8.75 knots submerged	
Range	11,265 nm at 8.8 knots surfaced, 66 nm at 4 knots submerged	
Armament	6 × 21 in (533 mm) torpedo tubes (bow)	
	12 torpedoes carried	
	50 × Mk. XVI mines (later additional mines could replace torpedoes)	
	1 × 4 in (101 mm) gun	
Complement (Officers/Men)	59 (5/54)	
Data note		

Builder	Name	Pennant No.	Class	Launched	Fate	Date
Scott's	HMS *Cachalot*	84M, 84N, N84	Porpoise Class (Early)	2.12.1937	Lost – Enemy action	30.7.1941
HM Dockyard, Chatham	HMS *Grampus*	56M, 56N, N56	Porpoise Class (Early)	25.2.1936	Lost – Depth charge	16.6.1940
Vickers Armstrong	HMS *Narwhal*	45M, 45N, N45	Porpoise Class (Early)	29.8.1935	Lost – Enemy action	7.1940
Vickers Armstrong	HMS *Rorqual*	74M, 74N, N74	Porpoise Class (Early)	21.7.1936	PO – Scrapped	12.1945
HM Dockyard, Chatham	HMS *Seal*	37M, 37N, N37	Porpoise Class (Early)	27.9.1938	Captured	
Scott's	HMS *P.411*		Porpoise Class (Early)		Cancelled	
Scott's	HMS *P.412*		Porpoise Class (Early)		Cancelled	
Scott's	HMS *P.413*		Porpoise Class (Early)		Cancelled	

▲ HMS *Cachalot*. *(Glasgow University)*

▶ HMS *Rorqual* being launched by Vickers Armstrong in December 1936.

(HM Submarine Museum)

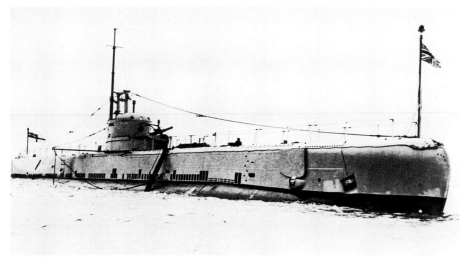

▲ HMS *Rorqual* entering Malta in 1942 with the T Class HMS *Taku*, in the foreground. She was the only one of the class to survive the war, during which she had laid a total of 1,284 mines. *(HM Submarine Museum)*

▲ HMS *Rorqual.* *(HM Submarine Museum)*

▼ The Jolly Roger from HMS *Rorqual* preserved at RN Submarine Museum at Gosport. In the top left corner a total of 1,165 mines laid is recorded. The white bars indicate the number of ships sunk by torpedoes, while the red ones are for warships. The one with a 'U' is for a submarine sunk. The crossed guns and stars show the number of ships sunk by gunfire, and the two daggers are for 'cloak and dagger' special operations. *(Jeremy Flack)*

◀ Mk XVI mines being loaded into the chute at the stern on HMS *Narwhal* at Immingham. Fifty of these mines could be carried in the specially designed casing. *(HM Submarine Museum)*

Unity and Undine (U Class)

The U Class were designed as unarmed target submarines for anti-submarine training, a role that was being filled by the remaining few obsolete H Class. With Europe in a state of re-arming, it was decided by the Admiralty to arm them so that they could also be used as a submarine training boat for crews that were to man the much larger T Class.

Initially six torpedo tubes were fitted, two incorporated in an external large bulbous bow, similar in appearance to that fitted to the early T Class. As with the Ts, this bow shape caused wake problems, reducing visibility when at the vital periscope depth. This resulted in a return to the more conventional streamlined profile by omitting the two extra tubes on the second batch.

Fuel and main ballast were all located within the pressure hull, and power was diesel-electric. The electric motor drove the shaft at all times, while the diesel engine would be used when on the surface to power the generator, which would top up the batteries and feed the motor.

Only three boats were completed before the outbreak of the Second World War, but their design was simple and so production was quickly stepped up. They were soon making a substantial contribution the the war effort despite their limited weapon load. Their small radius of action was not a problem either, owing to their being utilised primarily in coastal waters, where their small size was also an advantage.

HMS *Undine* was the first to be commissioned, but also the first to be lost when on 7 January 1940 she was undertaking her fourth patrol of the war. She spotted the German minesweepers *M.1201, M.1204* and *M.1207* in the Heligoland Bight, and closed in to attack, then fired her torpedoes. They failed to hit the enemy boats but the torpedo trail alerted the German crews and an immediate counter-attack took place. *Undine* dived and waited for it to go quiet. Once she felt it safe she returned to periscope depth, and suddenly another explosion thundered through the boat, wrecking the hydoplanes. Now unable to control herself, there was little alternative but to abandon ship, and once all were clear she was scuttled with an explosive charge.

In April 1940, HMS *Unity* was departing Blyth for a patrol off Norway. The crew were settling down for a routine passage in thick fog. Unknown to them, a Norwegian ship, the *Atle Jarl*, was on a collision course. She was spotted just a couple of minutes before the impact, and the boat was abandoned just before she sank. Four of her crew were lost.

In May, HMS *Undaunted* was to patrol off Tripoli, but failed to return. Two weeks later, HMS *Upholder* was also on patrol in the Mediterranean, commanded by Lt Cdr Wanklyn. On 24 May she was just off Sicily when, in failing light, an enemy troopship convoy was spotted, together with a strong escort of destroyers. The optics of the periscope were of little use in the rapidly approaching darkness, and her listening gear was already unserviceable. A surface attack would have been suicidal and so Wanklyn decided to move in and make a close attack. He manoeuvred the boat into position ready for firing, aware that he could not see any of the escorts. Suddenly, one of the destroyers appeared out of the gloom at high speed, and it was only with quick presence of mind that Wanklyn managed to avoid being rammed. As soon as it passed he took aim and fired torpedoes at one of the large troopships. At close range they could not miss, and the fatally damaged ship began to sink. The troopship was the 17,800 ton ex-liner *Conte Rosso*. She was sailing with 4,000 troops aboard, of whom some 2,300 perished.

The destroyers were determined to seek vengeance, and over the next twenty minutes a total of thirty-seven depth charges were counted exploding around *Upholder*. Unable to trace the whereabouts of the destroyers, Wanklyn used his skill and judgment to break clear of what would have seemed to the crew to have been endless hell, and returned the boat and crew safely to base.

HMS *Urchin* was loaned to the Polish Navy, of which part managed to escape during the German invasion. They brought with them a few ships and submarines, and were provided with some Royal Navy vessels, which they operated under British orders. *Urchin* was one of these vessels, which was handed over in January 1941 and named *Sokol*. She remained manned by a Polish crew until she was returned to the Royal Navy in 1946.

HMS *Usk* disappeared in April 1941 during a patrol that was planned to take her close to Palermo in Sicily. Intelligence sources reported a substantial anti-submarine operation in progress, and she was signalled to await further orders before proceeding. HMS *Usk* failed to respond to any further signals and did not return to Malta. HMS *Undaunted* also failed to return to Malta from her patrol that was to take her close to Tripoli the following month. The Italian torpedo boat *Pegaso* signalled that she had attacked a submarine on the 12th and had seen an oil patch indicating that she had been successful. However, this was the day after *Undaunted* should have arrived in Malta, casting some doubt on the tie-up.

The circumstances that let to the loss of HMS *Umpire* on 19 July 1941 can be accurately traced, and did not involve enemy forces. She was en route from Chatham to the Clyde and had made an overnight stop at Sheerness. The next day she tagged onto a convoy but encountered mechanical difficulties and soon lagged behind. That night, another ship convoy was heading south, and most had passed when the trawler *Peter Hendricks* sailed straight into her, ripping her open. She sank immediately and claimed the lives of 22 of her crew.

HMS *Union* was also lost in July when she was intercepted by the Italian torpedo boat *Circe* off Tunisia, while trying to attack a convoy making for Tripoli. HMS *P.32* and *P.33* were attempting to attack another convoy on 18 August. *P.32* transmitted a signal to Malta advising that following hearing a depth-charge attack lasting some two hours she was unable to regain contact with *P.33*. Later that day *P.32* moved into position for an attack, and as she slipped down to periscope depth she struck a mine, which fatally damaged her as well.

Lt Cdr Malcolm David Wanklyn had already been appointed a Companion of the Distinguished Service Order, and on 16 December 1941 he was awarded the Victoria Cross for his skill and relentless determination and bravery against the enemy. By then, Wanklyn, with the support of his crew, was responsible for the sinking of a destroyer, a U-boat, two 19,500 ton troopships, two tankers and three supply ships. In addition, he was also credited with probably destroying a further destroyer and a cruiser, and a possible hit on another cruiser.

In January 1942 HMS *Unbeaten* was on patrol near Sicily when she spotted and managed to successfully attack the Italian submarine *Guglielmotti*. On 23 February 1942, HMS *P.38* was manoeuvring to attack a convoy off Tripoli. Amongst the escorts was the Italian torpedo boat *Circe*. Her crew spotted the periscope, and she broke formation to commence her attack. The captain of *P.38* saw *Circe* approaching and dived, but not quickly enough, as the depth charges struck home. All of a sudden *P.38* emerged stern first before finally disappearing with oil and debris appearing on the surface.

HMS *Ultimatum* spotted the Italian submarine *Ammiraglio Enrico Millo* the following month off the southern coast of Italy and sank her. During March and April, German aircraft conducted a number of bombing attacks against various targets on Malta. HMS *P.39* was damaged beyond repair on 26 March, HMS *P.36* was sunk on 1 April, along with the Porpoise Class, HMS *Pandora*.

On 1 April 1942 HMS *Urge* attacked and sank the Italian cruiser *Giovanni dell Bande Nere* north of Sicily, but at the end of the month she had disappeared during a passage from Malta to Alexandria.

HMS *Upholder* was on patrol off Sicily when she was signalled to join HMS *Urge* and *Thrasher* to intercept a convoy. *Upholder* did not acknowledge the signal, and when she failed to return to harbour it was felt possible that she had already been lost before the signal was transmitted. Several theories have been put forward as to her fate. On 11 April a submarine was seen heading towards a minefield. Alternatively, and possibly more likely, the Italian torpedo boat *Pegaso* reported attacking a submarine near Tripoli on 14 April.

This was a major loss, not only in the Mediterranean Theatre, but also to the Royal Navy at large. During just fifteen months with the Tenth Submarine Flotilla based at Malta, Lt Cdr Wanklyn and the crew of HMS *Upholder* had sunk or damaged no fewer than 22 enemy ships, totalling well over 100,000 tons, of which the majority were supply ships – a major loss to the enemy by any count. In an unprecedented wartime announcement the Admiralty gave full credit to the whole crew for their arduous and dangerous duty.

Convoy *Pedestal* comprised a fleet of fourteen fast merchant ships which were carrying vital supplies to the beleaguered island of Malta. They were heavily escorted by another fleet of warships. They were subjected to a series of attacks by Axis naval and air forces. On 13 August 1942 the Italians aborted one attack and were returning to base with a number of destroyers. Unknown to them they were approaching HMS *Unbroken*. Patiently she waited for them to get even closer before she fired her last four remaining torpedoes. They struck the heavy cruiser *Bolzano* and the light cruiser *Muzio Attendolo*, which required substantial repairs after her bow was blown off, which were not completed before Italy surrendered.

The other destroyers made a substantial counter-attack, with over a hundred depth charges being counted. However, HMS *Unbroken* quietly slipped away undamaged to Malta. She had fared better than the Convoy *Pedestal*, of which only five transports survived the passage, while many of the escorts were sunk or damaged.

HMS *Unbending* successfully attacked the Italian destroyer *Giovanni de Verazzano* in October 1942 and damaged another a few months later. During the same month, HMS *Unique* departed Holy Loch for a patrol in the Bay of Biscay and was not seen again. The captain of HMS *Ursula*, which was on patrol in the same area, recorded hearing explosions on the 10th. Although remote, this could have been *Unique*, although no German records exist of an attack on that date. HMS *Unbeaten* was also lost with her whole crew in the Bay of Biscay when she was attacked in error by an RAF Wellington maritime patrol aircraft on 11 November.

HMS *Utmost* was on a Mediterranean patrol during November. On the 21st she attacked and badly damaged the Italian cruiser *Luigi di Savoia Duca Degli Abruzzi,* which managed to limp back to harbour but did not sail again. *Utmost* was returning to Malta, but was spotted by the Italian torpedo boat *Groppo*, which commenced a depth charge attack and sank her on the 25th.

HMS *P.222* departed Gibraltar on 30 November 1942 to patrol off Naples, and a signal was received from her on 7 December. On the 21st she was due in Algiers but she did not arrive. *Fortunale* of the Italian Navy claimed to have attacked a submarine in the Bay of Naples on the 12th, and it was assumed that she must have sunk *P.222*.

HMS *P.48* was depth-charged and sunk by the Italian torpedo boats *Ardente* and *Audace* on 25 December in the Gulf of Tunis while she was trying to attack a convoy.

HMS *United* sank the Italian destroyer *Bombardiere* off Sicily on 17 January

1943, and followed this up later in the year with *Olbia* in June and the submarine *Remo* in the Gulf of Taranto in July. On 28 May, HMS *Unshaken* successfully attacked and sank the Italian torpedo boat *Climen*e near Sicily.

Meanwhile, back in home waters during February 1943, HMS *Vandal* had been spending a couple of days on a training exercise in the Clyde when she vanished without trace. Later in May, HMS *Untamed* was exercising with HMS *Campbeltown* and other destroyers in the Clyde. On 30 May 1943 she was flooded when a routine repair which was being made while she was submerged went wrong. What wasn't appreciated was that a valve had been fitted incorrectly, probably during construction. As a result, when the Patent log was removed water gushed in. Various options were attempted before a decision to escape was made. With time now running short, it was discovered that they were unable to flood the compartment because another valve was found to be incorrectly fitted. The effect of the air pressure, together with a high carbon dioxide content, rapidly took its toll, and the crew would have quickly perished. Even those using the DSEA breathing pure oxygen would have died because of its toxicity under those conditions. She was salvaged on 5 July, and a comprehensive survey was made which led to improved escape techniques. Following a refurbishment, *Untamed* was recommissioned as HMS *Vitality*.

Action continued in the Mediterranean. HMS *Usurper* was on patrol around the port of La Spezia in Northern Italy during September and October. She was due to return to Algiers on 12 October but did not make it. *UJ-2208*, a German anti-submarine ship, had reported an attack that she had made on a submarine in the Gulf of Genoa on the 3rd, and it was concluded that this was probably the cause of her loss. Later that month HMS *Umbra* sank the *Amsterdam*. It turned out that this supply ship was transporting a valuable load of tanks and other vehicles for Rommel's Afrika Korps.

During the lead-up to the invasion of Sicily in 1943, HMS *Unrivalled*, *Unseen* and *Unison* were used to transport Chariots for beach reconnaissance. These boats were used instead of the usual larger T Class because of their better shallow water capabilities.

In July, HMS *Unruly* sank the Italian submarine *Acciaio* off the Italian coast, and HMS *Ultor* sank the torpedo boat *Lince* in the Gulf of Taranto in August. On 9 September HMS *Unshaken* captured the Italian submarine *Menotti* and escorted her to Malta. This was the night that Italy surrendered, but the war was far from over, and on 21 September, HMS *Unseen* sank the German *Brandenburg* (ex French Navy *Kita*) off Corsica.

In June 1944 HMS *Untiring* sank *Uj.6078* off Toulon, and HMS *Unsparing* sank *Uj.2106* in the Aegean on 26 June. HMS *Venturer* was making good use of her Asdic and sank *U-771* off Norway in November, followed by *U-864* the following February while both boats were submerged.

During 1944 HMS *Unbroken* was loaned to the Russian Navy as *V.2*, HMS *Unison* became *V.3* and HMS *Ursula V.4*. All were returned in 1949 and were scrapped. HMS *Untiring* and *Upstart* were loaned to the Greek Navy in 1945 and returned in 1952.

Once the war in Europe came to an end, the operational role of the U Class boats ceased, and the survivors reverted to their originally designed role of training.

HMS *P.52* managed to have a varied life. During the war she was operated by a Polish crew and named *Dzik*. In 1946 she was transferred to the Danish Navy as *U-1* and named HDMS *Springeren* in 1948. With her service life over, she was returned to the UK to be broken up at Faslane in 1958. Meanwhile, in 1946 HMS *Venture*r had been transferred to the Royal Norwegian Navy as *Utstein*. The majority of the survivors were broken up in 1946, with a few soldiering on until 1950.

Class	Unity/U Class
Role	Small Patrol Submarine

	IMPERIAL	METRIC
Sub Disp – surfaced	625 tons	635 tonnes
Sub Disp – submerged	728 tons	739.65 tonnes
Length	191 ft	58.21 m
Beam	16 ft	4.88 m
Draught	14 ft 6 in	4.42 m
Propulsion	2 × 400 bhp Davy Paxman diesel engines 2 × 412 ehp General Electric electric motors	
Speed	12.5 knots surfaced, 10 knots submerged	
Range	4,050 nm at 10 knots surfaced	
Armament	6 × 21 in (533 mm) torpedo tubes (bow, 2 of which external) 10 torpedoes carried 1 × 3 in (76 mm) gun (*Ursula* only, which could only carry 8 torpedoes)	
Complement (Officers/Men)	30 (3/27)	

Builder	Name	Pennant No.	Class	Launched	Fate	Date
Vickers Armstrong	HMS *Undine*	48C, 48N	Unity Class	5.10.1937	Lost – Attacked – Scuttled	7.1.1940
Vickers Armstrong	HMS *Unity*	66C, 66N	Unity Class	6.2.1938	Lost – Accident	29.4.1940
Vickers Armstrong	HMS *Ursula*	59C, 59N, N59	Unity Class	16.2.1938	PO – Scrapped	5.1950

▲ HMS *Ursula* with the two externally mounted torpedo tubes clearly visible.

(HM Submarine Museum)

Class	Unity/U Class, Group 1		
Role	Small Patrol Submarine		

	IMPERIAL	METRIC
Sub Disp – surfaced	546 tons	554.74 tonnes
Sub Disp – submerged	725 tons	736.6 tonnes
Length	191 ft	58.21 m
Beam	16 ft	4.88 m
Draught	14 ft 6 in	4.42 m
Propulsion	2 × 400 bhp Admiralty diesel engines	
	2 × 414 ehp General Electric electric motors	
Speed	12 knots surfaced, 10 knots submerged	
Range	4,050 nm at 10 knots	
Armament	4 × 21 in (533 mm) torpedo tubes (bow)	
	8 torpedoes carried	
	1 × 12-pdr AA gun	
Complement (Officers/Men)	30 (4/26)	

Builder	Name	Pennant No.	Class	Launched	Fate	Date
HM Dockyard, Chatham	HMS *Umpire* (ex *Umpire*, *P.31*)	N82	Undine/U Class	30.12.1940	Lost – Accident	19.7.1941
HM Dockyard, Chatham	HMS *Umpire* (ex *Una* then *P.32*)	N87	Undine/U Class	10.6.1941	Lost – Accident	4.1949
Vickers Armstrong	HMS *Unbeaten* (ex *Unbeaten*, *P.33*)	N93	Undine/U Class	9.7.1940	Lost – Sunk in error	11.11.1942
Vickers Armstrong	HMS *Undaunted* (ex *Undaunted*, *P.34*)	N55	Undine/U Class	20.8.1940	Lost – Unknown	5.1941
Vickers Armstrong	HMS *Union* (ex *Union*, *P.35*)	N56	Undine/U Class	1.10.1940	Lost – Depth charge	20.7.1941
Vickers Armstrong	HMS *Unique* (ex *Unique*, *P.36*)	N95	Undine/U Class	6.6.1940	Lost – Unknown	10.1942
Vickers Armstrong	HMS *Upholder* (ex *Upholder*, *P.37*)	N99	Undine/U Class	8.7.1940	Lost – Depth charge	14.4.1942
Vickers Armstrong	HMS *Upright* (ex *Upright*, *P.38*)	N89	Undine/U Class	21.4.1940	PO – Scrapped	3.1946
Vickers Armstrong	HMS *Urge* (ex *Urge*, *P.40*)	N17	Undine/U Class	19.8.1940	Lost – Unknown	4.1942
Vickers Armstrong	HMS *Usk* (ex *Usk*, *P.41*)	N65	Undine/U Class	7.6.1940	Lost – Mine	4.1941
Vickers Armstrong	HMS *Utmost* (ex *Utmost*, *P.42*)	N19	Undine/U Class	20.4.1940	Lost – Depth charge	25.11.1942
Vickers Armstrong	HMS *P.97* (ex *Urchin*, *Sokol*)	N97	Undine/U Class	30.9.1940	PO – Scrapped	1949

▲ HMS *Upright* with the streamlined bow. This resulted from the deletion of the pair of external torpedo tubes to improve periscope visibility, which had been obstructed by the wake in the earlier boats. *(HM Submarine Museum)*

▼ The crew of HMS *Upright* proudly display their Jolly Roger, which is traditionally flown on entering port to signify a successful patrol. *(HM Submarine Museum)*

	Class	Unity/U Class, Group 2
	Role	Small Patrol Submarine

	IMPERIAL	METRIC
Sub Disp – surfaced	626 tons	636.02 tonnes
Sub Disp – submerged	725 tons	736.6 tonnes
Length	196 ft 10 in	59.99 m
Beam	16 ft	4.88 m
Draught	14 ft 6 in	4.42 m
Propulsion	2 × 400 bhp Davy Paxman diesel engines 2 × 412 ehp General Electric electric motors	
Speed	12.5 knots surfaced, 10 knots submerged	
Range	4,050 nm at 10 knots surfaced, 120 nm at 2 knots submerged	
Armament	4 × 21 in (533 mm) torpedo tubes 8 torpedoes carried 3 in (76 mm) AA gun	
Complement (Officers/Men)	31 (4/27)	

Builder	Name	Pennant No.	Class	Launched	Fate	Date
Vickers Armstrong	HMS *Ultimatum* (ex *P.34*)	P34	U Class Group 2	11.2.1941	PO – Scrapped	2.1950
Vickers Armstrong	HMS *Ultor* (ex *P.53*)	P53	U Class Group 2	12.10.1942	PO – Scrapped	1.1946
Vickers Armstrong	HMS *Umbra* (ex *P.35*)	P35	U Class Group 2	15.3.1941	PO – Scrapped	7.1946
Vickers Armstrong	HMS *Unbending* (ex *P.37*)	P37	U Class Group 2	12.5.1941	PO – Scrapped	5.1950
Vickers Armstrong	HMS *Unbroken* (ex *P.42*)	P42	U Class Group 2	4.11.1941	PO – Scrapped	5.1950
Vickers Armstrong	HMS *Unison* (ex *P.43*)	P43	U Class Group 2	5.11.1941	PO – Scrapped	5.1950
Vickers Armstrong	HMS *United* (ex *P.44*)	P44	U Class Group 2	18.12.1941	PO – Scrapped	2.1946
Vickers Armstrong (Walker)	HMS *Universal* (ex *P.57*)	P57	U Class Group 2	10.11.1942	PO – Scrapped	6.1946
Vickers Armstrong	HMS *Unrivalled* (ex *P.45*)	P45	U Class Group 2	16.2.1942	PO – Scrapped	1.1946
Vickers Armstrong	HMS *Unruffled* (ex *P.46*)	P46	U Class Group 2	19.12.1941	PO – Scrapped	1.1946
Vickers Armstrong	HMS *Unruly* (ex *P.49*)	P49	U Class Group 2	28.7.1942	PO – Scrapped	2.1946
Vickers Armstrong	HMS *Unseen* (ex *P.51*)	P51	U Class Group 2	16.4.1942	PO – Scrapped	9.1949
Vickers Armstrong	HMS *Unshaken* (ex *P.54*)	P54	U Class Group 2	17.2.1942	PO – Scrapped	3.1946
Vickers Armstrong (Walker)	HMS *Unsparing* (ex *P.55*)	P55	U Class Group 2	28.7.1942	PO – Scrapped	2.1946

Builder	Name	Pennant No.	Class	Launched	Fate	Date
Vickers Armstrong (Walker)	HMS *Unswerving* (ex *P.63*)	P63	U Class Group 2	2.6.1943	PO – Scrapped	7.1949
Vickers Armstrong (Walker)	HMS *Untiring* (ex *P.59*)	P59	U Class Group 2	20.1.1943	PO – Expended as target	25.7.1957
Vickers Armstrong	HMS *Uproar* (ex *P.31, Ullswater*)	P31	U Class Group 2	27.11.1940	PO – Scrapped	2.1946
Vickers Armstrong	HMS *Upstart* (ex *P.65*)	P65	U Class Group 2	24.11.1942	PO – Expended as target	29.7.1957
Vickers Armstrong (Walker)	HMS *Usurper* (ex *P.56*)	P56	U Class Group 2	24.9.1942	Lost – Depth charge	10.1943
Vickers Armstrong (Walker)	HMS *Uther* (ex *P.62*)	P62	U Class Group 2	6.4.1943	PO – Scrapped	4.1950
Vickers Armstrong	HMS *Vandal* (ex *P.64*)	P64	U Class Group 2	23.11.1942	Lost – Accident	24.2.1943
Vickers Armstrong (Walker)	HMS *Varangian* (ex *P.61*)	P61	U Class Group 2	4.3.1943	PO – Scrapped	6.1949
Vickers Armstrong	HMS *Varne* (ex *P.66*)	P66	U Class Group 2	22.1.1943	PO – Transferred	28.3.1943
Vickers Armstrong (Walker)	HMS *Vitality* (ex *P.58, Untamed*)	P58	U Class Group 2	8.12.1942	PO – Scrapped	2.1946
Vickers Armstrong	HMS *Vox* (ex *P.67*)	P67	U Class Group 2	23.1.1943	PO – Scrapped	5.1949
Vickers Armstrong	HMS *P.32*	P32	U Class Group 2	15.12.1940	Lost – Mine	18.8.1941
Vickers Armstrong	HMS *P.33*	P33	U Class Group 2	28.1.1941	Lost – Depth charge	18.8.1941
Vickers Armstrong	HMS *P.36*	P36	U Class Group 2	28.4.1941	Damaged – Scrapped	1.4.1942
Vickers Armstrong	HMS *P.38*	P38	U Class Group 2	9.7.1941	Lost – Depth charge	23.2.1942
Vickers Armstrong	HMS *P.39*	P39	U Class Group 2	23.8.1941	Lost – Salvaged Scrapped	1954
Vickers Armstrong	HMS *P.41*	P41	U Class Group 2	24.8.1941	PO – Loan – Mine	2.1943
Vickers Armstrong	HMS *P.47*	P47	U Class Group 2	27.7.1941	PO – Transferred	11.1942
Vickers Armstrong	HMS *P.48*	P48	U Class Group 2	15.4.1942	Lost – Depth charge	25.12.1942
Vickers Armstrong	HMS *P.52*	P52	U Class Group	11.10.1942	PO – Scrapped	4.1958

▲ HMS *Ultimatum* alongside in her original configuration with the pair of external bow tubes. *(HM Submarine Museum)*

▼ HMS *Unseen*. *(HM Submarine Museum)*

▲ HMS *Unshaken*. *(HM Submarine Museum)*

▲ HMS *P.48* under way at Barrow-in-Furness during contractor's trials before she was commissioned. *(HM Submarine Museum)*

◄ HMS *P.36*. *(HM Submarine Museum)*

111

H.M.S. UMBRA

H.M.S. UNRUFFLED

◀ The Jolly Roger from HMS *Unruffled* preserved at the RN Submarine Museum, showing 13 ships sunk by torpedoes, including a warship, and four by gunfire, three cloak and dagger operations, a beacon or beach-marking operation for amphibious landings, a ship sunk using a demolition charge, a Chariot recovery operation, a train or rail line destroyed by gunfire. *(Jeremy Flack)*

V Class

As with most classes of submarine, the V Class was based on the previous class of boat – this time the U Class. It featured a partially welded hull which improved the diving capability. The V boats were visually very similar to the second batch of the U Class, although they did feature a more raked casing. The ADF (Aircraft Direction Finder) aerial was also relocated to just aft of the casing rather than on it. Their hull was slightly longer and they were fitted with more powerful diesel engines.

Once Italy capitulated in 1943, enemy activity in the Mediterranean declined, and the need for these boats reduced, resulting in a corresponding reduction in the construction programme, which included breaking up some boats already being built. When the war in Europe ended, all further construction halted, with twelve of the 34 boats ordered being cancelled.

The Royal Navy now had a surplus of the smaller patrol boats, and so was happy to release some to the reforming navies of Europe. Some had been partially transferred during the war, and were operated under control of the Royal Navy until the end of the war before being fully handed over.

HMS *Veldt* was transferred on loan to the Royal Hellenic Navy in 1943 and renamed *Pipinos*. She was joined by HMS *Vengeful* in 1945 as *Delfin*, with HMS *Virulent* as *Argonaftis* and HMS *Volatile* as *Triaina* in 1946. They were returned to the Royal Navy in 1957/8 and subsequently scrapped. *Virulent* was being towed back from Malta to the UK in 1958 and broke loose off Spain, where she ran aground and was finally scrapped. Also in 1943, HMS *Vox* (which was originally laid down as *P.67*) was loaned to the French Navy and renamed *Curie* until returned in 1949. Because a second HMS *Vox* was launched in 1943 and still existed when *Curie* was returned, she reverted to her original name of HMS *P.67*.

HMS *Untamed* had been exercising with the 8th Escort Group during their run-up for convoy escort duty in May 1943 off Campbeltown. On the 30th a number of attacks had been simulated when *Untamed* failed to respond to signals. A yellow smoke candle was released and the anti-submarine training yacht *Shemara* managed to locate her using her Asdic. When overhead they could hear noises as though she was trying to start her engine and struggling to blow the ballast tanks. HMS *Thrasher* tried to assist, but all response ceased shortly after she arrived. On the surface the weather had closed in and made it impossible to risk using divers. On 1 June the storm had slackened enough to get the divers down, but there was no response to their tapping on the hull. With no visible signs of damage, HMS *Untamed* was salvaged in July. It was then discovered that an open sluice valve had allowed water to flood in. Once the water had been pumped out and the bodies removed, a decision was made to refurbish HMS *Untamed* owing to the urgent need for more boats at that time, and she was renamed HMS *Vitality*.

HMS *Variance* and *Varne* were transferred to the Royal Norwegian Navy as *Utsira* and *Ula* shortly after they were completed. A second HMS *Varne* was built by Vickers yard on the Tyne and completed in 1944. They were joined by HMS *Viking* as *Utvaer* and HMS *Votary* as *Uthaug* in 1946. Also in 1944, HMS *Vineyard* was loaned to the French Navy as *Doris* and returned in 1947, and replaced by HMS *Vortex* as *Saelen* until 1958.

On 11 November 1944, HMS *Venturer* successfully attacked and sank the *U-771* near the Lofoten Islands of Norway. A few months later off Bergen, on 9 February 1945, while still under the command of Lt J. S. Launders, she sank *U-864* while both boats were submerged at periscope depth.

Thirty-five V Class boats were ordered in total, of which only twenty-two were built between 1942 and 1944. An additional boat was HMS *Vitality*, which was originally built as the U Class, *Untamed*, and sank and was recommissioned, as described above.

Some eleven of these boats were transferred to other European navies as they became surplus to Royal Navy requirements. Some were only on loan and were returned to the UK for scrapping.

A number of transfers have already been detailed, but one of the last was HMS *Vulpine*, which was loaned to the Royal Danish Navy in 1947 as *Storen*, joining *Saelen* (HMS *Vortex*). They were returned in 1958, and the last V Class were scrapped the following year.

Class	V Class (Late)
Role	Small Patrol Submarine

	IMPERIAL	METRIC
Sub Disp – surfaced	655 tons	665.48 tonnes
Sub Disp – submerged	733 tons	744.73 tonnes
Length	204 ft 6 in	62.33 m
Beam	16 ft	4.88 m
Draught	14 ft 9 in	4.50 m
Propulsion	2 × 400 bhp Dave Paxman diesel engines	
	2 × 412 ehp General Electric electric motors	
Speed	12.4 knots surfaced, 9 knots submerged	
Range	4,700 nm at 10 knots surfaced, 30 nm at 9 knots submerged	
Armament	4 × 21 in (533 mm) torpedo tubes (bow)	
	8 torpedoes carried	
	1 × 3 in (76 mm) AA gun	
Complement (Officers/Men)	36 (4/32)	

Builder	Name	Pennant No.	Class	Launched	Fate	Date
Vickers Armstrong	HMS Ulex (ex P.93)	P93	V Class (Late)		Cancelled	
Vickers Armstrong (Walker)	HMS Unbridled	P11	V Class (Late)		Cancelled	
Vickers Armstrong	HMS Upas (ex P.92)	P92	V Class (Late)		Cancelled – Scrapped	
Vickers Armstrong	HMS Upshot (ex P.82)	P82	V Class (Late)	24.2.1944	PO – Scrapped	11.1949
Vickers Armstrong (Walker)	HMS Upward	P16	V Class (Late)		Cancelled	
Vickers Armstrong	HMS Urtica (ex P.83)	P83	V Class (Late)	23.3.1944	PO – Scrapped	3.1950
Vickers Armstrong	HMS Utopia (ex P.94)	P94	V Class (Late)		Cancelled	
Vickers Armstrong (Walker)	HMS Vagabond	P18	V Class (Late)	19.9.1944	PO – Scrapped	1.1950
Vickers Armstrong	HMS Vampire (ex P.72)	P72	V Class (Late)	20.7.1943	PO – Scrapped	3.1950
Vickers Armstrong (Walker)	HMS Vantage		V Class (Late)		Cancelled	
Vickers Armstrong	HMS Variance (ex P.85)	P85	V Class (Late)	25.5.1944	PO – Transferred	8.1944
Vickers Armstrong (Walker)	HMS Varne (ex P.81)	P81	V Class (Late)	24.2.1944	PO – Scrapped	9.1958

Builder	Name	Pennant No.	Class	Launched	Fate	Date
Vickers Armstrong (Walker)	HMS Vehement	P25	V Class (Late)		Cancelled	
Vickers Armstrong	HMS Veldt (ex P.71)	P71	V Class (Late)	19.7.1943	PO – Scrapped	2.1958
Vickers Armstrong	HMS Vengeful (ex P.86)	P86	V Class (Late)	20.7.1944	PO – Scrapped	3.1958
Vickers Armstrong (Walker)	HMS Venom	P27	V Class (Late)		Cancelled	
Vickers Armstrong	HMS Venturer (ex P.68)	P68	V Class (Late)	4.5.1943	PO – Transferred	8.1946
Vickers Armstrong (Walker)	HMS Verve	P28	V Class (Late)		Cancelled – Scrapped	
Vickers Armstrong	HMS Veto (ex P.88)	P88	V Class (Late)		Cancelled – Scrapped	
Vickers Armstrong	HMS Vigorous (ex P.74)	P74	V Class (Late)	15.10.1943	PO – Scrapped	12.1949
Vickers Armstrong	HMS Viking (ex P.69)	P69	V Class (Late)	5.5.1943	PO – Transferred	8.1946
Vickers Armstrong	HMS Vineyard (ex P.84)	P84	V Class (Late)	8.5.1944	PO – Scrapped	6.1950
Vickers Armstrong	HMS Virile (ex P.89)	P89	V Class (Late)		Cancelled – Scrapped	
Vickers Armstrong	HMS Virtue (ex P.75)	P75	V Class (Late)	29.11.1943	PO – Scrapped	5.1946
Vickers Armstrong (Walker)	HMS Virulent (ex P.95)	P95	V Class (Late)	23.5.19443	PO – Foundered	4.1961
Vickers Armstrong	HMS Visigoth (ex P.76)	P76	V Class (Late)	30.11.1943	PO – Scrapped	4.1950
Vickers Armstrong	HMS Visitant (ex P.91)	P91	V Class (Late)		Cancelled	
Vickers Armstrong (Walker)	HMS Vivid (ex P.72)	P77	V Class (Late)	15.9.1943	PO – Scrapped	10.1950
Vickers Armstrong (Walker)	HMS Volatile (ex P.96)	P96	V Class (Late)	20.6.1944	PO – Scrapped	12.1958
Vickers Armstrong (Walker)	HMS Voradous (ex P.78)	P78	V Class (Late)	11.11.1943	PO – Scrapped	5.1946
Vickers Armstrong	HMS Vortex (ex P.78)	P87	V Class (Late)	19.8.1944	PO – Scrapped	8.1958
Vickers Armstrong (Walker)	HMS Votary	P29	V Class (Late)	21.8.1944	PO – Transferred	7.1946
Vickers Armstrong	HMS Vox (ex P.73)	P73	V Class (Late)	28.9.1943	PO – Scrapped	5.1946
Vickers Armstrong (Walker)	HMS Vulpine (ex P.79)	P79	V Class (Late)	28.12.1943	PO – Scrapped	6.1959

▲ HMS *Upshot.* (*HM Submarine Museum*)

▲ HMS *Vagabond.* (*HM Submarine Museum*)

▼ HMS *Vigorous.* (*HM Submarine Museum*)

T Class

The T Class of ocean-going submarines were built to replace the ageing O, P and R Classes. However, because of the 1935 London Naval Treaty, Britain was limited to a maximum of 15,500 submarine tonnage. As a result the number and size of submarines the Admiralty planned to build were smaller than required.

The T Class were the first British submarines to incorporate fuel tanks within the hull. This immediately resolved the leaking problem that had plagued previous classes and the tell-tale trace of fuel left on the surface.

Torpedo aiming remained primitive by modern standards, relying on accurate calculation of speed and distance of the target. It also had the unknown variable as to how alert the target's crew were to spot a torpedo trail and how quick to take evasive action. The Admiralty solution was to fire a salvo of torpedoes to increase the odds of a hit. To help achieve this, the initial batch of T Class boats had a further two torpedo tubes in the mid-ship position angled to fire forwards.

Although nearly 400 tons smaller than the boats they were replacing, the T Class were found to be superior in most respects. The armament was heavier, with an extra two torpedo tubes, the all-welded hull of the later boats was stronger, which meant that it could safely dive deeper to escape attack. They could also dive more quickly and had a greater range. Only their surface speed did not match their predecessors, owing to the space available for engines in the smaller hull, but this was only by a small margin. Various engines were used in the early boats to try to compare performance. However, the declaration of war stepped up production requirements, with only the Admiralty or Vickers diesel engines being fitted.

In the second batch the mid-ship torpedo tubes had their direction of fire changed to stern, and were located further aft. The bulbous bow that housed two external torpedo tubes was redesigned to a more streamlined shape to eliminate the problem with periscope visibility caused by the wake it produced. As a result the ends of the torpedo tubes could be seen projecting either side of the bow.

The third batch featured an eleventh torpedo tube fitted in the stern, and a 20 mm anti-aircraft gun on the rear of the conning tower to augment the .303 in machine-guns. They were also fitted with air-warning RDF equipment. Most of the features were added to the surviving earlier boats during refits.

Name changes could be quite confusing at times, especially when they changed boat as well. HMS *Talent* was originally built and launched as HMS *P.322*. When it was decided that all boats should have names, she was given the name *Talent*. In 1945 HMS *Tasman* was launched. Meanwhile, HMS *Talent* was sold to the Royal Netherlands Navy and a new HMS *Talent* was ordered. With the war ending, the need for new submarines halted and this third *Talent* was cancelled. Tradition is important within the Royal Navy, and where possible it tries to maintain historic links, and so *Tasman* was renamed *Talent*. She was finally paid off in 1967 and scrapped in 1970, but the name still continues with the current Trafalgar Class boats.

At the beginning of World War II, HMS *Tetrarch* was modified to carry mines in her saddle tanks in place of her beam torpedo tubes during a trial period.

Most of the all-welded hull boats that were prepared for Far East operations had some of their ballast tanks converted to take fuel, and the welded construction cured the leaks even for these tanks. The extra fuel proved invaluable where it could take a week's passage to get to the patrol area. One such patrol lasted for 56 days without support for HMS *Tantalus*, which spent a total of 40 days on patrol.

Probably the most infamous Royal Navy submarine was HMS *Thetis*. She was the third of the then new T Class of submarines, and had been built by Cammell Laird at Birkenhead. She was undergoing a series of trials prior to being handed over to the Royal Navy. On 1 June 1939 there was something of a party atmosphere with a number of workers from the yard on board for a rare opportunity for them to experience a submarine at sea. So on this occasion not only were there the naval crew and company trials crew, but also office staff and construction workers. Such was the occasion that a buffet had been laid on, together with catering staff. A total of 103 persons were on board – almost double her normal crew of 59.

Once everybody was aboard, final preparations were made and the crew of HMS *Thetis* cast off. They headed out into Liverpool Bay, where the plan was to make her first dive. Seemingly unknown to the crew, the outer bow cap of No. 5 torpedo tube was open. Not a major problem, but it meant that the tube was full of water. While positioning out to the diving area it was noticeable that the boat was not sitting upright in the water but had a slight list. Apparently she did not handle quite as expected. Again not a major problem, and it may have been put down to the extra 'visiting ballast'.

When it came to making the first dive, HMS *Thetis* proved reluctant. Then all of a sudden the bow dropped and she rapidly dived. Events are uncertain, but for some reason the inner door for No. 5 torpedo tube had been opened, allowing a 21 in (533 mm) column of sea water to gush into the forward weapons compartment. Whether the door had not been properly locked shut and the pressure had forced it open or someone had opened it is uncertain. However, one further minor incident may have had an implication. On each tube there is a test drain tap. If the tube is open and full of water, as No. 5 was, water would run out when it was turned on. By coincidence, a drop of paint had blocked the small pipe so that water would not run. It is therefore quite possible that someone was opening the inner door for whatever reason in the belief that it was safe to do so. What is certain is that once opened there would be no way that the door could be closed, because of the pressure of the water.

HMS *Thetis* rapidly sank just 170 ft (52 m) and hit the sea bed, which comprised soft mud. Having dived steeply with the bow down, her tail stuck out of the water. She desparately tried to release herself, but to no avail with the mud clinging to her like glue. Again this was not a fatal problem, as the boat would normally have had thirty-six hours' air, although with double the number of people aboard this would be nearer to eighteen.

Although the predicament they were in was not life threatening at that stage, there were probably a substantial number of injuries. With the large number of people being thrown about inside a hull and it being full of pipes, taps and machinery with numerous sharp edges, this was inevitable.

HMS *Thetis* was equipped with Davis Submarine Escape Apparatus aboard, but it was new. It was probable that the naval crew had not been trained in its use; the civilians certainly would not. Four of the crew did eventually manage to escape, but there should have been more.

Above them a rescue was being attempted, but it was disorganised, and without a set plan it failed. All sorts of recriminations have featured over the disaster, and it would appear that even today lessons have not been learned when one hears about the Russian nuclear submarine *Kursk* some sixty years later.

On 23 August, Diver Petty Officer Henry Otho Perdue, desperately working in extremely difficult conditions to rescue those trapped inside HMS *Thetis*, became a further victim when he died from the bends. Eventually, on 3 September, HMS *Thetis* was beached at Moelfre Bay, Anglesey, and those bodies that had not already been recovered were removed. It was also the day war was declared against Germany. Such was the desperate need for warships that HMS *Thetis* was refurbished and recommissioned at HMS *Thunderbolt* in 1940.

In September 1939, HMS *Triton* was on patrol off the Norwegian coast when she spotted a submarine. Signals were sent, but as she did not respond she was assumed to be German and torpedoes were fired. Only when two survivors were rescued was the dreadful error discovered. The victim was another British submarine HMS *Oxley*. At the board of enquiry it was discovered that *Oxley* had been trying to signal back, but with a lamp that had previously been reported faulty.

A total of 26 submarines were on standby to be deployed to the eastern side of the North Sea, as it appeared Germany was amassing an attack force against Scandinavia. British forces moved into position as the invasion of Norway commenced in April 1940, and numerous attacks ensued to hamper the Germans. HMS *Trident* attempted an attack on *Lützow*, and HMS *Truant* attacked the light cruiser *Karlsruhe* with torpedoes. The latter was more successful, as *Karlsruhe* was so badly damaged that she ended up having to be scuttled in the Kattegat. However, *Truant* was heavily depth-charged in a counter-attack but managed to escape by diving to over 300 ft (90 m).

The attack phase is when a submarine is most vulnerable. She must expose the periscope to monitor her target and might be spotted. The British torpedoes used a variety of air-powered motors, which left a trail of small bubbles visible to the keen lookout. The Germans had developed an electrically powered torpedo that left no trail. Once an attack has been made, an alert escort crew can mount a rapid counter-attack. There is also the possibility of being struck by another ship other than the target, either accidentally or on purpose.

In April 1940 HMS *Tetrarch* had just attacked a large merchant ship in the North Sea. A heavy counter-attack was made by the escorts and she was forced to dive deep, reaching 400 ft (120 m). Such was the ferocity of the attack that she remained submerged for a total of 43 hours.

HMS *Triton* attacked a German convoy which was taking part in the occupation of Norway on 10 April. She fired a salvo of six torpedoes and hit three ships, the *Friedenau*, *Wigbert* and *V1507*. It was believed that 900 of the German troops of occupation drowned in the attack.

Also in April HMS *Thistle* attacked the U-boat *U-4* in the North Sea, but was unsuccessful. A few days later, the tables turned, with *U-4* catching *Thistle* on the surface. She closed in, fired her torpedoes and sank *Thistle*, with the loss of all her crew. She became the first Allied submarine to become a victim of a U-boat, but it was the only U-boat success during the German battle to occupy Norway. About the same time HMS *Tarpon* also failed to hit her target – the Q-ship *Schiff 40*. This time there was an immediate counter-attack with depth charges, with fatal results for *Tarpon*.

In October 1940 HMS *Triad* failed to return to Alexandria from a patrol off Libya. During the same period HMS *Rainbow* also failed to return. At the same time, the Italians claimed to have sunk two British submarines. One sinking was during a gun battle with the submarine *Enrico Toti* off Colonne on the night of 14/15 October, and the other, a few days earlier, followed a ramming by the SS *Antoinetta Costa* in the Straits of Messina, off Calabria, when she was attacked. There is no conclusive evidence, and the positions are not far apart. She could have been lost on either or neither occasion.

In December, HMS *Triton* was yet another boat to be lost on patrol. She departed Malta to patrol the Southern Adriatic and Straits of Otranto at the end of November. It is believed that she made an attack on the Italian merchant ship *Olympia*, which was already in difficulties. Two torpedo boats that were also in the area reported making a counter-attack which they considered successful. A few days later another torpedo boat, the *Clio*, also claimed to have successfully attacked a submarine. Again either of these attacks could have been the answer, although the latter was considered to have been when *Triton* should have been returning to Malta.

On 5 July 1941, HMS *Torbay* successfully attacked and sank the Italian submarine *Jantina* in the Eastern Mediterranean. In November she took part in a covert operation when, together with *Talisman*, she landed a party of commandos near Apollonia. They were to undertake a raid against Rommel's HQ. Meanwhile, in October 1941, HMS *Tetrarch* disappeared during a passage from Malta to Gibraltar. She had been in contact with HMS *P.34* which was nearby on the 27th, but she failed to make Gibraltar.

HMS *Triumph* attacked and sank the Italian submarine *Salpa* off Mersa in June 1941 and damaged the heavy cruiser *Bolzano*. On Boxing Day she departed Alexandria with a party of commandos which she was to land near Athens. On the 30th she signalled that they had been successfully landed. *Triumph* was then to take up a patrol of the Aegean until 9 January, when she was to extract the commandos. When they arrived at the rendezvous the boat failed to appear, and it was later assumed that she must have already been lost.

In February, HMS *Tempest* had departed Malta and was to patrol the Gulf of Taranto. Intelligence discovered that the Italians were aware of her presence, and she was warned by signal. A couple of days later, on the 12th, *Tempest* and the Italian torpedo boat *Circe* spotted each other. *Tempest* dived and *Circe* rushed to the spot and fired depth charges. After a couple of runs oil was spotted on the surface, indicating some damage. After a number of hours had elapsed, *Tempest* rose back to the surface, only to find that *Circe* was patiently waiting and now opening fire. Unable to safely dive again, her captain instructed the crew to abandon ship, and they were taken prisoner by the Italians. A demolition charge had been left on the *Tempest*, but for some reason this did not detonate. The weather had deteriorated and the Italians were unable to board her and so decided to sink her by gunfire. Although a number of hits were seen, she defiantly remained afloat but had the last laugh when she sank as an attempt was made to get a line to her to take her under tow.

On 16 February 1942, HMS *Thrasher* had attacked and sunk a heavily escorted supply ship off Suda Bay. She was immediately counter-attacked by a total of 33 depth charges from the escorts, and was also bombed by aircraft. Two of the bombs dropped struck *Thrasher* but failed to explode. With the attack over, *Thrasher* surfaced, only to find that she began rolling. As soon as some of the crew climbed on the casing they discovered the cause. One of the bombs was lodged on the gun casing but the other had penetrated the casing and was trapped between it and the hull. Lt Roberts and PO Gould volunteered to try to dispose of the bombs, even though they did not know the type. According to PO Gould, he was responsible for keeping that part of the boat tidy and so it was his job to tidy it up! Having dealt with the 'easy' bomb, they proceeded to try to reach the second one. Because of the confined space they had to work flat and in darkness. Gradually, between them they pushed and dragged the bomb some twenty feet. Aware that they could be blown up at any time and the boat with the rest of the crew lost, the situation was not helped by the twanging sound from inside the bomb every time it was moved. While this occupied their minds, the crew was also very much aware that their position was known to the enemy and that it was close to the Italian coast with frequent patrols. Should an enemy attack be launched, they would have no alternative but to dive to protect the boat and the rest of the crew. A nervous lookout was maintained to scour the horizon. Fortunately for all, the bomb was eventually moved to a position from where it could be lifted and then dropped over the side. For valour, Lt Peter Scawen Watkinson Roberts and PO Thomas William Gould were both awarded the Victoria Cross on 9 June 1942.

Off the Norwegian coast, HMS *Trident* attacked the German heavy battleship *Prinz Eugen* in February. Although she did not sink, the damage inflicted was substantial, with her rudder and 30 ft (9 m) of her stern blown off. She managed to struggle home for repairs which lasted some eight months and kept her from attacking further convoys. However, worse was emerging in the form of the battleship *Tirpitz*. HMS *Seawolf* maintained a careful watch and signalled her position to the Home Fleet, enabling them to protect the valuable convoys more effectively.

The following month HMS *Torbay* was on patrol off the Greek coast when on 4 March an enemy convoy of four troopships was spotted entering the South Corfu Channel. As they were too far away to attack, Miers – her commander – decided to try to follow them and attack them in Corfu Harbour.

Under the cover of darkness, HMS *Torbay* approached the harbour, only to find that the convoy was not there. It had passed straight through the Channel. As light broke on a perfect sea, she attacked two stores ships that were present and then hastily made her escape. This was not without drama, as the waters were heavily patrolled and some forty depth charges were dropped during the attempt to destroy *Torbay*. After seventeen hours in enemy waters, she managed to escape safely. For this, Lt Cdr Anthony Cecil Chapel Miers DSO was awarded the Victoria Cross on 7 July 1942.

Luck was with HMS *Thrasher* again in June. She had just sunk Mussolini's yacht *Diane* when she was spotted and attacked and damaged by a Royal Navy Swordfish torpedo bomber. Fortunately, she managed to limp back to her base at Alexandria.

In August, HMS *Thorn* was not so lucky when she was seen by a patrolling aircraft which proceeded to machine-gun her. At the same time an Italian ship *Istria* was passing, escorted by the torpedo boat *Pegaso*. As *Pegaso* approached the area she detected a submerged submarine and instigated a series of depth-charge attacks. With no further contact, *Pegaso* rejoined *Istria*, but HMS *Thorn* failed to return to base and was believed to have been destroyed in the attack.

HMS *Talisman* was tasked with a patrol which would take her from Gibraltar to Malta in September 1942. She transmitted a signal a few days later but failed to arrive by the 18th. An Italian claim to have sunk a submarine on the 17th may well have been the answer, but could not be confirmed.

Towards the end of November, HMS *Traveller* was tasked to provide intelligence about the warships in Taranto Harbour. This was a preliminary to Operation *Portcullis*, in which Chariots would be used for an attack on the Italian battleships in Taranto Harbour. HMS *Traveller* failed to return to Malta after the reconnaissance.

On 6 December 1942, HMS *Tigris* spotted the Italian submarine *Porfido* off Sardinia. She managed to manoeuvre into position without being spotted, then fired her torpedoes with deadly accuracy and sank *Porfido*. Three months later, *Tigris* failed to return from another patrol in the same area.

HMS *P.311* had been modified to carry a pair of Chariots and departed the UK for Malta in late November. (A description and details of Chariot operations follows on page 128.) Towards the end of December she sailed from Malta as part of Operation *Principal* to attack Italian warships in Maddalena Harbour. Progress signals were received a couple of days later, but she failed to take part in the attack and never returned to Malta. HMS *Thunderbolt* and *Trooper* were also carrying Chariots (two and three respectively), and proceeded to the target, which by now had changed to Palermo. Despite heavy anti-submarine patrols the two boats arrived off Palermo and despatched five Chariots which attacked the Italian cruiser *Ulpio Traiano* and the troopship *Viminale*.

In February, HMS *Tigris* was on patrol near Naples. On 27 February, the German *UJ-2210* was escorting a convoy near Capri when she detected a submarine. She reported that she had made a number of depth charge attacks and finally broke off when oil and a large bubble broke the surface. A signal was transmitted to change *Tigris*'s destination to Algiers, which she failed to acknowledge, and she never arrived at Malta or Algiers.

HMS *Thunderbolt* had led a venturesome career. She had been built as *Thetis*, but sank before delivery. She was salvaged, refurbished, renamed *Thunderbolt* and commissioned in 1940. She attacked and sank the Italian submarine *Capitano Tarantini* in the Bay of Biscay on 15 December 1940, and on 12 March 1943 sank the Italian merchant ship *Esterel*. Unknown to the crew, her luck was now reverting to bad, as the Italian torpedo boat *Libra* was tasked with finding the submarine. She established a contact and made a number of depth-charge attacks, but *Thunderbolt* escaped. On 14 March the Italian corvette *Cicogna* arrived on the scene and she made contact. The periscope was briefly seen before she dived, only to reappear just ten feet away from *Cicogna*. The corvette immediately fired a pattern of depth charges, and shortly afterwards the tail of *Thunderbolt* rose vertically out of the water before sliding beneath the waves with her crew.

HMS *Turbulent* had also seen her fair share of action. On 29 May 1942 she successfully attacked and sank the Italian destroyer *Emanude Pessagno* north of Benghazi. On 8 August she caught the stranded Italian destroyer *Strale* off Cape Bonon and torpedoed her. On 1 March 1943 she torpedoed and sank the Italian steam ship *Vincenz*. On 11 March she attacked the mail ship *Mafalda*, but the following day the anti-submarine trawler *Teti II* spotted her and launched an attack. Although *Turbulent* failed to return to Algiers there appears to be some evidence that she survived the attack only to strike a mine shortly after. Whatever happened to HMS *Turbulent*, all her crew were lost with her. On 25 May 1943 her captain, Commander John Wallace Linton, was awarded the VC for great valour, having sunk a total of 31 enemy ships in his various commands.

In June, HMS *Truculent* successfully attacked and sank the German U-boat *U-308* off the Faroes, and the following month HMS *Tuna* sank *U-644*. However, in September, HMS *Trooper*, was lost, probably to a mine in the Aegean, although there is a German Q-ship claim to have sunk a submarine in that area at that time.

In the Far East progress was being made. On 13 November 1943, HMS *Taurus* successfully attacked and sank the Japanese submarine *I-34* in the Straits of Malacca.

In April 1944 two large task forces were assembled and departed from the Far East Fleet HQ at Trincomalee. Operation *Cockpit* was to attack various Japanese targets in Sumatra. Included with these task forces was HMS *Tactician*, which was to play the role of rescue boat. About a hundred miles from Sumatra some sixty aircraft were launched. They successfully carried out their attacks on various harbour and airfield targets with just a single casualty. A single-seat Hellcat fighter was hit and had to ditch, but HMS *Tactician* was in position not far off the coast and the pilot was quickly rescued.

On 8 June 1944 HMS *Trenchant* was undertaking a patrol by the entrance to the Banka Strait near Palembang in Sumatra. She was accompanied by HMS *Stygian*, who positioned herself out to sea. A Japanese destroyer emerged but spotted *Trenchant* as she fired a torpedo. *Trenchant* managed to withdraw in the darkness, and *Stygian* launched a follow-up attack which was also unsuccessful. The destroyer launched its own similarly unsuccessful counter-attack.

Meanwhile, HMS *Trenchant* spotted the 12,700 ton Japanese cruiser *Ashigara*. She carefully positioned herself, and as this was such a valuable target she fired all eight of her bow torpedoes at a range of 4,000 yards. Five were seen to hit the target, blowing off the cruiser's bow. Fire quickly spread and she developed a list and sank a couple of hours later.

This was a spectacular result for HMS *Trenchant*, but more importantly it removed the only Japanese heavy cruiser in that area. She had been in the process of transporting thousands of Japanese troops to Singapore on what was the eve of the Australian landings on Borneo, and it potentially saved many allied lives. For this Commander Hezlet was awarded the DSO and the Legion of Merit by the USA.

HMS *Tally Ho* attacked and sank the Japanese light cruiser *Kuma* in the Straits of Malacca in January 1944.

HMS *Truant* managed a couple of claims to fame during the war. She was the only Royal Navy submarine to sink enemy ships in three different theatres – Home, Mediterranean and Far East – during which she sank nearly 80,000 tons of enemy shipping. When returning from her refit in the USA in 1941, she spotted and stopped a Norwegian ship, the *Tropic Sea*, which was acting suspiciously. It transpired that she had already been stopped by the Germans and was being sailed by a German prize crew. She also had aboard the captured British survivors from the SS *Braxby*. The British crew were taken aboard *Truant*, along with the captain and his wife, to be taken to Gibraltar. The *Tropic Sea* was scuttled, and the captain's wife became the first woman to sail in a submarine.

On 27 February 1945, HMS *Tantalus* completed the longest wartime patrol, lasting 55 days, during which she had travelled over 11,500 miles. In May 1945 HMS *Terrapin* attacked a tanker in the Java Sea. She was badly damaged by the counter-attack from her escorts but managed to limp back to base. She was considered not to be worth repairing and was scrapped. HMS *Terrapin* was the last British submarine to be attacked and damaged in the Second World War.

In 1948, the second HMS *Talent* was used by Admiralty scientists to carry out a detailed gravitational survey of the English Channel. This was subsequently used to develop the precise Ship's Inertial Navigation System (SINS).

With the war over, a major refit was carried out on eight of the all-welded boats. This required the hull to be cut and a 20 ft (6.1 m) section to be added. The five external torpedo tubes were removed. Improvements were also made to the diesel and electric power-plants and the various sensors. They were also fitted with a fin-type conning tower. When completed it was found that those that underwent the full refit had increased their submerged speed from 9 knots to 15 knots.

In January 1950, HMS *Truculent* had completed her refit at Chatham and was undergoing trials before returning to service. Consequently, she had an extra eighteen dockyard workers on board to monitor the progress of the trials. She was heading down the Thames towards Sheerness in the early evening darkness when the navigation lights of a ship were spotted ahead. For some reason it was assumed that the extra light indicated that she was stationary, but in actual fact it was a dangerous cargo carried. Within a few minutes it was realised too late that they were about to collide, and virtually immediately *Truculent* sank. While most

managed to escape from the submerged boat, only fifteen of the sixty-eight aboard survived. The rest either drowned or died from exposure before being rescued.

During 1950–51 HMS *Taciturn* underwent her refit and emerged with a new streamlined shape. Similar to the US Guppy conversion programme, she was lengthened and fitted with a fin in addition to equipment upgrades.

During 1954 HMS *Talent* was one of the very few riveted boats to receive the Guppy upgrade. While in dock she had a lucky escape when a spring tide caused an incorrectly ballasted caisson to release itself. This flooded the dry dock, and *Talent* was washed out. Fortunately her damage was slight, but four men were killed in the accident.

Following her refit HMS *Thermopylae* underwent her trials fitted with a large dome on the bow. Loch Striven saw a number of boats sunk for various trials over the years. HMS *Thermopylae* and *Templar* were just two examples. They were subsequently raised in rescue training exercises before being scrapped.

This was the largest class of ocean going patrol boat in the Royal Navy, with a total of 62 T Class boats ordered, although the last seven were cancelled.

HMS *Tabard*, *Tactician*, *Telemachus* and *Thorough* were loaned to the Royal Australian Navy, and HMS *Tapir* was loaned to the Royal Netherlands Navy as *Zeehond* for five years, with HMS *Taurus* as *Dolfijn* to join *Tijgerhaai* (previously HMS *Tarn*), which had been transferred in 1945.

HMS *Totem* made a visit to Canada during which members of the Cowichan Indian tribe visited the boat. As is custom with the Indians, gifts were exchanged, and the boat was appropriately presented with a small totem pole. This totem pole apparently had magic properties provided by the Thunderbird, the Grizzly Bear, the Killer Whale and the Fire God which were carved on it. These spirits would ensure that harm would not come to the boat as long as it remained aboard. In 1964 HMS *Totem* was transferred to the Israeli Navy as *Dakar*, along with *Truncheon* and *Turpin* (they became *Dolphin* and *Leviathan* respectively). The totem pole was handed over to the RN Submarine Museum at Gosport to be placed on display. On 26 January 1968, *Dakar* was lost in the Eastern Mediterranean – cause unknown! Her wreck was discovered in 1999 between Crete and Cyprus and parts were recovered; despite various sinister theories it would appear that she may have been the victim of an accidental collision.

On 16 December 1957, HMS *Thorough* returned to HMS *Dolphin* after becoming the first submarine to circumnavigate the world, and in 1962. HMS *Tiptoe* took part in escape trials off Malta during which an officer and six men ascended from 260 ft (80 m). HMS *Tiptoe* was the last of the T Class boats to be operated by the Royal Navy, and was paid off on 29 August 1969. Her anchor is preserved as a memorial at Blyth.

| Class | T Class, Group 1 |
| Role | Patrol Submarine |

	IMPERIAL	METRIC
Sub Disp – surfaced	1,306 tons	1,326.90 tonnes
Sub Disp – submerged	1,572 tons	1,597.15 tonnes
Length	275 ft	83.82 m
Beam	26 ft 6 in	8.08 m
Draught	14 ft 3 in	4.34 m
Propulsion	1 × 1,250 bhp Sulzer diesel engine	
	1 × 725 ehp Laurence & Scott electric motor	
Speed	16.25 knots surfaced, 9.25 knots submerged	
Range	8,000 nm at 10 knots surfaced, 80 nm at 4 knots submerged	
Armament	10 × 21 in (533 mm) torpedo tubes (8 bow, 2 beam of which 5 external)	
	16 torpedoes carried	
	1 × 4 in (101 mm) gun	
Complement (Officers/Men)	53 (5/48)	

Builder	Name	Pennant No.	Class	Launched	Fate	Date
Cammell Laird	HMS *Taku*	38T, 38N, N38	Triton Class	20.5.1939	PO – Scrapped	11.1946
Cammell Laird	HMS *Talisman*	78T, 78N, N38	Triton Class	29.1.1940	Lost – Unknown	9.1942
Scott's	HMS *Tarpon*	17T, 17N, N17	Triton Class	17.10.1938	Lost – Depth charge	10.4.1940
Vickers Armstrong	HMS *Tetrarch*	77T, 77N, N77	Triton Class	14.11.1939	Lost – Unknown	10.1941
Cammell Laird	HMS *Thetis*	11T	Triton Class	29.6.1938	Accident – Renamed	1.6.1939
Vickers Armstrong	HMS *Thistle*	24T, 24N, N24	Triton Class	25.10.1938	Lost – Torpedo	10.4.1940
Cammell Laird	HMS *Thunderbolt* (ex *Thetis*)	(11T), 25N, N25	Triton Class	29.6.1938	Lost – Depth charge	14.3.1943
HM Dockyard, Chatham	HMS *Tigris*	63T, 63N, N63	Triton Class	31.10.1939	Lost – Unknown	2.1943
HM Dockyard, Chatham	HMS *Torbay*	79T, 79N, N79	Triton Class	9.4.1949	PO – Scrapped	12.1945
Vickers Armstrong	HMS *Triad*	53T, 53N, N53	Triton Class	5.5.1939	Lost – Unknown	10.1940
Scott's	HMS *Tribune*	76T, 76N, N76	Triton Class	8.12.1938	PO – Scrapped	7.1947
Cammell Laird	HMS *Trident*	52T, 52N, N52	Triton Class	7.12.1938	PO – Scrapped	2.1946
Vickers Armstrong	HMS *Triton*	15T, 15N, N15	Triton Class	5.10.1937	Lost – Enemy action	18.12.1940
Vickers Armstrong	HMS *Triumph*	18T, 18N, N18	Triton Class	16.2.1938	Lost – Unknown	1.1942
Vickers Armstrong	HMS *Truant*	68T, 68N, N68	Triton Class	5.5.1939	PO – Foundered	12.1945
Scott's	HMS *Tuna*	94T, 94N, N94	Triton Class	10.5.1940	PO – Scrapped	4.1946

▲ The launch of HMS *Thetis* at Cammell Laird's yard at Birkenhead in June 1938. A year later she was undergoing her final contractor trials when she sank with the loss of 99 souls. *(HM Submarine Museum)*

▶ HMS *Triumph* slides down Vickers' slipway at Barrow-in-Furness. *(HM Submarine Museum)*

▲ HMS *Tribune*, still being fitted out by Scott's, alongside HMS *Punjabi*, which was also built at their yard. She has externally mounted forward-facing bow torpedo tubes just visible below the conning tower. *(Glasgow University)*

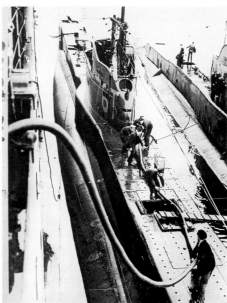

▲ On 26 December 1939, HMS *Triumph* was on patrol in the North Sea when she struck a mine. This blew away some 18 feet (5.5 metres) of the bow, but fortunately did not set off any of the eight torpedoes that were loaded and ready to fire. The layout of the tubes can clearly be seen, with six tubes reloadable from inside the pressurised hull and a further two external tubes visible above. *(HM Submarine Museum)*

▶ HMS *Tribune* refuels from the Depot Ship HMS *Forth*, while HMS *Trident* awaits outside her. *(HM Submarine Museum)*

Class	T Class, Group 2
Role	Large Patrol Submarine

	IMPERIAL	METRIC
Sub Disp – surfaced	1,308 tons	1,328.93 tonnes
Sub Disp – submerged	1,572 tons	1,597.15 tonnes
Length	273 ft 5.75 in	83.25 m
Beam	26 ft 6 in	8.08 m
Draught	12 ft	3.66 m
Propulsion	1 × 1,250 bhp Sulzer diesel engine	
	1 × 725 ehp Laurence & Scott electric motor	
Speed	16.25 knots surfaced, 9.25 knots submerged	
Range	8,000 nm at 10 knots surfaced, 80 nm at 4 knots submerged	
Armament	11 × 21 in (533 mm) torpedo tubes (8 bow, 3 stern of which 5 external)	
	17 torpedoes carried	
	1 × 4 in (101 mm) gun	
Complement (Officers/Men)	57 (5/52)	

Builder	Name	Pennant No.	Class	Launched	Fate	Date
Cammell Laird	HMS *Tempest*	N86	T Class, Group 2	10.6.1941	Lost – Depth charge	13.2.1942
Cammell Laird	HMS *Thorn*	N11	T Class, Group 2	18.3.1941	Lost – Depth charge	7.8.1942
Cammell Laird	HMS *Thrasher*	N37	T Class, Group 2	28.11.1940	Scrap	3.1947
Scott's	HMS *Traveller*	N48	T Class, Group 2	27.8.1941	Lost – Unknown	12.1942
Scott's	HMS *Trooper*	N91	T Class, Group 2	5.3.1942	Lost – Unknown	10.1943
Vickers Armstrong	HMS *Trusty*	N45	T Class, Group 2	14.3.1941	Scrap	7.1947
Vickers	HMS *Turbulent*	N98	T Class,	12.5.1941	Lost – Unknown	3.1943

▲ HMS *Trooper*. *(Glasgow University)*

▼ HMS *Trooper* modified for special operations for which she could carry four Chariot containers. One of the containers is open and shows a Chariot partially emerged down the launch rail, while the Chariot for the other one is fully out. *(HM Submarine Museum)*

Class	T Class, Group 3
Role	Large Patrol Submarine

	IMPERIAL	METRIC
Sub Disp – surfaced	1,412 tons	1,434.59 tonnes
Sub Disp – submerged	1,571 tons	1,596.14 tonnes
Length	273 ft 5.75 in	83.35 m
Beam	26 ft 6 in	8.08 m
Draught	14 ft 3 in	4.34 m
Propulsion	1 × 1,250 bhp Admiralty diesel engine	
	1 × 725 ehp Laurence Scott electric motor	
Speed	15.25 knots surfaced, 8.75 knots submerged	
Range	11,000 nm at 10 knots surfaced, 80 nm at 4 knots submerged	
Armament	11 × 21 in (533 mm) torpedo tubes (8 bow, 3 stern of which 5 external)	
	17 torpedoes carried	
	1 × 4 in (101 mm) gun	
	1 × 20 mm gun	
Complement (Officers/Men)	63 (5/58)	

Builder	Name	Pennant No.	Class	Launched	Fate	Date
Scott's	HMS *Tabard* (ex *P.342*)	P342, S42	T Class, Group 3	21.11.1945	PO – Scrapped	3.1974
Vickers Armstrong	HMS *Taciturn* (ex *P.334*)	P334, S34	T Class, Group 3	7.6.1944	PO – Scrapped	8.1971
Vickers Armstrong	HMS *Tactician* (ex *P.94*)	P314, S34, S74	T Class, Group 3	29.7.1942	PO – Scrapped	12.1963
Vickers Armstrong	HMS *Talent* (ex *P.322*)	P322	T Class, Group 3	17.7.1943	PO – Sold	6.12.1943
Scott's	HMS *Talent* (ex *Tasman*)	P343	T Class, Group 3		Cancelled	
Vickers Armstrong	HMS *Talent* (ex *P.337*, *Tasman*)	P337, S37	T Class, Group 3	13.2.1945	PO – Scrapped	2.1970
Vickers Armstrong	HMS *Tally Ho* (ex (*P.97*), *P.317*)	P317, S87	T Class, Group 3	23.12.1942	PO – Scrapped	2.1967
Vickers Armstrong	HMS *Tantalus* (ex (*P.98*), *P.318*)	P318	T Class, Group 3	24.2.1943	PO – Scrapped	11.1950
Vickers Armstrong	HMS *Tantivy* (ex (*P.99*), *P.319*)	P319	T Class, Group 3	6.4.1943	PO – Expended as target	1951
Vickers Armstrong	HMS *Tapir* (ex *P.335*)	P335, S35	T Class, Group 3	21.8.1944	PO – Scrapped	2.1966
Vickers Armstrong	HMS *Tarn* (ex *P.336*)	P336	T Class, Group 3	29.11.1944	PO – Sold	6.4.1945
Vickers Armstrong	HMS *Taurus* (ex (*P.93*), *P.313*, *P.339*)	P313, P339	T Class, Group 3	27.6.1942	PO – Scrapped	4.1960

Builder	Name	Pennant No.	Class	Launched	Fate	Date
Vickers Armstrong	HMS *Telemachus* (ex *P.321*)	P321, S21	T Class, Group 3	19.6.1943	PO – Scrapped	8.1961
Vickers Armstrong	HMS *Templar* (ex (*P.96*), *P.316*)	P316	T Class, Group 3	26.10.1942	PO – Exp as target – Scrap	7.1959
Vickers Armstrong	HMS *Teredo* (ex *P.338*)	P338, S38	T Class, Group 3	27.4.1945	PO – Scrapped	6.1945
Vickers Armstrong	HMS *Terrapin* (ex *P.323*)	P323	T Class, Group 3	31.8.1943	Damaged – Scrapped	6.1946
Vickers Armstrong	HMS *Theban*	P341	T Class, Group 3		Cancelled	
HM Dockyard, Chatham	HMS *Thermopylae* (ex *P.355*)	P355, S55	T Class, Group 3	27.6.1945	PO – Exp as target – Scrap	7.1970
HM Dockyard, Portsmouth	HMS *Thor* (ex *P.349*)	P349	T Class, Group 3	18.4.1944	Cancelled – Scrapped	
Vickers Armstrong	HMS *Thorough* (ex *P.324*)	P334, S24	T Class, Group 3	30.10.1943	PO – Scrapped	6.1961
Vickers Armstrong	HMS *Threat* (ex *P.344*)	P344	T Class, Group 3		Cancelled	
HM Dockyard, Devonport	HMS *Thule* (ex *P.325*)	P325, S25	T Class, Group 3	22.10.1942	PO – Scrapped	9.1962
HM Dockyard, Portsmouth	HMS *Tiara*	P351	T Class, Group 3	18.4.1944	Cancelled – Scrapped	6.1947
Vickers Armstrong	HMS *Tiptoe* (ex *P.332*)	P332, S32	T Class, Group 3	25.2.1944	PO – Scrapped	1975
HM Dockyard, Portsmouth	HMS *Tireless* (ex *P.327*)	P327, S77	T Class, Group 3	19.3.1943	PO – Scrapped	11.1968
HM Dockyard, Portsmouth	HMS *Token* (ex *P.328*)	P328, S28	T Class, Group 3	19.3.1943	PO – Scrapped	3.1970
HM Dockyard, Devonport	HMS *Totem* (ex *P.352*)	P352, S52	T Class, Group 3	28.9.1943	PO – Sold	10.11.1967
HM Dockyard, Chatham	HMS *Tradewind* (ex *P.329*)	P329, S29	T Class, Group 3	11.12.1942	PO – Scrapped	12.1955
HM Dockyard, Chatham	HMS *Trenchant* (ex *P.331*)	P331, S31	T Class, Group 3	24.3.1943	PO – Scrapped	7.1963
Vickers Armstrong	HMS *Trespasser* (ex (*P.92*), *P.312*)	P312, S12	T Class, Group 3	29.5.1942	PO – Scrapped	9.1961
Vickers Armstrong	HMS *Truculent* (ex (*P.95*), *P.315*)	P315	T Class, Group 3	12.9.1942	Accident – Scrapped	8.5.1950
Vickers Armstrong	HMS *Trump* (ex *P.333*)	P333, S33	T Class, Group 3	25.3.1944	PO – Scrapped	8.1971
HM Dockyard, Devonport	HMS *Truncheon* (ex *P.353*)	P353, S53	T Class, Group 3	22.4.1944	PO – Sold	1.1968
HM Dockyard, Devonport	HMS *Tudor* (ex *P.326*)	P326, S126	T Class, Group 3	23.9.1942	PO – Scrapped	7.1963
HM Dockyard, Chatham	HMS *Turpin* (ex *P.354*)	P354, S54	T Class, Group 3	5.8.1944	PO – Sold	19.5.1967
Vickers Armstrong	HMS *P.311* (ex *P.91* (*Tutankhamen*))	P311	T Class, Group 3	5.3.1942	Lost – Unknown	1.1943
Vickers Armstrong	HMS *P.345*	P345	T Class, Group 3		Cancelled	
Vickers Armstrong	HMS *P.346*	P346	T Class, Group 3		Cancelled	
Vickers Armstrong	HMS *P.347*	P347	T Class, Group 3		Cancelled	
Vickers Armstrong	HMS *P.348*	P348	T Class, Group 3		Cancelled	

▲ HMS *Tabard* with her stern and an aft-facing external bow torpedo tubes visible. *(Glasgow University)*

▲ HMS *Tireless.* *(HM Submarine Museum)*

▶ The totem pole from HMS *Totem* on display at the RN Submarine Museum. *(Jeremy Flack)*

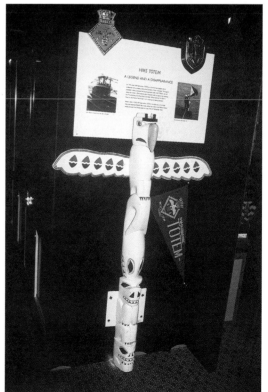

◀ HMS *Tally Ho.* *(HM Submarine Museum)*

R Class (ex USN)

Three boats of the US Navy R Class were loaned to the Royal Navy in 1941/2 to assist in the training role.

HMS *P.514* was lost during the passage when heading for St John's, Newfoundland. During darkness of 21 June 1942 she was seen by the *Georgian*. The minesweeper was awaiting the arrival of a convoy for which she was to be the escort. Not having been advised of any Allied submarines in her waters, *Georgian* signalled for an identification request, and with no response rammed the boat, which was on the surface. *P.514* sank immediately, and when *Georgian* signalled her action the mistake was realised. Despite a search, no survivors were found.

HMS *P.511* and *P.512* spent most of their time training at Holy Loch, and were eventually returned to the US Navy in 1944/5. *P.511* did not make it back to the USA as she foundered in the Thames Bay on 21 November 1947. As a result she was subsequently sold to West of Scotland Shipbreaking, and arrived at Troon in February 1948.

	IMPERIAL	METRIC
Class	R Class (ex USN)	
Role	Training Submarine	
Sub Disp – surfaced	569 tons	578.10 tonnes
Sub Disp – submerged	680 tons	690.88 tonnes
Length	186 ft 5 in	56.82 m
Beam	18 ft 1 in	5.51 m
Draught	14 ft 5 in	4.39 m
Propulsion	2 × 440 bhp New London Ship & Engine diesel engines	
	2 × 467 ehp Electric Dynamics electric motors	
Speed	13.5 knots surfaced, 10.5 knots submerged	
Range	3,700 nm at 10 knots surfaced	
Armament	4 × 21 in (533 mm) torpedo tubes (bow)	
	8 torpedoes carried	
	1 × 3 in (76 mm) gun	
Complement (Officers/Men)	33 (4/29)	

Builder	Name	Pennant No.	Class	Launched	Fate	Date
Fore River Shipbuilding Co.	HMS *P.511* (ex USN *R.3*)	P511	R Class (ex USN)	18.1.1919	PO – Returned	20.12.1944
Union Iron Works	HMS *P.512* (ex USN *R.17*)	P512	R Class (ex USN)	24.10.1917	PO – Transferred	19.7.1942
Union Iron Works	HMS *P.514* (ex USN *R.19*)	P514	R Class (ex USN)	28.1.1918	Lost – Sunk in error	21.6.1942

◄ USS *R-3* was originally launched in 1919, and although operationally obsolete she was useful for training new crew members. She was commissioned into the Royal Navy in 1941 as HMS *P.511*. (*Submarine Force Museum*)

S Class (ex USN)

Six of the US Navy S Class boats were transferred to the Royal Navy in 1941/2. As with the the three R Class, these were all built in the 1920s, and they were primarily used in the training role, although they were also used for some operational purposes.

HMS *P.551* was allocated to the Polish Navy as *Jastrazab* almost immediately on arrival in the UK. She was accidentally sunk by the destroyer HMS *St Albans* and minesweeper HMS *Seagull* on 2nd May 1942 when the submarine was located North of Norway; she was assumed to be German and was attacked with depth charges.

All the other boats of this batch were handed back to the US Navy in 1944–6. However, HMS *P.555* was used for trials at Portsmouth and was sunk as a target during Asdic trials on 25 August 1947 in the English Channel. HMS *P.556* became stranded at Porchester in 1949, and was not salvaged and scrapped until 1965.

Class	S Class (ex USN)	
Role	Training Submarine	

	IMPERIAL	METRIC
Sub Disp – surfaced	854 tons	867.66 tonnes
Sub Disp – submerged	1,062 tons	1,078.99 tonnes
Length	219 ft 5 in	66.88 m
Beam	20 ft 8 in	6.30 m
Draught	15 ft 9 in	4.80 m
Propulsion	2 × 600 bhp New London Ship & Engine diesel engines	
	2 × 750 ehp Ridgeway Dynamo & Electric electric motors	
Speed	13 knots surfaced, 11 knots submerged	
Range	8,000 nm at 10.5 knots surfaced	
Armament	4 × 21 in (533 mm) torpedo tubes (bow)	
	12 torpedoes carried	
	1 × 4 in (101 mm) gun	
Complement (Officers/Men)	42 (4/38)	

Builder	Name	Pennant No.	Class	Launched	Fate	Date
Bethleham Steel	HMS *P.551* (ex USN *S.25*)	P551	S Class (ex USN)	29.5.1922	PO – Lost – Sunk in error	2.5.1942
Fore River Shipbuilding Co.	HMS *P.552* (ex USN *S.1*)	P552	S Class (ex USN)	26.10.1918	PO – Returned	26.10.1944
Bethleham Steel	HMS *P.553* (ex USN *S.21*)	P553	S Class (ex USN)	18.8.1920	PO – Returned	11.7.1944
Bethleham Steel	HMS *P.554* (ex USN *S.22*)	P554	S Class (ex USN)	15.7.1920	PO – Returned	11.7.1944
Bethleham Steel	HMS *P.555* (ex USN *S.24*)	P555	S Class (ex USN)	27.6.1922	PO – Sunk	22.12.1944
Bethleham Steel	HMS *P.556* (ex USN *S.29*)	P556	S Class (ex USN)	9.11.1922	PO – Scrapped	26.1.1946

◀ USS *S.25* was loaded to the Royal Navy during the Second World War, but lost when she was sunk in error. *(Submarine Force Museum)*

Chariot Craft

The Chariot is not a submarine, but the two were so entwined during the Second World War that it is appropriate that they are included in this book.

The Chariot Craft evolved after a raid by Axis forces against British warships during December 1941 at the port of Alexandria. There, the Italian Maiale managed to break through the defences and severely damage the battleships HMS *Queen Elizabeth* and *Valiant*. Although the Maiale had been used on numerous previous attempts to attack Royal Navy ships in the Mediterranean, they had nearly always failed. One craft was recovered at Malta and examined. But it was the success of the attack at Alexandria that led the Admiralty to investigate the possibility of a similar type of craft for its own use.

The Chariot Craft was not to be a submarine, but the design looked very much like a torpedo with two seats. It was armed with a detachable 964 lb (438 kg) warhead on the nose. The crew wore a Sladen suit, which was also referred to as the 'Clammy Death', owing to it being uncomfortable and the dangerous pure oxygen system. An initial batch of Chariots were built in haste, and they proved to be less than ideal, as was the research into the diving suit safety. However, the world was at war and time was not available to produce the ideal solution.

The Chariots were first used in Operation *Title* during October 1942 for an attack on the German battleship *Tirpitz*. She was operating out of the Trondheim fjord when Chariots *VI* and *VIII* were loaded onto a small fishing boat, covered by tarpaulins and set sail. The plan was to enter the entrance of the fjord, crane the Chariots over the side and continue until closer to the target with them bolted submerged to the fishing boat's hull. The weather was extremely harsh, and the Chariots broke away from their mounts in the rough water only a few miles short of the target. With the loss of the Chariots the operation was halted and the fishing boat scuttled. The crews had to walk to the Swedish border to escape. All reached the border except Able Seaman Bob Evans, who was injured by a bullet from a German guard before he could cross over, and was later shot as a spy.

Improvement to the Chariots and their transport resulted in their being stored in watertight containers. These were welded on the deck of T Class boats, aft of the conning tower. Once in the area of operations, the submarine would surface, and with careful flooding of the the ballast tanks the Chariot could be floated out of the container. Once the crew had mounted the craft, the submarine would gently submerge further to allow the Chariot to float away.

Because of the harsh conditions of the North Sea, the Chariots were put to greater use in the Mediterranean, which was a less hostile environment for the exposed crews. Two months after the aborted attack on the *Tirpitz*, a small force was assembled at Malta. Operation *Principal* required eight Chariot teams,

together with the submarines HMS *Thunderbolt*, *Trooper* and *P.311*, to depart over 28/29 December for Sicily, where a concentration of Italian warships had been reported. *P.311*, with *X* and *XVIII*, signalled her position on the 31st but was never heard of again. It was presumed that she had hit a mine and was lost. Although they were initially briefed to attack Cagliari and Palermo, the target was later changed to just Palermo. The hazardous journey through the Sicilian Passage was delayed until the enemy patrols were reduced on 31 December, to increase the odds for the less manoeuvrable boats with the large cylinders. HMS *Thunderbolt* and *Trooper* launched a total of five Chariots (Nos *XV*, *XVI*, *XIX*, *XXII* and *XXIII*) on 2 January before they withdrew. A further boat – HMS *Unruffled* – was tasked with remaining on station to recover the crews once the task was over.

As with most of these types of operation, mechanical failure was a major feature in the event. A battery explosion in one craft resulted in a flooded buoyancy tank and its rapid sinking. One of the crew drowned and the other managed to struggle ashore and was later taken prisoner. A second Chariot abandoned the operation because of a faulty breathing bag, and managed to return to HMS *Unruffled*. The pilot of the third had suffered sea sickness during the passage but continued with the task. Unfortunately, while they penetrated the nets he tore the diving suit. The Number Two managed to beach the craft but was unable to save his colleague. He was later captured after scuttling the Chariot in deeper water.

The other two Chariots' crews from *Thunderbolt* had better luck. Lt R. T. G. Greenland with Leading Signalman A. Ferrier were aboard *XXII*, while *XVI* was manned by Sub Lt R. G. Dove and Leading Seaman J. Freel. They made their way towards the harbour, the entrance of which was guarded by a heavy wire net. The crew of *XXII* managed to force their Chariot underneath. They continued towards the target, and despite an unreliable compass, they dived under an anti-torpedo net and reached the new Italian Navy cruiser *Ulpio Traiano*. Fortunately, security appeared to be lax. Once alongside the huge warship, they dived once more to attach the explosive charge against the hull. A two-hour delay was set on the clockwork detonator, and the crew withdrew, but not before they had attached limpet mines on some nearby smaller ships. Meanwhile the other crew aboard *XVI* had made a similar attack on the *Viminale*, which was a commercial liner that had been converted to a troopship.

Both crews were suffering the effects of breathing pure oxygen and were exhausted, and so they independently decided that they would be unable to make the rendezvous with HMS *Unruffled*, and scuttled their Chariots and struggled ashore. Shortly after dawn those at the harbour were startled by the two charges detonating, but it was to the great satisfaction of the exhausted Chariot crews. They were captured shortly afterwards, and sent to Germany, apparently on the orders of Adolf Hitler, where they spent the rest of the war in a Prisoner of War camp.

The Chariots were involved in a number of other operations to attack enemy shipping. These included German merchant ships that were sunk at Tripoli in January 1943 by Chariots (*XII* and *XIII*) from HMS *Thunderbolt* in Operation *Welcome*. Use of the Chariots was not restricted to the war in Europe. Two Chariots that were operating with HMS *Trenchant* (*LXXIX* and *LXXX*) entered Phuket harbour in Siam and sank a merchant ship and damaged another on 28 October 1944.

Although not the ideal craft, the Chariots found themselves also used for intelligence gathering. During May and June 1943 three Chariots were used in Operation *Husky* to conduct reconnaissance of the beaches in preparation for the invasion of Sicily. This time they were transported by HMS *Unrivalled*, *Unseen* and *Unison*, as these smaller boats had a better capability for operating in the shallower coastal waters.

One unusual operation took place in June 1944. Italy had capitulated, but the Germans still controlled the port of La Spezia. Operation *QWZ* was instigated to attack the U-boats that operated from another port nearby, but was changed at the last moment to concentrate on two Italian cruisers which had been seized by the Germans. It was feared that the Germans would use these as block-ships. In a bizarre joint operation, the two Royal Navy Chariot crew were to proceed aboard an Italian motor torpedo boat escorted by a destroyer – both manned by Italian Navy crews. They were also accompanied by three Italian 'assault swimmers'. La Spezia had been the base for the Italian equivalent to the Chariot – the Maiale – and the Italians were eager to get their own back on the Germans. One of the Chariots was abandoned when it broke down, while the other one, with Sub Lt M. Causer and Able Seaman H. Smith, managed to navigate through the obstructions and reach the *Bolzano*. The charge was attached and set, and the crew beat a hasty retreat. With the batteries running low, the Chariot had to be scuttled and the crew made for the shore. They were assisted by local partisans, who had already located the other crew and were able to watch *Bolzano* capsize.

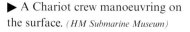
► A Chariot crew manoeuvring on the surface. *(HM Submarine Museum)*

▲ King George VI inspecting a Chariot crew wearing the Sladen suit which was also referred to as the 'Clammy Death'. *(HM Submarine Museum)*

▼ A crewman sat on a Chariot with no charge fitted. *(HM Submarine Museum)*

Welman Craft

The Welman Craft was an alternative solution to the Chariot Craft, and was designed by Colonel Dolphin of the Interservice Research Board. Intended for Army use, his design was for a very small, single-crew submarine. The midget submarines were built at Welwyn Garden City. They were armed with a 1,200 lb (544.8 kg) charge that was fitted on the bow and could be released from inside the craft. One hundred and fifty were ordered, and despite the fact that this was reduced to twenty, there are reports that approximately a hundred may have been built

The extremely cramped craft suffered from various problems, one of which was that because of its size there was no depth to incorporate a periscope. As a result, the only way the crewman could check his position was to gently surface and look through viewing ports on the mini-conning tower. When operating in the confines of a harbour, this would alert the enemy.

The first operational use of the Welman Craft was in an attack on Bergen by four of the craft (Nos 45 to 48) on 20 November 1943. They were transported to the target area by motor torpedo boats, but owing to the restrictive visibility they found it impossible to penetrate the harbour defences, and one of the craft was captured. As a result of the lack of any success, all further plans to use the Welman Craft were halted.

The designer was not to be outdone, and a further design was built for a Welfreighter. It had a range of 600 nm and a speed of 6 knots. Construction of a prototype began in November 1942, and an order for forty was placed, but it would appear that they were also unsuccessful. Twelve were shipped to Australia in 1945, along with six XE-Craft, but were scrapped a short time later.

Class	Welman Craft	
Role	Midget Submarine	
	IMPERIAL	METRIC
Sub Disp – surfaced	4,600 lb	2,091 kg
Sub Disp – submerged	5,740 lb	2,606 kg
Length	20 ft 2 in	6.15 m
Beam	3 ft 6 in	1.07 m
Draught	4 ft 2 in	1.27 m
Propulsion	1 × 2.5 hp petrol engine	
	1 × electric motor	
Speed	3 knots	
Range	12 hours	
Armament	1 × 1,200 lb (544.8 kg) charge	
Complement (Officers/Men)	1	

▶ A Welman under way with the mini-conning tower exposed to enable the crewman to navigate. (*HM Submarine Museum*)

▲ A Welfreighter. *(HM Submarine Museum)*

▲ A Welman midget submarine. *(HM Submarine Museum)*

X Craft Midget Submarines

Lt Godfrey Herbert had served on, or was a captain of, various vessels during the First World War, and made a number of proposals for several midget submarines, including the Devastator. These were turned down by the then First Lord, Winston Churchill, and the First Sea Lord, Prince Louis of Battenburg, as this form of weapon, apart from being dangerous, was considered to be the type of weapon that would be used by the weaker power. The Admiralty did not consider that Great Britain was second to any world power!

In the mid-1920s Captain Max Horton, Captain of the First Submarine Flotilla, proposed Herbert's latest idea for a two man craft, but the Admiralty still hung on to the idea that this was not a fair weapon. At the same time Robert Davis had designed and patented two midget submarines and a human torpedo.

In 1940, the Germans had invaded Norway and positioned some of their capital ships in occupied ports which were protected by the fjords. Across the North Sea the British warships became threatened, as did the convoys, and the idea of mini-submarines came to the surface as a solution.

The trials with the Chariot craft led to an ex-submarine captain, Cromwell H. Varly DSC, to produce a design for a mini-submarine as a private venture. The boat was similar in design to a conventional submarine but reduced in size to 35 tons – not unlike those of Robert Davis. This boat was capable of accommodating just three crew, although this was increased to four later. A second diver was accommodated after a diver had been lost during a training exercise. There were no torpedo tubes fitted. The weapon load comprised two shaped charge-containers.

For long-distance passage, the X Craft, as these midget submarines were known, would be carried aboard a ship. Once in theatre, for operations they had two crews. One would man the boat, which would be towed to the operating area while the other would remain aboard the towing vessel. Once within range of the target, the crews would change, enabling the rested 'attack' crew to carry on the mission.

If, on approach to the target(s), anti-submarine nets were encountered, the midget submarine was equipped with a 'wet-and-dry' compartment which would enable a diver to emerge and make a suitable hole. It could also be used to enable divers to attach smaller charges to hulls.

HMS *X.3* was the first of the Midget submarines, and was launched on 15 March 1942 in great secrecy at Varly Marine Works near Southampton. She incorporated several features similar to the original Holland Class. Her armament comprised a pair of 3,570 lb (1,620 kg) side cargo panels which were filled with Amatex explosive. These were released when under a target, and detonated by a timing device. Alternative cargo panels could be fitted to carry limpet mines.

HMS *X.3* was well designed and manoeuvred well in trials. A few of the systems proved a little temperamental at times, especially the electrically operated items. A second boat – HMS *X.4* – was laid down in Portsmouth Dockyard and a further six were ordered to be built by Vickers. With the trials over, *X.3* was transported by train to Faslane in August 1942, and operational training began. A few months later, on 11 November, a crew had a lucky escape when she sank in 100 feet (30 m) of water when a valve jammed open. When recovered, the boat required delivery to Portsmouth for checks and repairs. In the meantime, *X.4* had been completed and delivered to Faslane, and the six Vickers-built operational-standard boats followed in January 1943.

Intensive training continued, and eventually the six production boats plus the Chariots were formed into the Twelfth Submarine Flotilla in April 1943.

During 1942/3 the German heavy battleships *Tirpitz* and *Scharnhorst* were using the Norwegian fjords for cover, and were causing a constant threat to the convoys to Russia. The Admiralty decided that something needed to be done and following the failure of the Chariots, the midget submarines had to be the answer. Despite pressure from various quarters, the raid was deferred from March until September to enable the crews to be fully trained.

Eventually, Operation *Source* was under way, with all six boats being despatched under tow for the 1,000-mile passage assisted by four S and two T Class boats from Lock Cairnbawn to a position off Altenfjord. The X Craft were to remain submerged for six hours at a time, then surface for fresh air. The mother ships would remain on the surface unless there was a threat of attack. Communications were via a wire in the towing rope. Unfortunately, HMS *X.9*, which had been detailed to attack the *Scharnhorst*, lost her 600 ft (180 m) tow line when it parted during the passage, unknown to HMS *Syrtis*. The first that was known of this was when she was due to surface on the 16th. No trace was ever found of her or her passage crew.

The target allocated to HMS *X.8* was the pocket battleship *Lützow*. However, she had problems with ballast in one of the explosive panels during the passage and had to release it. Shortly after, the same happened with the other panel. This time, although it was detonated at a greater distance, the explosion severely damaged the boat, and this resulted in her having to be scuttled while still crossing the North Sea.

The remaining four boats left their parent boats on 20 September as planned. Eventually, after a further 50-mile passage lasting two days, during which they encountered minefields and nets, and were in full knowledge of the existence of listening devices, patrol boats and gun defences, they entered Kaa Fjord.

HMS *X.5* had Lt Henry Creer as her captain. She was reported to have been spotted by the German guards on *Tirpitz*. Guns were fired at the boat as she dived, and this was followed by the firing of a pattern of depth charges by a destroyer. She was never heard of again and was presumed lost owing to the enemy action.

HMS *X.6*, with Lt Donald Cameron RNR as her captain suffered problems that put both her periscope and compass out of action. However, they still managed to pass through the outer protective nets by following a small vessel in broad daylight. They then managed to enter the double row of torpedo nets that protected the *Tirpitz,* despite the elaborate protection.

Once inside the protective screen, Cameron kept HMS *X.6* just below the still surface as they approached the battleship. Without warning, they struck some rocks which forced the boat to briefly break the surface. Fortunately, it was over so quickly that the German guards thought it was a dolphin. Cautiously, they proceeded further but became entangled in another net. Struggling to get untangled, they eventually broke free when under full astern power. This caused *X.6* to break the surface with great commotion, and her cover was blown. Luckily for the crew, they were so close to the *Tirpitz* that the Germans were unable to train any significant gun power onto her. Cameron continued with the mission despite the shower of bullets and hand grenades that were bouncing off the boat. They dropped the charges and then proceeded to abandon the scuttled boat. They were immediately captured and taken aboard the *Tirpitz.*

Meanwhile, HMS *X.7* was in the hands of Lt Basil Place. He had also managed to enter the inner nets, and proceeded to try to place her charges after a brief encounter with the inner nets. Eventually, they dropped both charges but became entangled in the nets once again as they attempted to withdraw. Like *X.6*, they also broke surface and were subjected to rifle and machine-gun fire. Diving to continue their escape, they became caught up in the protective nets yet again. This time they were freed by the effect of the charges exploding. But being so close, *X.7* was severely damaged by the blast. Place managed to scramble out of his boat before she sank and Sub Lt Bob Aitkin managed to escape and surface some hours later, but the other two members did not survive. Their attack had been successful and resulted in the *Tirpitz* requiring repairs lasting until April 1944, thus giving Allied shipping some respite from her devastating attacks.

The Germans recovered part of the wreck of HMS *X.7* and it was transported back to Germany for examination. The rest of the remains were located in 1974 and are now on display at the Imperial War Museum at Duxford near Cambridge.

HMS *X.10*, under the command of Lt K. R. Hudspeth, was detailed to attack the *Scharnhorst*, but also lost her periscope and compass. She managed to return to the waiting parent boat, HMS *Sceptre*, but had to be scuttled on the return home because of dangerous weather. As it turned out, the *Scharnhorst* had

already left the fjord before the attack was launched.

As a result of the efforts of the team of six X Craft, the *Tirpitz* was never to attack Allied shipping again. Following over twelve months of repairs, the RAF managed to hit the 42,000 ton (42,673 tonne) battleship with a 12,000 lb (5,558 kg) Tallboy bomb, thus ending any chance of her putting to sea again.

The courage of this team, who all knew the risks, was immense. All six of the X Craft were lost, and more importantly, the passage crew of HMS *X.9* and the attack crew of HMS *X.5* were all drowned in a valiant attempt to halt these powerful German warships. Lt Basil Charles Godfrey Place and Lt Donald Cameron RNR were awarded the Victoria Cross for valour on 22 February 1944.

On 7 February 1944, HMS *Syrtis* was involved in a training towing exercise with HMS *X.22* around the Pentland Firth. The weather was foul, with the sea being blown up by gale-force winds. The Officer of the Watch of *Syrtis* was washed overboard, and so she was quickly turned to effect a rescue. Unfortunately, *X.22* struck *Syrtis* and sank.

Despite the high loss rate of the X Craft, production of further boats progressed, which enabled further attacks.

In April 1944 HMS *X.24* was towed to a position off Bergen by HMS *Sceptre* during Operation *Guidance*. With the attack crew aboard, she entered the port on the 14th with the plan to destroy an 8,000 ton (8,128 tonne) floating dock. Once in the port it was decided to attack another target, and the charge was placed under the 7,800 ton (7,925 tonne) *Barendels*. The successful attack resulted in the coaling wharf being put out of action for the rest of the war.

In September the team returned to Bergen on Operation *Heckle*, again with HMS *X.24*, and successfully destroyed the floating dock. The explosion also damaged two ships that happened to be alongside. Besides the damage caused, the effect was felt long after, because of the restricted facilities left available and the tying up of increased resources required to prevent any further attacks.

HMS *X.20* and *X.23* were used during the first week of June 1944 for Operation *Gambit*. Here they were used for the vital job of surveying and marking the Sword and Juno beaches in preparation for the D-Day landings.

Because of the extensive training of the crews a very similar design of unarmed midget submarine (HMS *XT.1* to *19*) was designed and ordered in 1943, specifically for this role. Of the eighteen ordered, only six were completed and the balance cancelled.

A further design of midget submarine (HMS *XE.1* to *12*) were designed for use in Far East waters. With longer distances and higher temperatures to be encountered, they were slightly larger and fitted with air conditioning, and they had a greater stowage space than the earlier boats. To facilitate the releasing of the side charge-panel, the improved X boats were fitted with three spring legs which helped them to remain upright when resting on the sea-bed. A total of twelve XE boats were ordered during 1943 and 1944. A further six were ordered later on in 1944 but were cancelled. HMS *XE.10* was never completed.

HMS *XE.11* was the first to be lost when she was hit while submerged by a trawler in Loch Striven. Two of the crew managed to escape, but *XE.11* sank in over 200 feet (61 m) of water

As soon as a sufficient force could be made available they were ordered to pre-position in the Far East. In July 1945, Midget Submarine Operations were based aboard HMS *Bon Adventure*, located in Brunei Bay together with a number of the XE boats to organise and carry out attacks on Japanese targets in the Far East in Operation *Struggle*.

Towed by HMS *Spark* and *Stygian*, HMS *XE.1* and *XE.3* were towed to the Johore Straits, where they had been tasked to attack Japanese warships in Singapore harbour. On 31 July, Lt Ian Frazer managed to get *XE.3* in position under the 9,580 ton cruiser *Takao* to deposit her two charge panels. Leading Seaman Magennis swam out from *XE.3* with limpet mines and attached them to the hull of the cruiser. This proved difficult owing to a build up of barnacles on the hull.

While this was happening, not only had one of the charge panels failed to release clear, but the cruiser had moved enough to trap HMS *XE.3* beneath her. Once again Magennis swam out and cleared the charge panel, which enabled *XE.3* to manoeuvre, and she returned to HMS *Stygian* – a return passage of some eighty miles through Japanese and Allied minefields, hydrophone listening devices, as well as controlled mines and anti-submarine nets.

Meanwhile, HMS *XE.1* had been similarly tasked, but to attack the *Myoko*; however, because of a delay, this proved impossible, so she also laid her charges near the *Takao*. When the charges exploded, the *Takao* was severely damaged.

Lt Ian Edward Frazer RNR and Leading Seaman James Joseph Magenniss were both awarded a Victoria Cross for valour on 13 November 1945.

The attacks on the Japanese continued. The Allies had managed to break the Japanese codes, and were therefore able to monitor radio messages, but they could not listen to telephone calls. Underwater cables linked several major locations, and a plan was compiled. To maintain the element of surprise, a simultaneous attack was conducted by HMS *XE.4* and *XE.5* against the underwater telephone cable that linked Saigon and Hong Kong, as well as another linking Saigon and Singapore. These cables were located in 40 ft (12 m) of water. Despite atrocious conditions and strong currents, *XE.4* completed her task and returned with a section of cable as proof. Towed by HMS *Selene*, HMS *XE.5* had been positioned close to Hong Kong to cut the cable link to Singapore Here she also found difficult conditions, with her four divers having to work in deep mud. As a result they spent three and a half days trying to complete their task. On 3 August they had

to withdraw before they thought they had completely cut the cable. Later it was discovered that they had in fact been successful.

These attacks at Singapore and Hong Kong were planned to be the prelude to a large amphibious landing on the west coast of Malaya codenamed Operation *Zipper*. However, the dropping of the atom bomb on Japan brought about her surrender and the end of the war in the Far East.

The X boats had proved to be an effective force which could produce results that were substantial when compared with its resources.

In the mid-1950s four X Craft midget submarines (HMS *X.51* to *X.54*) were built, and although they were improved, with newer technology, they were not as effective as their predecessors with their more basic systems.

HMS *X.53* was loaned complete with her British crew to the US Navy from June to September 1958 for trials in harbour defence. Following refurbishment, HMS *X.51* (*Stickleback*) was sold to the Swedish Navy, with which she was operated as *Spiggen*, mainly in the training role. Once her service life ended, she was presented to the Imperial War Museum in 1976, and can be seen on display at its museum at Duxford near Cambridge.

When cuts in the Royal Navy submarine force were required, it was the X boats that suffered the axe. While they had a real purpose in wartime, it was considered that their safety margin was unacceptable in peacetime. As a result the unit was disbanded in 1958.

Such were the dangers and devotion to duty by the crews of the various Chariot and X Craft during the Second World War that between them the crews amassed the following in recognition of their efforts:

4	Victoria Crosses (VC)
3	Commander of the British Empire (CBE)
11	Distinguished Service Orders (DSO)
1	Order of the British Empire (OBE)
10	Members of the British Empire (MBE)
17	Distinguished Service Crosses (DSC)
6	Conspicuous Gallantry Medals (CGM)
12	Distinguished Service Medals (DSM)
4	British Empire Medals (BEM)
26	Mentions in Despatch (MiD)

Preserved
HMS *X.7* (remains)	Imperial War Museum, Duxford
HMS *X.24*	RN Submarine Museum, Gosport
HMS *Stickleback*, *X.51*	Imperial War Museum, Duxford

	Class	X Craft prototype
	Role	Midget Submarine

	IMPERIAL	METRIC
Sub Disp – surfaced	30 tons	30.48 tonnes
Sub Disp – submerged	32.5 tons	33.02 tonnes
Length	43 ft 6 in	13.26 m
Beam	8 ft	2.44 m
Draught	5 ft 6 in	1.68 m
Propulsion	1 × 42 bhp Perkins diesel engine	
	1 × 25 ehp electric motor	
Speed	6.5 knots surfaced, 4.5 knots submerged	
Range	1,300 nm at 4 knots surfaced, 80 nm at 2 knots submerged	
Armament	2 × containers with 3,570 lb (1,620 kg) Amatex	
	Limpet mines	
Complement (Officers/Men)	7 (3/4)	

Builder	Name	Pennant No.	Class	Launched	Fate	Date
Varley Marine	HMS *Piker* (ex *X.3*)	X3	X Craft prototype	15.3.1942	Accident – Scrapped	1945
HM Dockyard, Portsmouth	HMS *X.4*	X4	X Craft prototype	1942	PO – Scrapped	1945

	Class	X5 Class
	Role	Midget Submarine

	IMPERIAL	METRIC
Sub Disp – surfaced	27 tons	27.43 tonnes
Sub Disp – submerged	30 tons	30.48 tonnes
Length	51 ft 7 in	15.72 m
Beam	8 ft 6 in	2.59 m
Draught	7 ft 5 in	2.26 m
Propulsion	1 × 42 bhp Gardner diesel engine	
	1 × 30 ehp electric motor	
Speed	6.5 knots surfaced, 5.5 knots submerged	
Range	1,300 nm at 4 knots surfaced, 80 nm at 2 knots submerged	
Armament	2 × containers with 4,000 lb (1,816 kg) Amatex	
	Limpet mines	
Complement (Officers/Men)	4	

Builder	Name	Pennant No.	Class	Launched	Fate	Date
Vickers Armstrong	HMS *Platypus* (ex *X.5*)	X5	X5 Class	31.12.1942	Lost – Unknown	22.9.1943
Vickers Armstrong	HMS *Piker II* (ex *X.6*)	X6	X5 Class	11.1.1943	Lost – Scuttled	22.9.1943
Vickers Armstrong	HMS *Pdinichthys* (ex *X.7*)	X7	X5 Class	1943	Lost – Unknown	22.9.1943
Vickers Armstrong	HMS *Expectant* (ex *X.8*)	X8	X5 Class	1943	Lost – Unknown	18.9.1943
Vickers Armstrong	HMS *Pluto* (ex *X.9*)	X9	X5 Class	1943	Lost – Foundered	16.9.1943
Broadbent	HMS *X.10*	X10	X5 Class	1943	Lost – Scuttled	22.9.1943
Broadbent	HMS *Exemplar* (ex *X.20*)	X20	X5 Class	1943	PO – Scrapped	1945
Broadbent	HMS *Exultant* (ex *X.21*)	X21	X5 Class	1943	PO – Scrapped	1945
Markham	HMS *Exploit* (ex *X.22*)	X22	X5 Class	1943	Lost – Accident	7.2.1944
Markham	HMS *Xiphias* (ex *X.23*)	X23	X5 Class	1943	PO – Scrapped	1945
Marshall	HMS *Expeditious* (ex *X.24*)	X24	X5 Class	1943	PO – Preserved	
Marshall	HMS *Xema* (ex *X.25*)	X25	X5 Class	1943	PO – Scrapped	1945

▲ Remains of the front section of HMS *Pdinichthys*, which was used to attack the German battleship *Tirpitz*. *(Jeremy Flack)*

▼ HMS *Expeditious*, on display at the RN Submarine Museum, took part in two attacks on German shipping at the Norwegian port of Bergen in 1944. *(Jeremy Flack)*

	Class	XE Class
	Role	Midget Submarine

	IMPERIAL	METRIC
Sub Disp – surfaced	30 tons	30.48 tonnes
Sub Disp – submerged	34 tons	34.54 tonnes
Length	53 ft	16.15 m
Beam	8 ft 6 in	2.59 m
Draught	5 ft 8 in	1.73 m
Propulsion	1 × 42 bhp Garner diesel engine	
	1 × 30 ehp electric motor	
Speed	6.5 knots surfaced, 5.5 knots submerged	
Range	1,300 nm at 4 knots surfaced, 80 nm at 2 knots submerged	
Armament	2 × 5.5 ton (5.59 tonne) charges	
	Limpet mines	
Complement (Officers/Men)	5	

Builder	Name	Class	Launched	Fate	Date
Vickers Armstrong	HMS *Executioner* (ex *XE.1*)	XE Class	1944	PO – Scrapped	1945
Vickers Armstrong	HMS *Xerxes* (ex *XE.2*)	XE Class	1944	PO – Scrapped	1945
Vickers Armstrong	HMS *Sigyn* (ex *XE.3*)	XE Class	27.11.1944	PO – Scrapped	1945
Vickers Armstrong	HMS *Exciter* (ex *XE.4*)	XE Class	1944	PO – Scrapped	1945
Vickers Armstrong	HMS *Perseus* (ex *XE.5*)	XE Class	1944	PO – Scrapped	1945
Vickers Armstrong	HMS *Excalibur II* (ex *XE.6*)	XE Class	1944	PO – Scrapped	1945
Broadbent	HMS *Exuberant* (ex *XE.7*)	XE Class	1944	PO – Scrapped	1953
Broadbent	HMS *Expunger* (ex *XE.8*)	XE Class	1944	PO – Scrapped	1955
Marshall	HMS *Unexpected* (ex *XE.9*)	XE Class	1944	PO – Scrapped	
Marshall	HMS *XE.10*	XE Class		Cancelled – Scrapped	1945
Markham	HMS *Lucifer* (ex *XE.11*)	XE Class	1944	Accident – Scrapped	6.3.1945
Markham	HMS *Excitable* (ex *XE.12*)	XE Class	1944	PO – Scrapped	1952
Marshall	HMS *XE.14*	XE Class		Cancelled	
Marshall	HMS *XE.15*	XE Class		Cancelled	
Marshall	HMS *XE.16*	XE Class		Cancelled	
Marshall	HMS *XE.17*	XE Class		Cancelled	
Marshall	HMS *XE.18*	XE Class		Cancelled	
Marshall	HMS *XE.19*	XE Class		Cancelled	

Builder	Name	Pennant No.	Class	Launched	Fate	Date
Vickers Armstrong	HMS *Extant* (ex *XT.1*)	XT1	XT Class	1944	PO – Scrapped	1945
Vickers Armstrong	HMS *Sandra* (ex *XT.2*)	XT2	XT Class	1944	PO – Scrapped	1945
Vickers Armstrong	HMS *Herald* (ex *XT.3*)	XT3	XT Class	1944	PO – Scrapped	1945
Vickers Armstrong	HMS *Excelsior*	XT4	XT Class	1944	PO – Scrapped	1945
Vickers Armstrong	HMS *Extended* (ex *XT.5*)	XT5	XT Class	1944	PO – Scrapped	1945
Vickers Armstrong	HMS *Xantho* (ex *XT.6*)	XT6	XT Class	1944	PO – Scrapped	1945
Broadbent	HMS *XT.7*	XT7	XT Class		Cancelled	
Broadbent	HMS *XT.8*	XT8	XT Class		Cancelled	
Broadbent	HMS *XT.9*	XT9	XT Class		Cancelled	
Broadbent	HMS *XT.10*	XT10	XT Class		Cancelled	
Broadbent	HMS *XT.11*	XT11	XT Class		Cancelled	
Broadbent	HMS *XT.12*	XT12	XT Class		Cancelled	
Broadbent	HMS *XT.14*	XT14	XT Class		Cancelled	
Broadbent	HMS *XT.15*	XT15	XT Class		Cancelled	
Broadbent	HMS *XT.16*	XT16	XT Class		Cancelled	
Broadbent	HMS *XT.17*	XT17	XT Class		Cancelled	
Broadbent	HMS *XT.18*	XT18	XT Class		Cancelled	
Broadbent	HMS *XT.19*	XT19	XT Class		Cancelled	

▲ HMS *Expunger* plus two others alongside. *(HM Submarine Museum)*

▼ HMS *Extended* was used to train X Class boat crews. *(HM Submarine Museum)*

▼ HMS *Exciter* was used to cut the underwater phone cable between Saigon and Hong Kong being used by the Japanese. *(HM Submarine Museum)*

Class	XT Class
Role	Midget Submarine Trainer

	IMPERIAL	METRIC
Sub Disp – surfaced	27 tons	27.43 tonnes
Sub Disp – submerged	30 tons	30.48 tonnes
Length	51 ft 4 in	15.65 m
Beam	5 ft 9 in	1.75 m
Draught	5 ft 8 in	1.73 m
Propulsion	1 × 42 bhp Garner diesel engine	
	1 × 30 ehp electric motor	
Speed	6.5 knots surfaced, 5.5 knots submerged	
Range	1,300 nm at 4 knots surfaced, 80 nm at 2 knots submerged	
Armament	None	
Complement (Officers/Men)	5	

Class	X51 Class
Role	Midget Submarine

	IMPERIAL	METRIC
Sub Disp – surfaced	36 tons	36.58 tonnes
Sub Disp – submerged	40 tons	40.64 tonnes
Length	53 ft 10.5 in	16.42 m
Beam	6 ft 3.5 in	1.92 m
Draught	5 ft 9 in	1.75 m
Propulsion	1 × 42 bhp Perkins 6 cylinder diesel engine	
	1 × 30 ehp electric motor	
Speed	7 knots surfaced, 6 knots submerged	
Range		
Armament	2 × containers with 2 tons (2.03 tonnes) of explosives	
Complement (Officers/Men)	5	

Builder	Name	Pennant No.	Class	Launched	Fate	Date
Vickers Armstrong	HMS *Stickleback* (ex *X.51*)	X51	X51 Class	1.10.1954	PO – Sold – Preserved	15.7.1958
Vickers Armstrong	HMS *Shrimp* (ex *X.52*)	X52, S102	X51 Class	30.12.1954	PO – Scrapped	1958
Vickers Armstrong	HMS *Sprat* (ex *X.53*)	X53, S103	X51 Class	1.3.1955	PO – Scrapped	1965
Vickers Armstrong	HMS *Minnow* (ex *X.54*)	X54, S104	X51 Class	5.5.1955	PO – Scrapped	1958

▼ HMS *X.51 Stickleback* with side containers fitted. *(HM Submarine Museum)*

▼ HMS *X.51 Stickleback*. *(HM Submarine Museum)*

◄ HMS *X.51 Stickleback* on display at the Imperial War Museum at Duxford, near Cambridge (the torpedo is Japanese). *(Jeremy Flack)*

► HMS *X.52 Shrimp*. *(HM Submarine Museum)*

Foreign Submarines

A number of foreign submarines have been operated in various guises by the Royal Navy. Some of these were captured enemy boats, such as the German U-boats, while others have included some French Navy boats which served under British operational control when France fell during the Second World War.

Vickers Armstrong received an order for four submarines from the Turkish Navy in March 1939. These were similar in construction to the S Class, some of which were then in service with the Royal Navy. When war broke out all four were requisitioned by the Admiralty. However, in 1942 it was decided that two would be supplied, and so *Muratreis* (HMS *P.612*) and *Orucreis* (HMS *P.611*) were delivered by a Royal Navy crew. *Burakreis* and *Ulucalireis* continued to serve as HMS *P.614* and *P.615* until the latter was hit by a torpedo from the German *U-123* off West Africa and sank on 18 April 1943. *P.614* was finally commissioned into the Turkish Navy at the beginning of 1946.

On 19 June 1940, the Italian Navy submarine *Galileo Galilei* was detected by the trawler *Moonstone* using Asdic, and attacked using depth charges. She lost contact but waited patiently and was rewarded when the enemy submarine was detected again. More depth charges were let off, which resulted in her surfacing. *Moonstone* quickly opened fire and hit the conning tower. As a result of the successful attack the Italian crew surrendered and the destroyer *Kandahar* towed her to Aden. Documents found on board gave rendezvous positions, and as a result a further three Italian Navy submarines were ambushed and destroyed.

Galileo Galilei was brought back to the UK and commissioned with the Royal Navy and named HMS *X.2*. This was subsequently changed to *Moonstone*. She was used for tests and evaluation, and was eventually scrapped in 1946.

On 9 July 1942, the Italian Navy boat *Perla* was captured in the Eastern Mediterranean. After some evaluation, she was transferred to the Greek Navy as *Matrozos*. They continued to operate her until she was eventually scrapped in 1954. On 12 July 1943, another Italian boat, *Bronzo*, was captured off Syracuse and handed over for use by French Navy crews operating with the Royal Navy. and named *Narval*.

The French Navy's *Surcouf* was laid down in 1927, and at 110 m (361 ft) long and 3,250 tons surfaced she became the world's largest submarine. She had a 15,000 km (9,320 mile) range at a cruise of 10 knots, and was capable of 20 knots. She featured a pair of 204 mm (8 in) guns and carried over 600 shells. She had two external rotating triple torpedo racks with one 550 mm (21.67 in) and two 440 mm (17.34 in) torpedoes on each. Four 550 mm torpedo tubes were fitted internally in the bow, and 22 torpedoes were carried in total. A Beeson MB floatplane could be carried in a watertight hangar for reconnaissance purposes.

When the Second World War broke out, *Surcouf* was in the West Indies, and moved to Kingston, Jamaica, to help escort a convoy to England. This was to be of mutual benefit, as she was in urgent need of a refit and would need some support during the crossing. On reaching the Western Approaches she broke off from the convoy to make for Brest, arriving in October 1939. By June she had almost completed the refit, but on the 18th she was forced to leave port to avoid capture by the advancing Germans, and headed for Plymouth. On arriving, the crew were unsure what they should do. When the Vichy Government started to negotiate an armistice, the crew were split as to their loyalty. Hitler insisted that all French Navy ships were to return to base. The British government, which was expecting an imminent German invasion, was extremely concerned about the addition of French warships to the German Navy.

The British government had already prepared a plan for any French Navy ships in British waters, and *Surcouf* obviously fell in this category. On 3 July Commander Sprague, captain of HMS *Thames*, and Lieutenant Griffiths of HMS *Rorqual* led a party of officers, ratings and Royal Marines and boarded the *Surcouf* to confront the Captain. With the situation read out to them by Sprague that they were under arrest and could be returned to France or stay to fight the Germans, the French captain requested that he discuss the matter with his admiral, who was also at Plymouth, aboard the battleship *Paris*. Sprague agreed and escorted the captain up to the casing.

Meanwhile, below in the wardroom, two ratings were left to guard the five French officers. One of the officers requested a visit to the heads. There he located a pistol, and a shot was heard by Sprague. Straight away Sprague returned to the wardroom and was hit six times before the French gunnery officer hit him fatally in the head. Griffiths, who was following, hit the gunnery officer but tripped over Sprague as he turned for help, and was shot by the submarine's doctor in the back. The doctor then fired at one of the British ratings, who bayoneted another crew member before he died. Shortly after this brief skirmish the boarding crew regained control.

Most of the French crew of the *Surcouf* were replaced, and a Royal Navy officer, a Signalman and a Telegraphist were drafted to ensure that all signals were correctly interpreted and sent. She was recommissioned on 15 September, went to sea on 20 December and undertook a work-up in Holy Loch in February. However, with so many of her crew new to the boat she remained at low efficiency. After escorting a convoy across the Atlantic she sustained some damage from bombs.

The characteristics of the *Surcouf* made it difficult to find a proper role for the boat, which did not help the low morale of the crew. In December she was deployed to Halifax to join forces with several ships to annex St Pierre and the Miquelon Islands, which had radio stations operated by the Vichy and were thought to be passing information on Allied convoys. Once the situation had settled down, *Surcouf* was in need of some maintenance, but her lack of tasking continued. Problems in defending Tahiti and the other Free French Pacific Islands seemed to provide an ideal answer, and orders were given for her to head south and transit the Panama Canal. Sadly *Surcouf* did not make it. A US Army transport reported considerable damage after a collision on 18 February 1942 with an unidentified vessel that immediately sank. All 129 crew were lost.

In 1940 the French Navy's *Junon*, a Diane Class submarine, was taken under Royal Navy control. At the end of the war she returned to France.

On 28 August 1941, *U-570*, a Type VIIC U-boat, was spotted by an RAF Hudson of No 269 Sqn on the surface in the North Atlantic towards Iceland. The RAF crew immediately pressed home an attack and managed to damage the enemy boat with bombs. Unable to dive, she surrendered and a Royal Navy warship took the crew prisoner. *U-570* was initially towed to Iceland, underwent some minor repairs and sailed to the UK under escort. *U-570* was commissioned into Royal Navy service as HMS *Graph*. She was given the pennant number P715, which was later changed to N46. Having initially been studied to evaluate her capabilities, she was used operationally for a short time, during which she unsuccessfully attacked *U-333* in October 1942. Subsequently, HMS *Graph* was utilised for anti-submarine training, and was usually seen flying a White Ensign to ensure she was not attacked for real in error. In March 1944 she was under tow off Scotland when she broke the line and ran aground. She was subsequently salvaged and scrapped in 1947.

The Polish Navy operated *Jastrab*, *Wilke* and *Orzel* with the Royal Navy. *Orzel* attacked and sank the troopship *Rio de Janeiro* on 8 April 1940 off Lillesand. A hundred or so survivors were rescued, and it was discovered that they were en route to Bergen. As a result, Norway's small military forces requested full mobilisation, but her pacifist government would do nothing that could be interpreted as hostile to nearby Germany, who subsequently invaded her.

When hostilities in Europe ended, Admiral Dönitz ordered all the U-boats to return to base, but it was August before the last finally surrendered. Over 150 U-boats were handed over to the Royal Navy. Between November 1945 and early 1946 some 120 boats that had been moved to Loch Ryan were taken out to sea and scuttled some thirty nautical miles north of Malin Head during Operation *Deadlight*. A number of others were used for assessment trials, while some were transferred to other countries for use by their navies, such as Norway and Russia.

A Royal Navy team found *U-1407* scuttled at Cuxhaven. She had only been commissioned on 13 March 1945 and was scuttled as Germany surrendered. She was a Type XVIIB U-boat built by Blohm und Voss for trials with a Walther HTP (High Test Peroxide) turbine. She was considered a valuable prize, and so she was salvaged and then delivered to Vickers for refurbishment.

The Germans had been experimenting with various fuels, including hydrogen peroxide, which is available in various strengths. At the weak end it can be used to bleach hair, but at the other end is the enriched HTP (High Test Peroxide). It was found that when diesel was ignited it burnt fiercely in an HTP spray, and the exhaust gases could be used to power a turbine. However, the process was unstable and potentially dangerous.

Professor Walther came over to Vickers with some of his staff from Germany and assisted with the rebuilding of *U-1407*. Once complete, she was commissioned into the Royal Navy as HMS *Meteorite* and the propulsion system was evaluated. Although highly volatile, with a number of explosions sustained, it was decided to develop the trial further, and two boats were designed as the Explorer Class and built by Vickers using experience from this German experimental boat. HMS *Meteorite* was scrapped at Barrow in 1949.

The list of ships shows the number of foreign boats that were operated by the Royal Navy. The majority were surrendered German U-boats, most of which were only used for trials for a short time, and not formally commissioned with names and pennant numbers.

Builder	Name	Pennant No.	Class	Launched	Fate	Date
Nordseewerke	HMS *N.16* (ex *U-1105*)	N16	VIIo/41 U-boat	1944	PO – Transferred	1946
Danziger Werft	HMS *N.19* (ex *U-1171*)	N19	VIIo/41 U-boat	1944	PO – Scrapped	4.1949
Blohm & Voss	HMS *Meteorite* (ex *U-1407*)	N25	XVIIB U-boat	1945	PO – Scrapped	1949
Blohm & Voss	HMS *N.27* (ex *U-2529*)	N27	XXI U-boat	1944	PO – Transferred	1946
AG Weser	HMS *N.28* (ex *U-3035*)	N28	XXI U-boat	1945	PO – Transferred	1945
AG Weser	HMS *N.29* (ex *U-3041*)	N29	XXI U-boat	1945	PO – Scrapped	1945
Schichau	HMS *N.30* (ex *U-3515*)	N30	XXI U-boat	1944	PO – Transferred	1945
Deutsche Werft	HMS *N.31* (ex *U-2353*)	N31	XXIII U-boat	1944	PO – Transferred	1947
Deutsche Werft	HMS *N.35* (ex *U-2326*)	N35	XXIII U-boat	1944	PO – Transferred	1946
Deschimage	HMS *N.41* (ex *U-3017*)	N41	XXI U-boat	1944	PO – Scrapped	1949
Blohm & Voss	HMS *Graph* (ex *U-570, P715*)	N715, N46	VIIc U-boat	20.3.1941	PO – Scrapped	1947
Kriegsmarinewerft	HMS *N.65* (ex *U-776*)	N65	VIIC U-boat	1944	PO – Scuttled	3.12.1945
Blohm & Voss	(*U-1023*)	N83	VIIc/41 U-boat	1944	PO – Scuttled	7.1.1946

Builder	Name	Pennant No.	Class	Launched	Fate	Date
Germaniawerft	(*U-249*)	N86	VIIc U-boat	1943	PO – Scrapped	11.1945
Krupp-Germania	(*U-86*)		VIIB U-boat	WW1	PO – Foundered	1921
Blohm & Voss	(*U-126*)		IXC U-boat	WW1	PO – Scrapped	1923
AG Weser	(*U-190*)		IXC/40 U-boat	1942	PO – Transferred	1945
HC Stülcken	(*U-712*)		VIIC U-boat	1941	PO – Scrapped	1950
Germaniawerft	(*U-795*)		XVIIC U-boat	1944	PO – Scrapped	1947
AG Neptun-Werft	(*U-926*)		VIIC U-boat	1943	PO – Transferred	1947
Blohm & Voss	(*U-953*)		VIIC U-boat	1942	PO – Scrapped	1949
Blohm & Voss	(*U-995*)		VIIC U-boat	1943	PO – Transferred	10.1948
Blohm & Voss	(*U-1023*)		VIIC U-boat	1944	PO – Scuttled	7.1.1946
Germaniawerft	(*U-1057*)		VIIC U-boat	1944	PO – Transferred	1945
Germaniawerft	(*U-1058*)		VIIC U-boat	1944	PO – Transferred	1945
Germaniawerft	(*U-1064*)		VIIC U-boat	1944	PO – Transferred	1945
Nordseewerke	(*U-1108*)		VIIc/41 U-boat	1944	PO – Scrapped	1949
Schichau	(*U-1202*)		VIIC U-boat	1943	PO – Transferred	7.1947
Deutsche Werft	(*U-1231*)		IXC/40 U-boat	1943	PO – Transferred	1946
Blohm & Voss	(*U-2518*)		XXI U-boat	1944	PO – Transferred	1946
Germaniawerft	(*U-4706*)		XXIII U-boat	1945	PO – Transferred	10.1948
Vickers Armstrong	HMS *P.611*	P611	S Class	19.7.1940	PO – Transferred	9.5.1942
Vickers Armstrong	HMS *P.612*	P612	S Class	20.7.1940	PO – Transferred	25.5.1942
Vickers Armstrong	HMS *P.614*	P614	S Class	19.10.1940	PO – Transferred	17.1.1946
Vickers Armstrong	HMS *P.615*	P615	S Class	1.11.1940	Lost – Torpedo	18.4.1943
Cant Nav. Franco Tosi	HMS *P.711* (ex INS *Gallilei*, *X.2 Moonstone*)	P711	Archimede Class	19.3.1934	PO – Scrapped	1.1946
Cant Riuniti dell' Adriatico	HMS *P.712* (ex *Peria*)	P712	Perla Class	3.5.1936	PO – Transferred	1943
Cant Nav. Franco Tosi	HMS *P.714* (ex *Peria*)	P714	Acciaio Class	28.9.1941	PO – Transferred	29.1.1944

▲ Surrendered U-boats at Liskhally awaiting their fate. *(HM Submarine Museum)*

▼ HMS *Graph* was previously *U-570*, and was used operationally. *(HM Submarine Museum)*

▲ HMS *Meteorite* was previously *U-1407*, and was used to trial a Walther HTP turbine. *(HM Submarine Museum)*

◀ Most surrendered U-boats were towed out to sea off the Northern Ireland coast and scuttled. *(HM Submarine Museum)*

143

A Class

The A Class represented the only new class of submarine during the whole of the Second World War. The existing designs had been adequate for the needs in the home and Mediterranean theatres with improvements carried out during construction or refit. However, the war in the Far East required a new boat with better range, speed and conditions, and work on a new design commenced in 1942.

The A Class were specifically designed for use in Pacific. They were based on the successful and proved T Class, but modified to take advantage of the lessons learned with wartime experience. In addition, the war in Europe appeared to be drawing to an end, so emphasis was given for Far East operations. As a result the hull was fully welded and fitted with air conditioning. They were heavily armed with six forward-firing torpedo tubes and a further four firing aft. An advance for this class was the fitting of an air-warning radar that could be operated while the submarine was submerged. They were all fitted with a 'Snort' breathing capability.

Being based on the T Class, a large number of components needed for the A Class were either already available or could be quickly built. However, although the design was rushed through, orders were only placed when builders advised that they had capacity, making deliveries somewhat protracted. Orders for 46 A Class boats were placed, and the first boat was laid down at Vickers in November 1943. HMS *Amphion* was launched the following August, but it was only *Amphion* and *Astute* that were delivered before hostilities ceased. Initially, they proved to be rather unstable, but this was fixed by the addition of an extra buoyancy tank in the bow.

When Japan finally surrendered, cancellations were already being made throughout the armament industries, and submarine builders were not to be missed. Thirty of the 46 A Class boats ordered were cancelled. Some of them had already been launched and were almost complete, but with no requirement, they were scrapped or used for destructive trials.

Although the war was over, the subsequent Cold War meant that the military were to be kept on their toes. The sixteen serving A Class boats were involved in a number of different trials in a continual quest for improvement.

HMS *Ace* had been launched in 1945, but was still being fitted out. Rather than scrap her immediately she was towed up to Scotland and used for trials in Loch Striven. During trials with HMS *Orion* and *Ashanti*, she was subjected to various underwater explosions while she was on or below the surface. She was eventually sold in June 1950 and scrapped at Port Glasgow.

HMS *Alliance* and *Ambush* took part in capability demonstrations during which they remained submerged for lengthy periods. On 9 October 1947 HMS *Alliance* commenced a snort cruise which lasted for 30 days before she surfaced again. In February 1948 HMS *Ambush* departed Rothesay for a submerged patrol that would last six weeks. Like the *Alliance*, she was fitted with a British version of the German Schnorkel. She had also been fitted with a pair of fore-and-aft control planes to trial. Their route was to take them as far north as they were able. Medical staff were carried for this trial to monitor the crew, as little was known about the effect of lengthy snorts in adverse weather. Apart from the automatic plane control failing, the rest of the patrol was successful, although a little uncomfortable.

In 1950 HMS *Anchorite* was used for testing the Type 169 Asdic. HMS *Achates* was virtually completed by HM Dockyard, Devonport, when she was cancelled and a decision was made to use her for trial purposes. She was taken to Gibraltar later that year, where she was joined by four lifting craft and taken out to deep water. The hull was then lowered until it failed. She was then recovered and examined. Once the trial was completed she was then sunk for use as a sonar target.

HMS *Affray* disappeared overnight of 16/17 April 1951. She was participating in a training course and took with her, not only her crew of 69, but 23 junior officers, as well as a detachment of Royal Marines. She reported that she was diving off the Isle of Wight but failed to report in at her designated surfacing time. Within a short time of a SUBSUNK being declared, search aircraft were joined by some forty British ships, as well as a visiting US Navy destroyer flotilla.

On 19 April the search was called off as it was considered that there could no longer be any survivors. However, the Royal Navy continued to utilise considerable resources to continue the search. She was eventually found two months later in 280 ft (85 m) of water near Guernsey – nearly 40 miles (64 km) from where she was known to have dived. Indications were that she had been at periscope depth when her snort mast had fractured. The mast was found and investigation showed that it had suffered metal fatigue. Such a failure should not have caused a major problem, as an induction valve should have quickly halted any water entering the boat.

An Admiralty statement said that the cause was an explosion of the battery gases, which had allowed water to flood the batteries, and that the crew would have died almost instantly. HMS *Affray* was never salvaged and was left as a watery grave for those souls that had perished aboard her.

In 1953, HMS *Andrew* managed to gain substantial publicity with her exploits when she completed a record-breaking first ever submerged Atlantic passage from Bermuda to the English Channel, covering the 2,500 miles (4,023 km) in 15 days. She later appeared in a number of films, including 'On the Beach'. HMS *Andrew* was the last Royal Navy submarine to be fitted with a permanent deck gun. However, not all the headlines were positive, as in 1973 she was 'caught' by a trawler.

HMS *Artemis* was not so fortunate – in 1954 she was sabotaged when a stoker placed a signal grenade in the engine. In 1963, she caused a rescue plan to be put into operation when she failed to surface on time while on temporary loan to the RCN. Fortunately, her predominantly Royal Navy crew managed to bring her safely to the surface an hour and a half later.

Commencing in 1955, during their refit, nearly all the A Class were subjected to a major programme to improve their streamlining. This reduced their underwater noise and thereby increased the performance of the Asdic. HMS *Artful* became the first to undergo the modernisation, which included a 26 ft 6 in (8.09 m) higher conning tower and the hull being lengthened to 283 ft (86.26 m). The gun was removed, as well as the pair of bow-mounted external torpedo tubes. The overall effect was to increase her range by a further 500 nautical miles.

In 1956 HMS *Aurochs* became the second Royal Navy submarine to circumnavigate the world, while in 1965 HMS *Amphion* and *Finwhale* took part in communications trials under the Arctic ice. Before returning home from the Far East, HMS *Alliance* tested a new camouflage paint scheme. She gained an insight of a future public life when she became a tourist attraction for those on the Isle of Wight. She had run aground just off the island, and it was a few days before the tide allowed her to be towed off. *Alliance* also suffered a couple of battery explosions before she was paid off and became a permanent exhibit at the Royal Navy Submarine Museum in Gosport.

In July 1971, HMS *Artemis* was being refuelled at Gosport. She was alongside, but without her ballast being adjusted she began to take in water through her open aft torpedo hatch door. She was connected with cable through the hatch, which prevented it being sealed. Three crew were immediately trapped but they managed to escape through the forward escape tower. With the A Class boats gradually being paid off, a decision was made not to refurbish her, and she was sold for scrap and could be seen twenty years later still languishing at Pound's breakers yard at Portsmouth.

HMS *Aeneas* was fitted with the Short Blowpipe in 1972 for air defence trials. Blowpipe was normally used by the Army as a shoulder-launched surface-to-air missile. A launcher with four missiles was fitted on the periscope radar mast. It was intended that they could be fired remotely from inside the boat as a defence against anti-submarine helicopters and aircraft. Although the trials were considered successful, they did not materialise into the fitting of surface-to-air missiles to any other Royal Navy submarines.

Orders for 46 boats were placed with all the submarine builder yards with quantities appropriate to their available capacity, but when hostilities ended in the Far East, thirty of these boats that were not actually completed were cancelled. Those that were commissioned formed the backbone of the Royal Navy submarine fleet until the arrival of the Porpoise and Oberon Classes. HMS *Andrew* was the last operational boat of the class, being paid off in 1974.

Preserved
HMS *Alliance* S67   RN Submarine Museum, Gosport

Class	A Class (Late)
Role	Overseas Patrol Submarine

	IMPERIAL	METRIC
Sub Disp – surfaced	1,385 tons	1,407.16 tonnes
Sub Disp – submerged	1,620 tons	1,645.92 tonnes
Length	281 ft 8 in*	85.85 m
Beam	22 ft 8 in	6.78 m
Draught	17 ft	5.18 m
Propulsion	2 × 4,300 bhp Admiralty or Vickers diesel engines	
	2 × 1,250 ehp English Electric electric motors	
Speed	18.5 knots surfaced, 8 knots submerged	
Range	10,500 nm at 11 knots surfaced, 90 nm at 3 knots submerged	
Armament	10 × 21 in (533 mm) torpedo tubes (6 bow, (2 external), 4 stern (2 external))	
	20 torpedoes carried or 26 mines	
	1 × 4 in (101 mm) gun	
	1 × 20 mm Oerlikon anti-aircraft gun	
Complement (Officers/Men)	60 (5/55)	
Data note	*After additional buoyancy tank fitted	

Builder	Name	Pennant No.	Class	Launched	Fate	Date
HM Dockyard, Portsmouth	HMS *Abelard*	P451	A Class (Late)		Cancelled	
HM Dockyard, Portsmouth	HMS *Acasta*	P452	A Class (Late)		Cancelled	
HM Dockyard, Devonport	HMS *Ace*	P414	A Class (Late)	14.3.1945	Cancelled – Scrapped	6.1950
HM Dockyard, Devonport	HMS *Achates*	P433	A Class (Late)	20.9.1945	Cancelled – Scrapped	1950
HM Dockyard, Chatham	HMS *Acheron*	P414, S11, S61	A Class (Late)	25.3.1947	PO – Scrapped	2.1972
HM Dockyard, Chatham Vickers	HMS *Adept*	P412	A Class (Late)		Cancelled	
Armstrong (Walker) Vickers	HMS *Admirable*	P434	A Class (Late)		Cancelled	
Armstrong (Walker)	HMS *Adversary*	P457	A Class (Late)		Cancelled	

Builder	Name	Pennant No.	Class	Launched	Fate	Date
Cammell Laird	HMS *Aeneas*	P427, S27, S72	A Class (Late)	25.10.1945	PO – Scrapped	12.1974
Cammell Laird	HMS *Affray*	P421	A Class (Late)	12.5.1945	Sunk – Accident	16.4.1951
Cammell Laird	HMS *Agate*	P448	A Class (Late)		Cancelled	
Cammell Laird	HMS *Aggressor*	P446	A Class (Late)		Cancelled	
Cammell Laird	HMS *Agile*	P443	A Class (Late)		Cancelled	
Cammell Laird	HMS *Aladdin*	P454	A Class (Late)		Cancelled	
Cammell Laird	HMS *Alaric*	P441, S41	A Class (Late)	18.2.1946	PO – Scrapped	7.1971
Cammell Laird	HMS *Alcestis*	P453	A Class (Late)		Cancelled	
Vickers Armstrong	HMS *Alcide*	P415, S15, S65	A Class (Late)	12.4.1945	PO – Scrapped	1974
Vickers Armstrong	HMS *Alderney*	P416, S16, S66	A Class (Late)	25.6.1945	PO – Scrapped	8.1972
Vickers Armstrong	HMS *Alliance*	P417, S17, S67	A Class (Late)	28.7.1945	Preserved	1.1.1981
Vickers Armstrong	HMS *Ambush*	P418, S18, S68	A Class (Late)	24.9.1945	PO – Scrapped	7.1971
Vickers Armstrong	HMS *Amphion* (ex *Anchorite*)	P439, S43	A Class (Late)	31.8.1944	PO – Scrapped	7.1971
Vickers Armstrong	HMS *Anchorite* (ex *Amphion*)	P418, S18, S64	A Class (Late)	22.1.1946	PO – Scrapped	8.1970
Vickers Armstrong	HMS *Andrew*	P423, S23, S63	A Class (Late)	6.4.1946	PO – Scrapped	5.1977
Vickers Armstrong	HMS *Antagonist*	P424	A Class (Late)		Cancelled	
Vickers Armstrong	HMS *Answer*	P425	A Class (Late)		Cancelled	
Vickers Armstrong	HMS *Antaeus*	P429	A Class (Late)		Cancelled	
Vickers Armstrong	HMS *Andromache*	P428	A Class (Late)		Cancelled	
Vickers Armstrong	HMS *Anzac*	P431	A Class (Late)		Cancelled	
Vickers Armstrong	HMS *Aphrodite*	P432	A Class (Late)		Cancelled	
Vickers Armstrong	HMS *Approach*	P435	A Class (Late)		Cancelled	
Vickers Armstrong	HMS *Arcadian*	P436	A Class (Late)		Cancelled	
Vickers Armstrong	HMS *Ardent*	P437	A Class (Late)		Cancelled	
Vickers Armstrong	HMS *Argosy*	P438	A Class (Late)		Cancelled	
Scott's	HMS *Artemis*	P449, S49	A Class (Late)	26.8.1946	Accident – Scrapped	4.1972
Scott's	HMS *Artful*	P456, S96	A Class (Late)	22.5.1947	PO – Scrapped	6.1972
Scott's	HMS *Asgard*	P458	A Class (Late)		Cancelled	
Vickers Armstrong	HMS *Asperity*	P444	A Class (Late)		Cancelled	
Scott's	HMS *Assurance*	P462	A Class (Late)		Cancelled	
Scott's	HMS *Astarte*	P461	A Class (Late)		Cancelled	
Vickers Armstrong	HMS *Astute*	P447, S47	A Class (Late)	30.1.1945	PO – Scrapped	10.1970
Vickers Armstrong	HMS *Atlantis*	P442	A Class (Late)		Cancelled	
Vickers Armstrong	HMS *Auriga*	P419, S19, S69	A Class (Late)	29.3.1945	PO – Scrapped	2.1975
Vickers Armstrong	HMS *Aurochs*	P426, S26, S62	A Class (Late)	28.7.1945	PO – Scrapped	2.1967
Vickers Armstrong (Walker)	HMS *Austere*	P445	A Class (Late)		Cancelled	
Vickers Armstrong (Walker)	HMS *Awake*	P459	A Class (Late)		Cancelled	
Vickers Armstrong (Walker)	HMS *Aztec*	P455	A Class (Late)		Cancelled	

▲ HMS *Affray* with the additional bow buoyancy tank fitted. These were fitted to improve stability at sea. *(HM Submarine Museum)*

▼ HMS *Affray* prepares to come alongside at HMS *Dolphin*. *(HM Submarine Museum)*

▲ HMS *Ambush*. *(HM Submarine Museum)*

▲ HMS *Acheron* with her gun removed and conning tower modified.
(HM Submarine Museum)

▼ HMS *Aeneas* modified with the larger fin, but still with a gun fitted.
(HM Submarine Museum)

▼ HMS *Aeneas* with the gun removed. *(HM Submarine Museum)*

▲ HMS *Aeneas* photographed in 1972 with the Submarine Launched Airflight Missile (SLAM) fitted to the top of a mast. The photo also shows her flying her paying-off pennant. *(HM Submarine Museum)*

▲ HMS *Alaric*. *(HM Submarine Museum)*

▶ HMS *Alliance* on display at the RN Submarine Museum, Gosport. *(Jeremy Flack)*

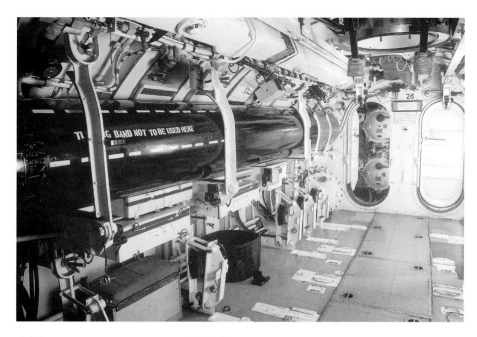

▲ The weapons compartment on HMS*Alliance*. *(Jeremy Flack)*

▼ The control room aboard HMS *Alliance*. *(Jeremy Flack)*

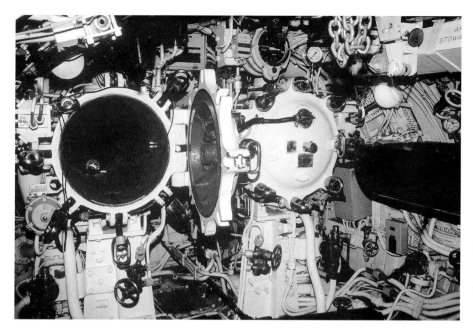

▲ The pair of internally mounted stern torpedo tubes. *(Jeremy Flack)*

▼ HMS *Artemis* at Pound's yard, Portsmouth, in 1992. *(Jeremy Flack)*

Porpoise Class (Late)

The Porpoise Class was the first post-Second World War submarine design to enter operational service with the Royal Navy, and was the subject of numerous advances. This new design was capable of high underwater speed and substantial diving depths, as well as being very quiet. They were fitted with extremely large main batteries to store the necessary power. With their advanced snort and replenishment systems, they could operate independently, without support in any part of the world, for months.

The Porpoise Class featured both an air- and a surface-warning radar that could be operated at periscope level as well as when surfaced. They also had an advanced snort system that allowed maximum charging capability, even in rough sea conditions. This also helped to provide effective air conditioning to allow operations in arctic or tropical seas, as well as keeping the boat dry internally. This class of boat also featured oxygen replenishment, together with carbon dioxide and hydrogen eliminators, which made submerged periods lasting six weeks possible.

To enable lengthy periods without support, the Porpoise Class had sufficient stowage area for substantial quantities of stores. They were also equipped to distil fresh water from sea water.

HMS *Sealion* was the last of the Porpoise Class to remain operational, and was decommissioned on 18 December 1987. A proposal was accepted for her to be preserved, and she was sold to a charity, but this never came to fruition and she remained laid up at Chatham. In 1990 she was finally sold for breaking up at Blyth.

Class	Porpoise Class (Late)	
Role	Overseas Patrol/Attack Submarine	

	IMPERIAL	METRIC
Sub Disp – surfaced	2,030 tons	2,062.48 tonnes
Sub Disp – submerged	2,405 tons	2,443.48 tonnes
Length	295 ft 3 in	89.99 m
Beam	26 ft 6 in	8.08 m
Draught	15 ft	4.57 m
Propulsion	2 × 1,650 bhp Admiralty Standard Range diesel engines	
	2 × 5,000 ehp electric motors	
Speed	12 knots surfaced, 17 knots submerged	
Range	9,000 nm at 12 knots surfaced	
Armament	8 × 21 in (533 mm) torpedo tubes (6 bow, 2 stern)	
	30 torpedoes carried	
Complement (Officers/Men)	71 (6/65)	

Builder	Name	Pennant No.	Class	Launched	Fate	Date
Scott's	HMS *Cachalot*	S06	Porpoise Class (Late)	11.12.1957	PO – Scrapped	2.9.1977
Cammell Laird	HMS *Finwhale*	S05	Porpoise Class (Late)	21.7.1959	PO – Sold	6.11.1978
Cammell Laird	HMS *Grampus*	S04	Porpoise Class (Late)	30.5.1957	PO – Expended as target	1978
Vickers Armstrong	HMS *Narwhal*	S03	Porpoise Class (Late)	25.10.1957	PO – Scuttled	1981
Vickers Armstrong	HMS *Porpoise*	S01	Porpoise Class (Late)	25.4.1956	PO – Expended	20.10.1985
Vickers Armstrong	HMS *Rorqual*	S02	Porpoise Class (Late)	5.12.1956	PO – Scrapped	1977
Cammell Laird	HMS *Sealion*	S07	Porpoise Class (Late)	31.12.1959	PO – Scrapped	1990
Scott's	HMS *Walrus*	S08	Porpoise Class (Late)	22.9.1959	PO – Sold	1987

▲ *HMS Finwhale* being launched at Cammell Laird's yard in Birkenhead in 1959. *(HM Submarine Museum)*

▲ HMS *Narwhal* being towed for her final fitting out, following her launch on 25 October 1957. *(HM Submarine Museum)*

▶ HMS *Porpoise* surfaces after a post-maintenance test dive. *(HM Submarine Museum)*

▲ HMS *Rorqual.* (*HM Submarine Museum*)

▲ Loading a Mk.VIII torpedo. (*HM Submarine Museum*)

◀ An aft three-quarters view of HMS *Sealion* in dry dock with one of the pair of stern torpedo tubes visible. (*HM Submarine Museum*)

▶ In this front three-quarters view of HMS *Sealion*, three of the six torpedo doors are visible. *(HM Submarine Museum)*

◀ HMS *Sealion*. *(HM Submarine Museum)*

Explorer Class

The Explorer Class were designed to trial a new diesel electric power-plant that incorporated hydrogen peroxide in its fuels. The main propelling machinery comprised turbines powered by steam and carbon dioxide. This was produced by burning the diesel in an atmosphere of steam and oxygen (the latter being produced from HTP (High Test oxygen Peroxide). This enabled the boat to produce full power while submerged, independent of any external air source. The Explorer Class were also fitted with a conventional diesel engine when on the surface, and battery-powered electric motors for normal submerged operations.

Only two of the Explorer Class were built. Most of the fittings were retractable, and this helped to improve her already streamlined shape, enabling a high submerged speed, and they were easily manoeuvrable. At the time they were thought to be the fastest submarines in the world.

The engine continued the development of the Walther engine that powered German *U-1407*. This had been salvaged and rebuilt before entering service with the Royal Navy as HMS *Meteorite*. The fuel was highly unstable, and several explosions of various magnitude were experienced.

The boats were purely experimental, and as such no armaments were fitted to the Explorer Class. Space was still limited, resulting in their crews being accommodated in the ex-minesweepers *Miner I* and *Miner VII*, which was also safer.

The Explorer Class were certainly fast boats when submerged – capable of 25 knots. However, when the Americans succeeded in building a nuclear reactor for a submarine, the experiment became superseded and the project was quickly run down. Although *Excalibur* survived until she was put up for disposal in 1970, *Explorer* was disposed of in 1965.

Class	Explorer Class
Role	Experimental Submarine

	IMPERIAL	METRIC
Sub Disp – surfaced	1,100 tons	1,117.6 tonnes
Sub Disp – submerged	1,197 tons	1,216.15 tonnes
Length	225 ft 6.5 in	68.74 m
Beam	15 ft 7.5 in	4.76 m
Draught	11 ft	3.35 m
Propulsion	15,000 shp Vickers Armstrong hydrogen peroxide plant 2 × diesel engines + 2 × electric motors	
Speed	15 knots surfaced, 25+ knots submerged	
Range	500 nm at 6 knots surfaced, 75 nm at 25 knots submerged	
Armament	None	
Complement (Officers/Men)	41 (6/35)*	
Data note	*49 crew on *Explorer*	

Builder	Name	Pennant No.	Class	Launched	Fate	Date
Vickers Armstrong	HMS *Explorer*	S40	Explorer Class	5.3.1954	PO – Scrapped	2.1965
Vickers Armstrong	HMS *Excalibur*	S30	Explorer Class	25.2.1955	PO – Scrapped	2.1970

▲ HMS *Excalibur* being launched at Vickers' yard at Barrow-in-Furness in 1955. *(HM Submarine Museum)*

▶ HMS *Explorer* during trials to explore the use of hydrogen peroxide as a fuel, but it was too volatile. *(HM Submarine Museum)*

▶ HMS *Excalibur* makes speed – at one time they were thought to be the fastest in the world. They were prone to explosions in the engine room, and the trials ceased with the advent of nuclear energy. *(HM Submarine Museum)*

Oberon Class

The Oberon Class were almost identical to the previous Porpoise Class. The differences were mainly internal. They were fitted with improved detection equipment and were equipped for firing homing torpedoes. Some adjustments were made to the positioning of the hull frames.

Plastic was used for the first time in a Royal Navy submarine, and glass fibre was used on part of the bridge superstructure and casing, although aluminium was used on HMS *Orpheus*. HMS *Otter* was a little different in that her casing was reinforced with steel, which enabled her to perform a role of target boat.

Two HMS *Odin*s were built, the first being sold to the Royal Canadian Navy shortly before she was due to be completed for the Royal Navy. A second replacement was ordered and commissioned in 1964.

In 1965, the first of three Oberon Class were commissioned into the Royal Canadian Navy. Having been refitted several times, they have remained operational into the twenty-first century until replaced by the four ex-Royal-Navy Upholder Class. The Royal Australian Navy bought six, and although they are now being replaced by the Collins Class, these have performed sterling service, and recent refits have enabled them to include the Harpoon missile in their inventory.

In 1970 Vickers were building an Oberon Class submarine for Brazil (their third). During its fitting out a fire started in the cabling and resulted in a significant delay on its delivery. It also had an implication for the Royal Navy order for Oberon submarines, as they all required rewiring.

Also in 1970, trials were being held in the Mediterranean with a submarine escape training team. Led by Lt Cdr Todd, they established a world record when they surfaced from HMS *Osiris* while she was moving at a depth of 600 feet.

In 1982 HMS *Onyx* became the only Oberon Class to see active service, when she was tasked as the only diesel submarine to be deployed to the Falklands as part of Operation *Corporate*. She is now preserved at Birkenhead by Historic Warships.

In the 1980s their performance was enhanced by fitting 2051 sonar and adding the capability of firing Tigerfish torpedoes and Sub-Harpoon anti-ship missiles. The Triton sonar modernisation programme gave the boats the capability of guiding two torpedoes simultaneously.

In July 1987 HMS *Otus* was used for a series of trials to try to establish from what depth a submariner could safely be expected to escape. These were conducted at Bjornafjordan in Norway with a team of British, Norwegian and Swedish divers. Escapes commenced at 30 metres (98 ft) and gradually increased. While some dropped out at 90 metres (295 ft), two submariners continued until they reached 183 metres (600 ft).

In 1993, HMS *Opossum* became the last of the Oberon Class boats to be paid off. It also meant the end of 90 years of continuous submarine operations at HMS *Dolphin*. Appropriately, this location has now become the home of the Royal Navy Submarine Museum.

Preserved
Ocelot S17   1962   Oberon class   Historic Dockyard, Chatham Kent
Onyx S21   1966   Oberon class   Historic Warships, Birkenhead

A further three ex-RAN O boats are preserved in Australia
Otway S59
Ovens S70
Onslow S60

Class	Oberon Class
Role	SSK Submarine

	IMPERIAL	METRIC
Sub Disp – surfaced	2,030 tons	2,062.48 tonnes
Sub Disp – submerged	2,410 tons	2,448.56 tonnes
Length	295 ft 3 in	89.99 m
Beam	26 ft 6 in	8.08 m
Draught	15 ft	4.57 m
Propulsion	2 × 3,000 bhp Admiralty Standard Range Diesel	
	2 × 1,280 kW electric motors	
Speed	12 knots surfaced, 17 knots submerged	
Range	9,000 nm at 12 knots surfaced	
Armament	8 × 21 in (533 mm) torpedo tubes	
	Mk. 8 torpedo	
	Tigerfish torpedo	
	UGM-84B Sub-Harpoon	
Complement (Officers/Men)	71 (6/65)	

Builder	Name	Pennant No.	Class	Launched	Fate	Date
HM Dockyard, Chatham	HMS *Oberon*	S19, S09	Oberon Class	18.7.1959	PO – Scrapped	10.10.1986
HM Dockyard, Chatham	HMS *Ocelot*	S17	Oberon Class	5.1962	PO – Preserved	1992
Cammell Laird	HMS *Odin*	S20, S10	Oberon Class	1962	PO – Scrapped	1991
Vickers Armstrong	HMS *Olympus*	S46, S12	Oberon Class	6.1961	PO – Sold	28.7.1989
HM Dockyard, Chatham	HMS *Onslaught*	S57, S14	Oberon Class	24.9.1960	PO – Scrapped	1990
Cammell Laird	HMS *Onyx*	S21	Oberon Class	18.8.1966	PO – Preserved	14.12.1990
Cammell Laird	HMS *Opossum*	S19	Oberon Class	23.5.1963	PO – Scrapped	9.1993
Scott's	HMS *Opportune*	S20	Oberon Class	14.2.1964	PO – Scrapped	1993
Cammell Laird	HMS *Oracle*	S60, S16	Oberon Class	26.9.1961	PO – Scrapped	7.1993
Vickers Armstrong	HMS *Orpheus*	S11	Oberon Class	17.11.1959	PO – Scrapped	1996
Vickers	HMS *Osiris*	S50, S13	Oberon Class	29.11.1962	PO – Scrapped	5.1992
Scott's	HMS *Otter*	S59, S15	Oberon Class	15.5.1961	PO – Scrapped	31.7.1991
Scott's	HMS *Otus*	S18	Oberon Class	17.10.1962	PO – Scrapped	4.1991

▲ HMS *Otter* with her crew at Harbour Stations as she approaches Devonport with her original shorter conning tower. *(Courtesy DML)*

► HMS *Opossum* undergoes maintenance in dry dock at Devonport. *(Courtesy DML)*

▲ HMS *Opportune* makes a test dive in the safety of a basin to check her systems and to adjust the balance of her ballast tanks to ensure she is level when under way.

(Courtesy DML)

▲ HMS *Opportune* prepares to leave Devonport for her post-major refit trials.

(Courtesy DML)

▲ HMS *Opossum* departing Devonport after successfully completing her refit.
(Courtesy DML)

► HMS *Oberon* alongside at Subic Bay in the Philippines, with other submarines of the
US Navy. *(HM Submarine Museum)*

◀▲▶ Sequence of an O Class boat slipping below the waves with just bubbles showing as the last air empties from her ballast tanks and casing.

(Jeremy Flack)

▼ HMS *Otus* and *Opossum* await scrapping at Pound's breaker's yard, Portsmouth.
(Jeremy Flack)

▲ HMS *Opportune* being cut up at Pound's breaker's yard at Portsmouth, while HMS *Otus* and *Osiris* wait in the queue. *(Jeremy Flack)*

Dreadnought Class

The existence of a planned Dreadnought Class of atomic-powered submarine was announced in the 1957/8 Navy Estimates. It stated that progress was being made with the design of the submarine and the UK Atomic Energy Authority (UKAEA) were working on the problems associated with building a radiation shield.

The UKAEA at Harwell began designing a prototype reactor for a nuclear submarine in 1954. Although the pace was accelerating, by 1958 it was decided that the programme was insufficiently advanced, and negotiations were entered into with the Americans to buy a Pressurised Water Reactor (PWR). This was the same reactor that powered the USS *Skipjack*. Rolls Royce were contracted to manage the purchase and to integrate the reactor with the turbines to produce the fully functioning powerplant.

The hull was a joint design by the Admiralty and Vickers, and when HMS *Dreadnought* was commissioned in 1963 she was the first Royal Navy nuclear submarine. In 1971 she became the first Royal Navy submarine to surface through the ice at the North Pole. In 1980 HMS *Dreadnought* was modified to carry the Sub-Harpoon missile before she was finally paid off in 1982.

Class	Dreadnought Class	
Role	Fleet Submarine (SSN)	
	IMPERIAL	METRIC
Sub Disp – surfaced	3,556 tons	3,613 tonnes
Sub Disp – submerged	4,064 tons	4,129 tonnes
Length	265 ft 9 in	81 m
Beam	32 ft 3 in	9.83 m
Draught	26 ft	7.93 m
Propulsion	1 × S5W Pressurised water reactor with 15,000 hp geared steam turbines	
	Emergency drive batteries and electric motor	
Speed	25 knots surfaced, 30 knots submerged	
Range	N/a	
Armament	6 × 21 in (533 mm) torpedo tubes	
	Mk. 8 torpedo	
	Tigerfish torpedo	
	UGM-84B Sub-Harpoon	
Complement (Officers/Men)	99 (11/88)	

Builder	Name	Pennant No.	Class	Launched	Fate	Date
Vickers	HMS *Dreadnought*	S80, S101	Dreadnought Class	21.10.1960	PO – Laid up	1982

▲ HMS *Dreadnought* caught on the surface displaying her pennant number. Previously numbered S80, this was changed in 1961 to S101 during another renumbering exercise. This was to allocate post-war diesel-powered boats to the 1-99 range, and nuclear-powered from 101 onwards. *(HM Submarine Museum)*

▲ HMS *Dreadnought* shows off her amazing power when she accelerates to an 'on the step' condition. This is where the front of the boat almost lifts out of the water as she rides on the bow wave. *(Rolls Royce)*

▶ In 1965 the *Essenberger Chemist* became disabled. She started to drift into a shipping lane and become a potential hazard. As a result HMS *Dreadnought* was tasked with sinking her by torpedo. *(HM Submarine Museum)*

Valiant Class

The Valiant Class were the first all-British nuclear-powered submarine. The Admiralty Reactor Test Establishment (ARTE) site was built at Dounreay to house and test the new prototype naval nuclear propulsion plant – as it has done with all subsequent designs. A mock-up of the submarine with a full-scale working model of the engine included the construction of a hull. This was used to prove this radical new form of propulsion which would be developed to power all future British submarines.

The nuclear plant was developed and built by Rolls Royce from the original supplied by the USA for *Dreadnought*. The heat generated was used to produce steam, and English Electric were contracted to build the steam turbines.

HMS *Valiant* was completed in July 1966 at a cost of £24.9 million. It was later discovered, when the boats were in service, that the welding technique used to construct these two boats (and similar US Navy boats) resulted in hairline cracks appearing. The construction technique closely followed that used to build the SSNs for the US Navy, which had similar problems. While an alternative, improved welding-technique was evolved, these boats had frequently to be dry docked for repairs.

In April 1967 *Valiant* undertook a 28-day 12,000 nm submerged passage from Singapore to the UK, which established a world record.

In 1980 the armament was upgraded to include the Sub-Harpoon anti-ship missile.

Only two Valiant Class boats were built, and HMS *Valiant* was paid off on 12 August 1994 and laid up at Devonport. In 1997 she was displayed in the Plymouth Navy Days and for the first time was opened to the public.

	Class	Valiant Class
	Role	Fleet Submarine (SSN)

	IMPERIAL	METRIC
Sub Disp – surfaced	3,500 tons	3,556 tonnes
Sub Disp – submerged	4,500 tons	4,572 tonnes
Length	285 ft	86.86 m
Beam	33 ft 3 in	10.13 m
Draught	27 ft	8.23 m
Propulsion	1 × RR PWR1 nuclear reactor driving 15,000 shp English Electric steam turbine	
Speed	28+ knots submerged	
Range	N/a	
Armament	6 × 21 in (533 mm) torpedo tubes 26 torpedoes carried Mk. 8 torpedo Tigerfish torpedo UGM-84B Sub-Harpoon	
Complement (Officers/Men)	130 (18/112)	

Builder	Name	Pennant No.	Class	Launched	Reason
Vickers	HMS *Valiant*	S102	Valiant Class	3.12.1963	PO – Laid up 12.8.1994
Vickers	HMS *Warspite*	S103	Valiant Class	25.9.1965	PO – Laid up

▲ The rear ARTE hull mock-up at HMS *Vulcan* at Dounreay replicated the layout of a Valiant Class propulsion system. At the front is the Shield Tank which contains the reactor. In the centre is the Machinery Space which contains the turbines and gearbox. At the back is a Dynamometer which is not part of the propulsion system but is used to absorb and measure the power that would be output by the propeller. (*Rolls Royce*)

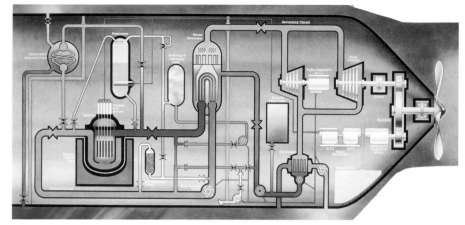

▲ A layout of the PWR propulsion system, showing the core at the bottom left superheating the water This is pumped around the sealed primary circuit.

The steam generator in the upper centre transfers the heat from the primary circuit to the sealed secondary system as steam. This is then used to turn the turbo-generator to provide electrical power for the boat's systems and the main turbine for propulsion. The steam is then condensed back to water and returned to the steam generator.

(*Rolls Royce*)

▶ HMS *Warspite* being launched at Vickers' yard in Barrow-in-Furness in 1965. (*HM Submarine Museum*)

▲ HMS *Valiant* at sea. *(HM Submarine Museum)*

▼ HMS *Warspite* returns to Devonport, streaming her paying-off pennant.
(HM Submarine Museum)

▲ HMS *Warspite* undergoes maintenance in one of the dry docks at Devonport.
(Courtesy DML)

▲ HMS *Valiant* alongside at Faslane. *(Jeremy Flack)*

Resolution Class

During the 1950s the US was concerned that, should the Soviets launch a pre-emptive strike at the US ICBM sites, their ability to launch a counter-strike could be significantly reduced. The USN promoted the solution of merging the capability of ICBM (Inter-Continental Ballistic Missile) with the performance of a nuclear submarine. In 1956 work began on a system capable of launching an IRBM (Intermediate Range Ballistic Missile). Known as Polaris, the missile system used the Ship Inertial Navigation System (SINS) to enable the SSBN to accurately compute its exact location, using accelerometers and gyroscopes to plot movement including drift. In 1960 the USS *George Washington* launched the first A-1 Polaris missile at a target 1,200 miles away.

While the US Navy aircraft carriers represent a visible, powerful force that can be projected close to a potential source of trouble in the old-style gunboat diplomacy, the nuclear armed submarine was rapidly becoming recognised as the new deterrent, able to operate in a medium that covers nearly three-quarters of the world's surface for months on end whilst remaining virtually undetectable. When armed with a load of devastating weapons, this was to be the deterrent of the future.

In the United Kingdom, the British nuclear deterrent was maintained by the RAF in the form of the Blue Steel missile carried by its ageing V bombers. A joint US/UK programme was being developed to improve the weapon delivery systems of both countries with the Skybolt missile programme. When it was cancelled by the US, the British Prime Minister, Harold Macmillan, and US President John F. Kennedy discussed the problem at Nassau in the Bahamas. An agreement was made that the US would provide Britain with the Polaris missile. Sixteen of these missiles would be fitted in a British-designed and built submarine. This included a British-designed and built nuclear propulsion plant and the warheads. This agreement was eventually formally announced in February 1963.

By 1966 the A-1 Polaris missile was replaced by the A-3, which had its range extended to 2,880 miles. Lake Bike in Central Asia is calculated to be the farthest inland position from the sea. At a distance of 1,720 miles this became the desired range of early missiles, but the A-3 ensured that anywhere could be capable of being targeted by a Polaris submarine-based IRBM. The contract was altered for Britain to have this latest version of the Polaris missile for her new 'bomber' submarines. The hull design was based on that of the Valiant Class, with the hull lengthened by some 140 feet to accommodate the missile tubes.

In May 1963 four boats were ordered – two to be built by Vickers and two by Cammell Laird. The fifth boat was planned to be a reserve boat should any of the four suffer an accident. When the Labour government came to power and cut most defence projects, plans for the fifth boat were also axed. Fortunately, such was the standard of design, construction and maintenance that the four boats managed to maintain the deterrent without any major problem.

HMS *Resolution* was the Royal Navy's first SSBN, and was laid down on 26 February 1964 and commissioned on 10 February 1967. She cost just over £40 million.

The first patrol by HMS *Resolution* commenced in June 1968. To enable each boat to maintain the maximum time at sea and to enable the crew to have a reasonable break, each boat was allocated two complete crews – referred to as port and starboard. These would alternate the manning of the boat, acting as relief for each other after each patrol, which lasted in the region of two to three months.

On 15 February 1968 HMS *Resolution* successfully launched the first UK Polaris missile on a range off the US east coast. This was the culmination of the efforts of the boat's crew to become operational. It was part of a shakedown in which the whole crew were tested to ensure that they could work as a team.

The key to the success of the Resolution Class boats was that they were able to operate very quietly and remain underwater for indefinite periods. The PWR1 reactor was capable of producing vast quantities of power in the form of heat which was converted to steam to provide motive power through a turbine as well as electrical power through turbo-generators.

The PWR1 reactor enabled the boats to achieve in the order of 25 knots while submerged. In practice, they were in no hurry, and with stealth being the prime consideration, they were more likely to travel quietly at just a few knots, causing less detectable disturbance below the waves. Besides providing power for the machinery and weapon systems, the electrical power enabled the working environment to be kept as comfortable as possible. Air conditioning plant monitored the air purity, removing any harmful gases. Carbon dioxide was removed and fresh oxygen produced from the sea water by electrolysers. Fresh water was also produced from the sea. As a result, these submarines could roam the seas or lie in wait for indefinite periods. The limiting factor now was crew endurance.

To maintain an efficient crew, the Resolution Class boats would operate on a two- to three-month patrol. At the end of the patrol they would return to RNAD Coulport to have their warheads removed before arriving at Faslane. The crew would go ashore and be replaced with the other crew. A period of maintenance and replenishment would take place before they returned to sea for the next patrol.

This system ensured that a workable cycle of refit, work-up, patrol, and maintenance would permit at least one boat to be on patrol at all times. The fact that the boat could be positioned anywhere in the vast oceans, without detection, and be able to launch a devastating attack on an enemy wherever in the world he might be, not only provided deterrent value to the UK but contributed to world peace through NATO.

In 1982 the Polaris missiles began an enhancement with the fitting of the British Chevaline independently targeted warheads. This resulted in the capability of each missile being increased, with the ability to hit each of three separate targets with a 60 kiloton nuclear weapon.

The commissioning of the first Vanguard Class SSBN meant the beginning of the end for the Polaris-armed bombers. HMS *Resolution* was the first to be withdrawn when she was paid off on 15 February 1968, having completed the 100th Polaris patrol. On 14 May 1966 HMS *Renown* returned to Coulport for de-arming at the end of her 60th patrol. This was the 229th and final patrol by a boat of the Resolution Class, and following decommissioning at Faslane she sailed on 6 September to Rosyth, where she is now laid up with the other three bombers.

Class	Resolution Class
Role	Polaris Submarine (SSBN)

	IMPERIAL	METRIC
Sub Disp – surfaced	7,500 tons	7,620 tonnes
Sub Disp – submerged	8,400 tons	8,534 tonnes
Length	425 ft	129.5 m
Beam	33 ft	10.01 m
Draught	30 ft	9.14 m
Propulsion	1 × RR PWR1 nuclear reactor driving 15,000 shp English Electric steam turbine	
Speed	20 knots surfaced, 28 knots submerged	
Range	N/a	
Armament	16 silos A-3 Polaris ICBM (later upgraded to A-3TK) 6 × 21 in (533 mm) torpedo tubes (bow) Tigerfish torpedoes	
Complement (Officers/Men)	143 (13/130)	

Builder	Name	Pennant No.	Class	Launched	Fate	Date
Cammell Laird	HMS *Renown*	S26	Resolution Class	25.2.1967	Laid up	2.1996
Vickers	HMS *Repulse*	S23	Resolution Class	4.11.1967	Laid up	28.8.1996
Vickers	HMS *Resolution*	S22	Resolution Class	15.9.1966	Laid up	22.10.1994
Cammell Laird	HMS *Revenge*	S27	Resolution Class	19.5.1965	Laid up	5.1992

▲ HMS *Resolution* and *Repulse* alongside at Faslane, undergoing routine maintenance between patrols. *(Jeremy Flack)*

169

▲ HMS *Renown* in Gare Loch. *(Jeremy Flack)*

▲ HMS *Renown* in Gare Loch. *(Jeremy Flack)*

◀ HMS *Renown* in Gare Loch.
(Jeremy Flack)

▲ HMS *Renown* with the port missile hatches clearly visible. *(Jeremy Flack)*

◀ HMS *Renown* in Gare Loch. *(Jeremy Flack)*

▼ HMS *Renown* is assisted to her berth at Faslane by three RMAS tugs. *(Jeremy Flack)*

▲ HMS *Renown* approaches Rosyth with her paying-off pennant flying, marking the end of the Resolution Class. *(Mike Tazioli Babcock Engineering Services)*

▲ The Polaris missiles are always launched while the boat is submerged. *(Lockheed)*

Churchill Class

The Churchill Class were effectively an improved Valiant Class. The same hull design was used but incorporated numerous internal modifications. Each of the three boats can carry a mixture of standard Mk.8 torpedoes, together with the more sophisticated Tigerfish torpedo and the Sub-Harpoon missile.

The Mk.8 torpedo requires to be aimed in the conventional way with a careful calculation of range and speed of the target to determine the correct intercept point. Consequently the range is fairly short – about 5,000 yards (4,500 m). The Tigerfish is an intelligent torpedo with built-in sensors which can detect and adjust its track to home in on the target. It is also fitted with a guide wire to enable communication to and from the submarine. It range is in the region of 20 miles (32 km). The Sub-Harpoon is a low-flying anti-ship missile which can home in on a target and carries a 500 lb (227 kg) warhead. It has a range of around 60 miles (96 km).

In 1982 HMS *Conqueror* was tasked with patrolling the waters around the Falkland Islands following the invasion by the Argentinians. During the patrol she located and shadowed the Argentinian battleship *Belgrano* for several days. On 2 May 1982 she spotted the Argentinian battleship near to the 100-mile exclusion zone. On instructions from London she launched an attack by firing two or three of her Mk.8 torpedoes. Within a hour the cruiser had rolled over and sunk. On her return to Faslane, HMS *Conqueror* hoisted the Jolly Roger, continuing the traditional signal of a successful patrol.

Following their decommissioning, HMS *Conqueror* and *Courageous* remain at Devonport awaiting disposal, while HMS *Churchill* is at laid up at Rosyth.

Class	Churchill Class	
Role	Fleet Submarine (SSN)	
	IMPERIAL	METRIC
Sub Disp – surfaced	4,400 tons	4,470 tonnes
Sub Disp – submerged	4,900 tons	4,978 tonnes
Length	285 ft	86.86 m
Beam	33 ft 2 in	10.11 m
Draught	27 ft	8.22 m
Propulsion	1 × RR PWR1 nuclear reactor driving 15,000 shp English Electric steam turbines	
Speed	25 knots surfaced, 30 knots submerged	
Range	N/a	
Armament	6 × 21 in (533 mm) torpedo tubes (bow) 26 torpedoes carried Mk. 8 torpedo Tigerfish torpedo UGM-84B Sub-Harpoon	
Complement (Officers/Men)	103 (13/90)	

Builder	Name	Pennant No.	Class	Launched	Fate	Date
Vickers Cammell Laird	HMS *Churchill*	S46	Churchill Class	20.12.1968	PO – Laid up	1991
Vickers	HMS *Conqueror*	S48	Churchill Class	28.8.1969	PO – Laid up	1992
	HMS *Courageous*	S50	Churchill Class	7.3.1970	PO – Laid up	1992

► HMS *Conqueror* being launched at Cammell Laird's yard at Birkenhead. *(HM Submarine Museum)*

▼ HMS *Conqueror* returns to Faslane after her patrol in the South Atlantic when she sank the *Belgrano*. *(HM Submarine Museum)*

175

▲ HMS *Conqueror* alongside at Devonport, undergoing maintenance. *(Courtesy DML)*

▶ HMS *Conqueror* and *Courageous* laid up at Devonport. *(Jeremy Flack)*

▲ The weapons compartment on HMS *Conqueror*. *(Courtesy BAE Systems)*

Swiftsure Class

The Swiftsure Class of submarine are nuclear-powered attack submarines (SSN) designed to locate and destroy enemy submarines and warships. Originally developed from the previous Valiant and Churchill Class SSNs, these newer Swiftsure Class boats have a distinctly different look from the previous nuclear boats, in that they have a parallel-sided hull compared to the humpback whale appearance of those earlier boats. This is the result of an Admiralty decision to change the shape and provide more internal space.

An improved weapon loading system has been fitted, which enables the torpedo tubes to be reloaded in just fifteen seconds. In 1995, the Royal Navy ordered 65 Tomahawk missiles for use by the Swiftsure and Trafalgar Class attack submarines.

The Strategic Defence Review of July 1998 announced the intention to reduce the attack submarine fleet from twelve to ten boats. However, the programme to upgrade the capability to launch the Tomahawk missile would be applied to all ten boats.

HMS *Splendid* was initially upgraded during her refit. On 18 November 1998, she became the first Royal Navy submarine to fire the Tomahawk cruise missile. She launched three missiles during proving trials off the South California coast, using the US Navy's Pacific Missile Test Range at Point Mugu.

These missiles are the Block III variant, and will enable the boats to surgically attack targets should they be required to conduct a force projection without revealing themselves. The missiles have a 1,000 lb (454 kg) high explosive/incendiary warhead and are capable of hitting a target with an accuracy of no less than ten feet owing to the GPS and contour-matching navigation. This now gives the boats a substantial capability against land targets in addition to their existing anti-ship and submarine performance.

On 24 March 1999, HMS *Splendid* claimed another Tomahawk first when she launched her first operational missile against a Serbian target during the NATO operation to protect the Albanians in Kosovo.

In 2000 HMS *Tireless* put into Gibraltar with a problem with her nuclear reactor. A check was made across all the Trafalgar and Swiftsure boats that were fitted with the same PWR1 reactor. Those that had recently completed a refit had already had the part replaced as a matter of routine. However, some boats were in the early stages of developing the same fault. These boats were withdrawn for safety, and during 2001 they were rectified. A further boat was discovered to have an underclad cracking problem, and remedial work commenced to rectify this.

The Swiftsure Class boats will gradually be replaced by the Astute Class once they start to enter service.

Class	Swiftsure Class
Role	Fleet Submarine (SSN)

	IMPERIAL	METRIC
Sub Disp – surfaced	4,200 tons	4,267 tonnes
Sub Disp – submerged	4,900 tons	4,978 tonnes
Length	272 ft	82.9 m
Beam	31 ft 3 in	9.52 m
Draught	27 ft	8.23 m
Propulsion	1 × RR PWR1 nuclear reactor driving 15,000 shp English Electric steam turbine	
	2 × Paxman 4,000 shp diesel engine	
Speed	20 knots surfaced, 30 knots submerged	
Range	N/a	
Armament	6 × 21 in (533 mm) torpedo tubes (bow)	
	20 torpedoes carried (Mk. 84, Tigerfish or Spearfish) or Tomahawk	
	UGM-84B Sub-Harpoon	
	Mines can also be carried in place of torpedoes	
Complement (Officers/Men)	97 (12/85)	

Builder	Name	Pennant No.	Class	Launched	Fate	Date
VSEL	HMS *Sceptre*	S104	Swiftsure Class	20.11.1976	Current	
VSEL	HMS *Sovereign*	S108	Swiftsure Class	17.2.1973	Current	
VSEL	HMS *Spartan*	S105	Swiftsure Class	7.4.1978	Current	
VSEL	HMS *Splendid*	S106	Swiftsure Class	5.10.1979	Current	
VSEL	HMS *Superb*	S109	Swiftsure Class	30.11.1974	Current	
VSEL	HMS *Swiftsure*	S126	Swiftsure Class	7.4.1971	PO – Laid up	1992

▲ The first Royal Navy Tomahawk flies on 18 November 1998, launched from HMS *Splendid*. *(Lockheed Martin)*

▲ An officer looks through the periscope on HMS *Sovereign*. *(Jeremy Flack)*

◄ A planesman at the controls of HMS *Sovereign*. *(Jeremy Flack)*

▲ Merlin HMA.1 hovers over HMS *Superb*.

▲ Fire control consoles on HMS *Sovereign*. *(Jeremy Flack)*

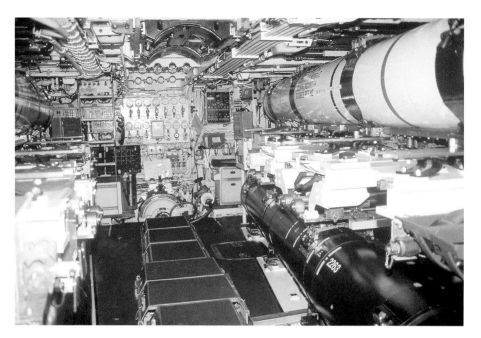

▲ Tigerfish torpedo and Sub-Harpoon missile in the weapons compartment of HMS *Superb*. *(Jeremy Flack)*

◄ HMS *Spartan* alongside at Faslane with cables encircling her hull during a deperming trial to remove her magnetic signature. *(Jeremy Flack)*

▲ A Tomahawk missile being launched from HMS *Splendid*. *(Courtesy BES)*

▶ HMS *Splendid, Superb* and *Sovereign* alongside at Faslane. *(Jeremy Flack)*

▲ HMS *Splendid* in dock. *(Mike Tazioli Babcock Engineering Services)*

Trafalgar Class

The Trafalgar Class of boats represent the continued modernisation of the Royal Navy Fleet Attack force. These are a substantially improved Swiftsure Class, and they have a similar role as a hunter-killer.

HMS *Trafalgar* was the first of the class to be ordered, on 7 April 1977. HMS *Triumph* was the last of the seven built and was completed in 1991. Being substantially newer than the Swiftsure Class, they will remain in service while the Swiftsure boats are paid off and replaced by the Astute Class which are currently under construction.

Although they are between ten and twenty years old, the Trafalgar Class continue to be updated during their refits with upgrades or replacement of their various sensors, countermeasures and fire control systems to ensure their maximum effectiveness.

In 1990 HMS *Trenchant* hit the headlines when she was accidentally caught in the net of the fishing boat *Antares* in the Firth of Clyde. Because of the immense power of these boats the captain was unaware of the accident, with the result that *Antares* was pulled under and four crew were drowned. Various trials followed, resulting, *inter alia*, in the fitting of sonar on nets to ensure that the accident could never be repeated.

After twelve years of service, including being the trials boat for the Spearfish torpedo service, in 1995 HMS *Trafalgar* underwent her first refit, which included her first refuelling – quite remarkable, considering the power consumption for the distance she had travelled. During her refit SMCS (Submarine Command System) was installed, together with the full Spearfish upgrade.

In 1998, HMS *Trafalgar* completed a further modernisation that enabled her to operate the US-built Hughes Tomahawk cruise missile. An improved version is currently being developed by Raytheon for their US customers. Initially being developed as a vertical-launch missile, the manufacturers anticipate a torpedo launch variant to be available soon. The advantages of this new version of the Tomahawk, referred to as Tacom, is that it can have a 4-hour loiter capability, plus an ability to transmit images of the target. One of the problems with firing the current missiles against land targets is that the co-ordinates need to be sent to the boat from PJHQ (Permanent Joint Headquarters) at Northwood before the missile can be launched. These new missiles will have the capability to have their target programmed while in flight. And the best thing about the new missile is that it will cost around half of the previous models.

During 1999 HMS *Trenchant* underwent a trial for which she was painted with a disruptive pattern camouflage. The two tones of blue paint were tested to try to make the boats less visible to aerial and satellite reconnaissance when they operate in shallower water.

In May 2000, while on the Task Group 2000 deployment, HMS *Tireless* suffered a primary coolant leak in her nuclear reactor and put into Gibraltar using her diesel power. Fine cracks were discovered in the surge line pintle weld of her propulsion system. As a result an immediate check was made on all other boats with the same system. In November it was announced that similar faults had been discovered in nearly all the rest of the Trafalgar Class, as well as the Superb Class, although to a lesser degree. The only boat that did not appear to have the fault was HMS *Triumph*. Consequently, all the Trafalgar vessels, as well as some of the Superb Class that were operational with the problem, were returned to their bases for rectification.

Because of the complicated nature of the fault, a protracted programme was immediately instigated, but it was over a year before the fleet were beginning to resume close to normal operations.

The Trafalgar boats are due to start decommissioning from 2010, and it is anticipated that they will be replaced by additional Astute Class vessels.

Class	Trafalgar Class
Role	Fleet Submarine (SSN)

	IMPERIAL	METRIC
Sub Disp – surfaced	4,730 tons	4,805 tonnes
Sub Disp – submerged	5,200 tons	5,238 tonnes
Length	280 ft 1 in	85.4 m
Beam	32 ft 1 in	9.83 m
Draught	31 ft 3 in	9.5 m
Propulsion	1 × RR PWR1 nuclear reactor driving 15,000 shp English Electric steam turbine 2 × Paxman 4,000 shp diesel	
Speed	32 knots submerged	
Range	N/A	
Armament	5 × 21 in (533 mm) torpedo tubes SLMC = Tomahawk missiles SSM = UGM-84B Sub-Harpoon Spearfish torpedoes Tigerfish torpedoes Mines can be carried in place of torpedoes	
Complement (Officers/Men)	130 (18/112)	

Builder	Name	Pennant No.	Class	Launched	Status
VSEL	HMS *Talent*	S92	Trafalgar Class	15.4.1988	Current
VSEL	HMS *Tireless*	S88	Trafalgar Class	17.3.1984	Current
VSEL	HMS *Torbay*	S90	Trafalgar Class	8.3.1985	Current
VSEL	HMS *Trafalgar*	S107	Trafalgar Class	1.7.1981	Current
VSEL	HMS *Trenchant*	S91	Trafalgar Class	3.11.1986	Current
VSEL	HMS *Triumph*	S93	Trafalgar Class	16.2.1991	Current
VSEL	HMS *Turbulent*	S87	Trafalgar Class	1.12.1982	Current

▲ HMS *Turbulent* and *Talent* alongside at Devonport. *(Courtesy of DML)*

▶ HMS *Tireless* in dry dock at Devonport with her anechoic tiles removed during a refit by DML. *(Courtesy of DML)*

▲ HMS *Trenchant*, with her crew at harbour stations, leaves Devonport for a patrol watched by the tug RMAS *Forceful*. A number of her anechoic tiles, which provide sound insulation, can be seen missing. *(Courtesy of DML)*

◀ HMS *Trafalgar* is carefully guided into a basin at Devonport by RMAS tugs. *(Courtesy of DML)*

▶ HMS *Tireless* floodlit while alongside at Devonport. *(Courtesy of DML)*

▲ Raytheon Tomahawk cruise missile being fitted to Trafalgar Class boats. This is a mock-up on display at the RN Submarine Museum at Gosport. *(Jeremy Flack)*

▲ A Spearfish torpedo being loaded into a Trafalgar Class boat. *(BAE Systems)*

◄ HMS *Trenchant* partially painted in grey and blue for a trial to evaluate a possible future camouflage scheme. *(John Brodie)*

▲ HMS *Torbay* departs Devonport. *(Jeremy Flack)*

▲ Sub-Harpoon being launched from a submarine. *(US Navy)*

Upholder Class

The Upholder Class represented a return to the diesel-powered submarine after the construction of a series of SSN classes. Originally designated as the Type 2400, these boats were designed to replace the earlier Oberon Class diesel-powered boats. A total of eighteen were planned, including a number of 'Super Upholder' boats of increased dimensions. Unlike the sleeker Oberon Class, the proportions of the Upholders were more akin to the Swiftsure/Trafalgar Class with a deeper hull containing two forward decks and a single engine space. The Upholder boats were designed to be very efficient, with a high degree of automation enabling a much reduced crew size.

Fate was not on the side of the Upholders. Industrial problems slowed their construction, and technical problems with their torpedo launch system resulted in protracted trials and delayed acceptance. With just four boats completed, the 1993 Defence Review resulted in all four boats being paid off with less than twelve months' service behind them, despite the problems being resolved and their actually becoming an effective boat.

The loss of these boats was more than just capability, since for the crews there are only a small number of nuclear SSN attack and SSBN bombers. There are no smaller boats for the junior and middle ranks to establish valuable experience and for officers to aspire to command.

Once the boats were paid off, they were put up for sale, which resulted in lengthy discussions with the Canadian government. Eventually, in 1998 an agreement was made for a $610m (Canadian) eight-year lease package which includes support and training plus an option to purchase them at the end. Following refurbishment and some modifications to meet their specific needs, the first boat, HMS *Unseen*, was delivered to the Canadian Navy and commissioned as HMCS/m *Victoria* on 2 December 2000.

Deliveries of the other three followed at approximately six-monthly intervals. The Canadian Navy plans call for two boats for operation on their east coast and a single on the west coast, with the fourth to be in overhaul.

HMS *Upholder* became HMCS *Chicoutimi* – SSK 879
HMS *Unicorn* became HMCS *Windsor* – SSK 877
HMS *Ursula* became HMCS *Cornerbrook* – SSK 878
HMS *Unseen* became HMCS *Victoria* – SSK 876

	Class	Upholder Class
	Role	Patrol Submarine (SSK)

	IMPERIAL	METRIC
Sub Disp – surfaced	2,185 tons	2,220 tonnes
Sub Disp – submerged	2,400 tons	2,438 tonnes
Length	230 ft 6 in	70.26 m
Beam	24 ft 11 in	7.6 m
Draught	18 ft	5.5 m
Propulsion	2 × 4,070 bhp Paxman Valenta 16 RPA 200SZ diesel generators	
Speed	12 knots surfaced, 20 knots submerged	
Range	10,000 nm surfaced	
Armament	6 × 21 in (533 mm) torpedo tubes Tigerfish torpedo Sub-Harpoon	
Complement (Officers/Men)	44 (7/37)	

Builder	Name	Pennant No.	Class	Launched	Fate	Date
Cammell Laird	HMS *Unicorn*	S43	Upholder Class	16.4.1992	PO – Sold	1995
Cammell Laird	HMS *Unseen*	S41	Upholder Class	14.11.1989	PO – Sold	1994
VSEL	HMS *Upholder*	S40	Upholder Class	2.12.1986	PO – Sold	1994
Cammell Laird	HMS *Ursula*	S42	Upholder Class	22.1.1991	PO – Sold	1994

▲ HMS *Upholder* in dry dock at Devonport during maintenance by DML.
(Courtesy DML)

▲ HMS *Ursula* being launched at Cammell Laird's yard at Birkenhead, with the position of her six torpedo tubes clearly visible. *(Hawker Siddeley)*

▶ HMS *Ursula* and *Unseen* in dry dock at Devonport during maintenance by DML.
(Courtesy DML)

▲ HMS *Upholder* approaching Devonport at the end of a patrol. *(Courtesy DML)*

▲ HMS *Upholder* departing HMS *Dolphin* with the assistance of an RMAS tug. *(Courtesy DML)*

◄ HMS *Unicorn* alongside at Portsmouth. *(Jeremy Flack)*

▲ HMS *Unseen* and *Ursula* laid up at Devonport awaiting their fate after being paid off. *(Jeremy Flack)*

◀ A planesman undergoing training in HMS *Upscot* – the Upholder Class simulator. *(Jeremy Flack)*

▼ HMS *Upholder* alongside at Faslane. *(Jeremy Flack)*

▲ The weapons compartment on HMS *Upholder*, with capacity for 18 torpedoes or missiles. *(Jeremy Flack)*

The Vanguard Class

The Vanguard Class of submarine is the most powerful warship in the Royal Navy. These nuclear-powered boats – usually referred to as bombers, or SSBNs – are armed with 16 Trident D5 missiles. Manufactured by Lockheed Martin, these SLBMs (Submarine Launched Ballistic Missile) have a range in excess of 6,000 nm, and each missile can be fitted with up to twelve MIRVs (Multiple Independently Targeted Re-entry Vehicles).

Each one of these MIRVs can have the equivalent yield of 100,000 tons of TNT. It was the UK government's stated policy that no more than 96 warheads would be fitted. However, following the Strategic Defence Review (SDR), the then Defence Secretary, George Robertson, stated that in acknowledgement of the changing strategic environment, the British self-limiting total number of warheads for the 16 missiles on a single boat would be no more than 48. In addition, the UK stockpile of warheads would be maintained at fewer than 200.

The mid-section of the boat with the 16 vertically mounted missile tubes is identical to the USN Ohio Class. In addition to the SLBMs, each of the Vanguard Class boats is armed with Spearfish torpedoes which have passive and active warheads and a range in excess of 60 km. Apart from the attack weapons, each of the boats is fitted with a comprehensive suite of sonars, providing a highly effective search and warning capability and fire control systems. The defensive capabilities include decoys and electronic countermeasures.

The Vanguard boats are powered by the Rolls Royce PWR2 reactor rated at 27,500 hp. Heat generated in the core is taken away by water under extreme pressure to prevent the water boiling. This heat is then transferred to a secondary system which produces steam to drive the main turbine engines and provides the power to the drive shaft. Additional steam is used to drive turbo-generators which provide the electrical power. A pair of Paxman diesel generators are fitted to produce emergency power.

HMS Vanguard was the first of the class; the order was placed with VSEL on 30 April 1986, and she was launched on 4 March 1992. Commissioned on 14 August 1993, HMS Vanguard was the first of this new class of SSBN to go on patrol. After exhaustive trials, she departed Faslane, and after a short period loading the live warheads at RNAD (Royal Navy Armament Depot) Coulport at Loch Long, slipped quietly away to assume her role as Britain's nuclear deterrent in December 1994.

As with the Resolution Class, a port and starboard crew enable the boat to be at sea for the maximum time while allowing the crew to have time ashore. Much of the machinery, especially in the engine room, is automated. TV monitors allow visible checks to be made, while sensors ensure the equipment operates within set parameters. Even the periscope is normally viewed via monitors with optical, thermal imaging and infra-red capabilities. Although the boat has similar displacement to the Invincible carriers, her crew is normally 132, compared to the carriers' 685, plus 366 for the attached air group.

Owing to the size of the missiles – 13 metres high – the Vanguard boats have four decks, providing ample space for equipment and living quarters. Compared to diesel-power boats the galley and mess are palatial. There is even an exercise room to help the crew keep fit on patrols that can last three months.

On 20 September 1998, HMS Vengeance became the fourth and last of the Vanguard Class SSBNs to be launched.

The capability of the SSBNs is awesome and the effect they have on a potential nuclear-powered aggressor must have a substantial deterrent value. However, these powerful boats, costing huge sums of money, must have a lesser deterrent power on smaller aggressors.

Over recent decades the Cold War has come to an end, and many now consider that the threat from the former Soviet Union has diminished substantially, as was recognised in the SDR. Some of the old Warsaw Pact countries have joined, or are in the process of joining, Nato. But who knows from where a future threat will emerge?

The conflicts that have arisen in the Falklands, the Gulf and the Balkans have posed no nuclear threat – although who knows the future! In their traditional role and for these conflicts the SSBNs are impotent. An answer would be to arm them with a conventional weapon. At one point it had been proposed to arm the Polaris missiles carried in the Resolution Class boats with a conventional warhead. However, the cost of the missile would require the target to be of a major value to justify its launch. It is possible that a single weapon could have the desired deterrent shock value in a rapidly deteriorating situation, but it would not be practical in an all-out conflict.

The British Strategic Defence Review (SDR) recognised the situation with the reduced threat from the Cold War adversaries, and so the SSBNs were given a wider tasking. Not only did this include an enhanced attack role with Spearfish torpedoes, but also other roles including hydrographic research, were given them.

Although there are no proposals, a weapon of the capability of the Raytheon Tomahawk could be considered. The test firing of Tomahawk from HMS Splendid in 1998 was successful enough for a batch of missiles to be bought for the Royal Navy, and modifications to ten of the attack submarines have enabled them to act as launchers. The Tactom (Tactical Tomahawk) is currently being developed in the USA with improved capabilities. This missile has been designed as a vertical-launch system, but it is being developed for launch from a torpedo tube.

The main obstacle to this scenario is how effective the politicians see this course of action to be, and at what cost. In terms of Allied casualties, this could have a real potential in helping to keep them to a minimum, and would enable these boats to have a greater tactical role, as opposed to a purely strategic one. It may be considered that the SSNs can provide enough tactical capability, but their defect problems of 2000/1 highlight the problem of operating with minimum numbers.

In their current role, the SSBN can be anywhere in the vast oceans. They can approach a trouble spot without heightening tension by being visible. They could strike the aggressor without warning. Where would he hit back? By the time the missile is detected the boat will have moved some distance! How many boats are out there? Who knows? The deterrent is out there – somewhere!

Class	Vanguard Class	
Role	Trident Submarine (SSBN)	
	IMPERIAL	METRIC
Sub Disp – surfaced		
Sub Disp – submerged	15,900 tons	16,154 tonnes
Length	491 ft 10 in	149.9 m
Beam	42 ft	12.8 m
Draught	39 ft 5 in	12 m
Propulsion	1 × RR PWR2 nuclear reactor driving 27,500 shp steam turbine	
Speed	25 knots submerged	
Range	N/a	
Armament	16 × silo Trident D5 missiles 5 × 21 in (533 mm) torpedo tubes Spearfish torpedoes	
Complement (Officers/Men)	135 (14/121)	

Builder	Name	Pennant No.	Class	Launched	Status
VSEL	HMS *Vanguard*	S05	Vanguard Class	4.3.1992	Current
VSEL	HMS *Vengeance*	S08	Vanguard Class	19.9.1998	Current
VSEL	HMS *Victorious*	S06	Vanguard Class	29.9.1993	Current
VSEL	HMS *Vigilant*	S07	Vanguard Class	14.10.1995	Current

▲ Artist's impression of a Vanguard Class boat launching a Spearfish torpedo. (*BAE Systems*)

▼ The SubMarine Command System (SMCS) receives data from the various sensors and weapon systems. This information is processed and presented to the Commanding Officer to enable him to make his tactical decisions. These are then fed into the SMCS and are then converted to action commands by the appropriate crew. (*Jeremy Flack*)

▲ HMS *Vengeance* emerges from her home at Faslane for another patrol, while HMS *Vanguard* can be seen alongside behind her bow. *(Jeremy Flack)*

▲ A Lockheed Martin Trident ICBM blasts off from an SSBN. *(Lockheed Martin)*

◄ HMS *Vanguard* is assisted in manoeuvring by the submarine berthing tugs RMAS *Impetus* and *Impulse* as she prepares to come alongside at Faslane. *(Jeremy Flack)*

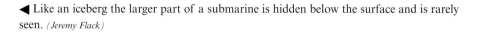

◄ Like an iceberg the larger part of a submarine is hidden below the surface and is rarely seen. *(Jeremy Flack)*

▼ It is only when seen like this and compared with the people around her that the full scale of her size can be appreciated. She is seen here being rolled out prior to being launched. *(Jeremy Flack)*

◀ An aerial view of HMS *Vanguard* fully emerged from VSEL's Devonshire Hall at Barrow-in-Furness. *(Jeremy Flack)*

▼ HMS *Vengeance* departs Faslane escorted by an RMAS tug and MOD Police RIB. *(Jeremy Flack)*

▶ Armed Royal Marines provide security. Visible are the circular hatch lids to the missile compartments. *(Jeremy Flack)*

▼ The weapons compartment aboard HMS *Vanguard* with Spearfish torpedoes held ready for use. *(Jeremy Flack)*

Astute Class

The Astute Class of attack submarines are the latest submarine ordered for the Royal Navy. Invitations to tender were issued on 14 July 1994 for a total of three submarines, with an option to build two more. GEC Marconi were selected as the prime contractor in July 1995, and the contract to build the initial three was placed on 17 March 1997. The Strategic Defence Review of July 1998 confirmed the decision to proceed with the additional two boats. A decision is expected in 2002 to place an order for a further three boats.

The hull of the Astute Class is being built by BAE SYSTEMS (previously Vickers) at Barrow-in-Furness, and is a development of the Trafalgar Class. It can be armed with an increased weapons load and will have a reduced radiated noise signature. Apart from being larger, the main recognition feature of the Astute Class from the Trafalgar and Swiftsure Class of submarines will be a slightly taller fin.

Following the successful completion of trials with the Raytheon Tomahawk TLAM (Tactical Land Attack Missile) launched from HMS *Splendid*, the design of the Astute Class boats has been modified to enable them to include the Tomahawk in their armoury. It is anticipated that they will eventually carry the Tactom (Tactical Tomahawk) missile. Currently, this is only being developed as a vertical-launch missile. The Astute design and construction has progressed too far to incorporate this new missile variant in its current form, but a torpedo-launched sub-variant will be produced.

A VSEL/MoD design for the SSN-20/W Class was an extension of the Swiftsure/Trafalgar design, but proved very expensive, especially when compared with the 30 per cent cheaper GEC consortium proposal. Various permutations of design were considered, ranging from a cheaper build with a higher operating cost through to higher initial cost but lower operating cost. A version of the latter was selected which will have an extended development 'whole life' core nuclear power-plant. What this means is that it is expected that the reactor will last the full 25 to 30 years life of the boat without refuelling.

As a result of their proposals, the GEC consortium were awarded the £2bn contract. GEC and VSEL are now part of BAE SYSTEMS Marine, and the design is currently being constructed at Barrow as the Astute Class.

The keel for HMS *Astute* was laid on 31 January 2001, and it is anticipated that she will be launched in 2004 and will begin replacing the five remaining Swiftsure Class boats soon after. The keel for HMS *Ambush* will also be laid in 2001.

Besides the Raytheon Tomahawk TLAM, the Astute Class will be armed with a submarine-launched Harpoon missile and the GEC Marconi Spearfish torpedo, as well as mines. The Spearfish is a wire-guided heavyweight torpedo with a 65 km range. It can travel at 60 knots and has a passive/active homing head enabling high-probability targeting. The substantial weapons compartment will have a capacity for 36 weapons, which can be in a variety of combinations depending on the role of the patrol.

A comprehensive range of sensors and countermeasures will be fitted to the Astute Class, ensuring they can navigate, communicate, detect and attack in the most hostile of environments. At the same time protective systems will help to disguise the boat by various means, including decoys.

The PWR2 reactor used to power the Astute Class was originally designed for the Vanguard Class SSBN, but is to be fitted with the latest 5th generation H core. Such have the advances been that this latest reactor has six and a half times the power output of that fitted to the Dreadnought and Valiant and that initially fitted to the Resolution Class boats, and four times the service life. In addition, improvements in the pumping power required to keep the reactor cool means that the reactor and therefore noise of the boat will be significantly reduced, making it even more difficult to detect. Although she is about 30 per cent larger than the Trafalgar Class, which she will also eventually replace, she will be approximately one-fifth faster. It is estimated that the whole-life cost of running Astute will be 10 per cent cheaper than the current Trafalgar boats, but with an increased capability.

	IMPERIAL	METRIC
Class	Astute Class	
Role	Attack Submarine (SSN)	
Sub Disp – surfaced		
Sub Disp – submerged	6,500 tons	7,200 tonnes
Length	300.9 ft	91.7 m
Beam	35.4 ft	10.8 m
Draught	32.8 ft	10 m
Propulsion	1 × 27,500 hp Rolls Royce PWR2 driving 2 × WH Allen turbo-generators 2 × 2,800 hp Paxman diesel engines	
Speed	29 knots submerged	
Range	N/a	
Armament	5 × 21 in (533 mm) torpedo tubes SLCM/Tomahawk SSM/Sub-Harpoon Spearfish torpedoes Mines	

Complement (Officers/Men)   100 (12/88)

Builder	Name	Pennant No.	Class	Launched	Status
BAE SYSTEMS Marine	HMS *Ambush*	S21	Astute Class	c.2005	Under Construction
BAE SYSTEMS Marine	HMS *Artful*	S22	Astute Class	c.2006	Under Construction
BAE SYSTEMS Marine	HMS *Astute*	S23	Astute Class	c.9.2004	Under Construction

▼ Artist's impression of an Astute Class boat. *(BAE Systems)*

Index

Page numbers in *italics* refer to illustrations.